Collins

History

GCSE Re

History

British

GCSE

Revision
Guide

Kelly Mellor, John Mitchell, and Steve McDonald

Contents

Contents

Crime and Punishment

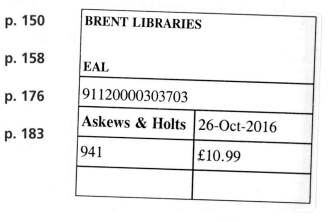

Anglo-Saxon Society on the Eve of Conquest

You must be able to:

- Describe the structure of Anglo-Saxon society before the Norman invasion
- Explain the key features of Anglo-Saxon religion, culture, language and law.

Society – the Rulers

- England was divided into seven separate kingdoms, each ruled by a king (the head of the most powerful family within the kingdom).
- By the later **Anglo-Saxon** period the separate kingdoms had been united under the rule of one king. Kings then allowed earls to look after areas of England known as **earldoms**.
- Earls were responsible for providing justice and ensuring law and order was maintained.
- In 1042 King Edward the Confessor was king of England but he left much of the ruling of the lands to the powerful Earl of Wessex.
- **Thegns** were given land in return (and as a reward) for their loyalty to the king. Thegns were responsible for protecting the villagers under their control and providing military assistance to the king when needed.
- The **Witan** (king's counsel) would be called together to give advice to the king. The king did not have to listen to or act upon the advice, but normally did so.

Society – Ordinary People

- Most ordinary people in the kingdom were **ceorls** (freemen).
- People who were **thralls** (slaves) usually came from one of three groups:
  - Prisoners of war
  - Criminals who couldn't pay their fines
  - Descendants of the original British people who inhabited the island before the Saxon invasion.
- In times of hardship ceorl parents sold their children into slavery.
- Society was not completely rigid; ceorls could become thegns.

Religion

- During Anglo-Saxon times kings in England had converted to Christianity. The conversion began in AD597 when Pope Gregory I sent missionaries to spread Christianity.
- People within England believed in one God rather than the many of the Pagan beliefs.
- The Saxons stopped being superstitious and believing in charms and magic and started to listen to the Christian Church under the guidance from Rome.

> ### Key Point
> England was divided into seven separate kingdoms; this was known as a heptarchy.

> ### Key Point
> English society was an amalgamation of settlers from north-west Europe (tribes from the Angles, Saxons and Jutes).

An 11th century church

- Religion became an important part of people's lives and the church held great power over them.
- Kings in England recognised the authority of the Pope as the head of the Roman Catholic Church. (There were no independent churches.)
- The vast majority of people loved the Church even though the Pope was very remote in Saxon England.
- The Pope and the king could appoint bishops and replaced Celtic monks with their chosen candidates.

Anglo-Saxon farming tools

Culture

- The majority of people's lives were based around the land.
- Each ceorl worked a **hide** of the thegns' land (the thralls also worked but as slaves). Ceorls paid food rent to the thegn.
- Some ceorls had specialised jobs such as shoemakers, bakers and merchants.
- For ordinary families, men and women had specific roles but both were considered important: boys would learn farming, fishing and how to hunt; girls would learn skills centred on the home, for example, how to cook and brew ale.
- It was rare for girls to be taught how to read and write. The sons of kings or rich thegns might be taught by a private teacher.
- The only schools were run by the Christian Church in monasteries.

Language

- The language spoken was Old English.
- This comprised a mixture of West Germanic languages.

Old English writing

Law

- Kings would give powers to local officials who would listen to cases. These were known as 'hundred' courts.
- Courts were becoming more important in deciding innocence or guilt (rather than people being punished on the say so of the king).
- Entire families could be punished for the actions of one individual.
- The Anglo-Saxons placed a high value on the word of a person (their solemn oath).
- Trials by ordeal were used to decide whether someone was innocent or guilty. Trials by iron or water were the most common.
- Everyone had a **wergild**. If the money could not or would not be paid then the family of the victim could pursue a blood feud.

Key Point

For the majority of people, life was very much structured by God and the social hierarchy.

Key Words

Anglo-Saxon
earldom
thegn
Witan
ceorl
thrall
hide
wergild

Quick Test

1. What religion were most people in England in 1066?
2. What were the most common trials to ascertain if a person was guilty of a crime?
3. Who usually received an education in Anglo-Saxon society?

The Succession Crisis of 1066

You must be able to:

- Explain why the House of Godwin was such a powerful family
- Explain why there was a crisis after the death of Edward the Confessor.

Edward the Confessor

- Edward spent much of his early life in Normandy.
- In the last stages of Harthacnut's reign, Edward was invited back to England to be **heir**.
- Edward became King of England in 1042.
- William of Normandy was a second cousin to Edward and the two men had spent time together in Normandy.
- Harold Godwinson's father was Godwine. He was the Earl of Wessex (a very powerful and important position in Anglo-Saxon England).
- In 1045 Edward married Godwine's daughter Edith.
- The marriage did not result in any children, which left a question over the **succession** of the English throne following Edward's death.
- In 1051 Edward allegedly nominated William as his heir. Sources state that Harold Godwinson had been sent to Normandy to relay this message and promised to support William's claim.
- In conflicting evidence, Edward allegedly nominated Harold Godwinson as his heir on his deathbed.

A statue of Edward the Confessor

The House of Godwin

- Harold Godwinson's father, Godwine, cemented the power of the family during the reign of Harold I and Harthacnut.
- Godwine proved himself to be a loyal statesman and the family became very wealthy and powerful.
- Godwine was the Earl of Wessex and two of his sons were earls in East Anglia and the West Country.
- In 1051 Godwine and his family were **banished** from England following disagreements with the king. They returned in 1052 and Edward agreed to return lands to them.
- When Godwine died in 1053, Harold Godwinson succeeded his father as Earl of Wessex. From this date Harold and his brothers gained and increased their power throughout Northumbria, East Anglia and Mercia.
- Harold had fought for King Edward and stopped a Welsh rebellion. He was a loyal servant to Edward.
- However, for all of Harold's power and influence he remained subordinate to King Edward and this was highlighted in the Northumbrian Crisis in 1065. The thegns in the area grew tired of the harsh rule of Tostig (Harold Godwinson's brother) and

> ### Key Point
>
> Edward had no children and therefore no clear heir when he died on January 5th 1066.

rebelled and overthrew him. Edward accepted this event, which emphasised that Harold's family, although important, were still outranked by the king's wishes.

- Tostig was exiled and spent some time in Scotland before uniting with Harald Hardrada and supporting his invasion of England and the Viking army at the Battle of Stamford Bridge.

Harold's Oath to William

- William had helped Edward when he had returned to England to be king by sending him soldiers. This resulted in a close relationship between Edward and William, and Edward promised William the throne because of this.
- In 1064 Harold became shipwrecked on the coast of Normandy.
- Different sources suggest alternative versions of events for Harold's oath to William.
- The first version of events holds that William seized the opportunity to make Harold swear an oath of allegiance to recognise him as the heir to the English throne.
- The Bayeux Tapestry shows Harold holding religious relics and making his oath while William watches (although this may be a post-invasion invention).
- Harold later argued that, because his oath was made under pressure, he did not have to honour it.
- The second version has it that Edward had sent Harold to Normandy to reaffirm William as the rightful heir and promise his support. However, Harold at the time had no intention of keeping his oath in the future.

Harold's oath to William

Quick Test

1. What year did Edward promise the throne to William?
2. What did Harold say Edward had promised on his deathbed?
3. Why was there a succession crisis after Edward's death?
4. When did Edward the Confessor die?

The Rival Claimants to the Throne in 1066

You must be able to:

- Recall who the claimants were to the English throne in 1066
- Explain the motives and claims of each contender.

Harold Godwinson

- Harold Godwinson was the Earl of Wessex (one of the most powerful men in England).
- He was brother-in-law to Edward the Confessor.
- The Godwin family had served Edward throughout his reign.
- Harold had proved himself a strong and effective leader and fighter.
- He had won the support of the **Witan** for his claim to the throne. The Witan had offered him the crown over all of the other **claimants** after Edward's death.
- The Witan could depose a king if they felt he was not right for England and so their support for Harold's claim was a big advantage.
- Harold claimed that Edward's dying wish was for him to take the throne.
- He was the only Anglo-Saxon contender.
- He argued that his oath to support William's claim was not to be honoured because he had been forced into making it.

> **Key Point**
>
> The only claimant who was supported by the Witan was Harold Godwinson.

Edgar the Aetheling

- Edgar had strong blood ties with Anglo-Saxon kings.
- He was the descendent of **Alfred the Great** (one of the most highly respected and successful Anglo-Saxon kings).
- He was the great nephew of Edward.
- He was only 10 years old when Edward died.
- As the closest living blood relative he was the rightful heir and should have been crowned king.
- He was deemed too young to control and protect England from the Viking and Norman threats.
- He could not realistically match Harold Godwinson's power and stake his claim to the throne.
- He did not have the support of the Witan to help his claim.

> **Key Point**
>
> All of the claimants argued that the English crown was rightfully theirs.

Harald Hardrada

- England had been ruled by Viking kings between 1016 and 1042 (Cnut 1016–1035 and Harthacnut 1035–1042).
- Harthacnut had no heir and promised the throne to King Magnus of Norway.
- Edward the Confessor had seized the throne from Harthacnut's named successor, King Magnus of Norway.

Harald Hardrada window in Kirkwall Cathedral

- Harald Hardrada was Magnus' son and therefore argued that he was the rightful heir to the English crown because of the promise made from Harthacnut to Magnus.
- Hardrada was already King of Norway so had experience of ruling a kingdom.
- He was a successful and very powerful warrior.
- His claim was supported by Tostig (Harold Godwinson's brother).

William of Normandy

- William of Normandy had been used to controlling lands since he was a young boy.
- He was the Duke of Normandy, a big and powerful part of northern France.
- He was a powerful, strong leader and fighter.
- He was a distant cousin of Edward the Confessor.
- Edward had spent a lot of time in Normandy and the relationship between William and Edward was close.
- Edward had invited many Normans to England to be part of his court when he was king.
- In 1051 Edward promised the throne to William.
- Edward had sent Harold Godwinson to Normandy to swear an oath to William that he would support his claim to the English crown.
- When Harold broke his oath, William gained **Papal** support for an invasion of England to claim the crown. He argued that he was the rightful heir.

William of Normandy

Edward's Death and the Crowning of Harold Godwinson

- Edward the Confessor died on 5 January 1066.
- Harold Godwinson declared himself king the day after Edward's death.
- He had an official coronation ceremony ten weeks later in Westminster Abbey.

> **Key Point**
>
> Once king, Harold's position remained unstable because the other claimants would not give up easily on their supposed right to be King of England.

> **Quick Test**
>
> 1. Name the claimant who was just 10 years old when Edward died.
> 2. What was the relationship between Edward and William?
> 3. Which king had Edward seized England from in 1042?

> **Key Words**
>
> Witan
> claimant
> Alfred the Great
> Papal

The Battles of Fulford and Stamford Bridge

You must be able to:

- Explain why the Battles of Fulford and Stamford Bridge occurred
- Explain what happened and the outcome of each battle.

The Battle of Fulford

- The earls in the north needed to defend York from the invading Vikings.
- The Vikings wanted to use York as a base for their conquest of England.
- Earl Morcar of Northumbria and Earl Edwin of Mercia led the Saxon defence.
- The Saxon earls used the time before the Vikings arrived to march south of York and choose **strategic** defensive positions.
- Morcar and Edwin used the natural obstacles in the area to help with the defence; they used the space between a stream and marsh ground.
- The battle was fought on 20 September 1066.

The Events of the Battle

- Harald Hardrada's army outnumbered the Saxon army.
- The battle started well for the Saxons. They pushed Hardrada's troops into the marsh but progress was slow.
- As Hardrada's troops continued to arrive, the Saxons were pushed back along the river.
- The Saxon army became trapped and had to fight the Vikings from three sides.
- The Vikings had slightly higher ground than the Saxons and they could see that the Saxon army was being pushed into a natural pit where their fate could be easily sealed.

Battle scene from the Bayeux Tapestry

Outcome

- The Saxon army was defeated and many men were killed or crushed in the pit.
- Sources from the battle state that the beck ran red with Saxon blood.

Key Point

The Vikings had a victory at Fulford.

Significance

- The way to York lay open for Harald Hardrada.
- The people of York were forced to accept Hardrada as their king and agreed to help and support his claim to the English throne against Harold Godwinson.
- The victory would have boosted the Vikings' confidence.

The Battle of Stamford Bridge

- In early September Harold Godwinson received news that Hardrada had landed in the north of England.
- Harold Godwinson was in a difficult position; he knew that the south of England was under threat from a Norman invasion in addition to the threat from the Vikings in the north.
- Harold took the decision to march north. He did not want to give Hardrada time to consolidate his control in the north.

The Events of the Battle

- The Saxon army surprised the Vikings early in the morning on 25 September 1066. The Saxon army had marched so quickly to Stamford Bridge that some Vikings were still asleep when they arrived and had left their armour in the boats.
- Accounts state that the Viking army had been split into two on either side of a small bridge.
- The bulk of the remaining Viking army held off the Saxon advance by creating a shield wall.
- Some sources tell the tale of a mighty Viking warrior who blocked the bridge and killed 40 or so Englishmen. He was killed when a Saxon soldier stabbed him with a spear from under the bridge.
- As the Saxon army crossed the bridge, the Vikings could not hold off their advances. Their shield wall was eventually broken and Hardrada was killed by an arrow in his neck.

A 13th century depiction of the Battle of Stamford Bridge

Outcome

- Harald Hardrada was killed.
- The Viking conquest of England was defeated.

Significance

- Although Harold Godwinson had been victorious, he still had to defend his crown from William.
- The Saxon army was tired and wounded from the battle.
- The march south after the battle did not help the Saxon chances at Hastings.

Key Point

Harold Godwinson defeated Harald Hardrada at Stamford Bridge.

Quick Test

1. Who led the Saxon forces at Fulford?
2. Why was the Battle of Fulford significant?
3. On what date did the Battle of Stamford Bridge occur?
4. What was the outcome of the Battle of Stamford Bridge?

Key Word

strategic

The Battle of Hastings

You must be able to:

- Explain the reasons for and the outcomes of the battle
- Describe the key events during the battle.

Background

- William had started preparing for the invasion as soon as he had heard that Harold Godwinson had been crowned king.
- William had received the Pope's blessing for an invasion because Harold had seemingly gone back on his oath to support William's claim. Even before the battle, the Pope was William's ally.
- William had prepared his army and resources well. He landed with his fleet at Pevensey Bay on 28 September 1066.

Scene of the Battle of Hastings, 1066

Tactics of Harold's Army

- Harold had marched his army quickly from Stamford Bridge to Hastings.
- He did not wait for reinforcements from London; instead he went straight for William's position.
- Harold's army included the **housecarls**, **thegns** and **fyrd**.
- The axe was the Saxons' most important weapon. It was mostly made from iron and could kill a man or horse easily.
- Before the battle, Harold took up position at the top of Senlac Hill. The road to London went across Senlac Hill and so, by positioning his troops on top of the hill, he blocked William's access to the city. William needed to get to London if he was going to be crowned king.
- Harold placed his housecarls at the front of the army on Senlac Hill. The Saxon army was protected by a strong shield wall.

> **Key Point**
>
> The fyrd were peasants. They were not trained soldiers.

Tactics of William's Army

- Because William's army had the support of the Pope, people supported and believed in this 'holy war'. This was a great morale booster for William's soldiers.
- William had travelled around neighbouring lands calling for men to fight with him and had received lots of willing volunteers.
- All of William's soldiers were professional, full-time soldiers.
- Within his army, William had **cavalry**, archers, crossbowmen and **infantry**.
- Due to the Saxon army being tired and weakened from their battle with Hardrada and their long march south, William's well-prepared and rested soldiers were arguably more battle-ready.
- William **pillaged** local villagers in an attempt to lure Harold straight to him.

Battle Abbey, near the site of the Battle of Hastings

The Main Events of the Battle (14 October 1066)

- During the morning's fighting, Harold had the upper hand. His army remained firm, packed tightly and protected behind the shield wall at the top of Senlac Hill.
- William had tried attacking with archers and infantry but could not make gains through the Saxon lines.
- During the battle a rumour started to spread that William had been killed. Fearing that the battle was lost, some of his men started to retreat down the hill.
- Seeing the retreating Norman army, some of the Saxon soldiers broke rank and ran after the Normans. This was possibly the fyrd thinking that they would be able to collect some 'spoils of war' (horses, swords, etc).
- When it was realised that William had not been killed, his army regrouped and killed the Saxons that had run out from the shield wall.
- William realised that the Saxons would chase the retreating Norman army. He decided to feign retreat to weaken the Saxon Shield wall.
- The Saxon line eventually became so weakened by this tactic that Harold was killed and his body so mutilated that it could not be identified.

Outcome of the Battle

- William was victorious. He was a step closer to making his claim for the English crown.
- William had been willing to make tactical changes during the battle, which helped his army gain victory.
- Luck had also helped William win. Harold's men were depleted and exhausted and at a mental disadvantage thanks to the belief that God was on the Norman side due to the **Papal** blessing given to William.
- William marched to London and was crowned king on 25 December 1066.

> **Key Point**
>
> Both sides fought well in the battle and at first it seemed as though Harold might win.

Battle scene from the Bayeux Tapestry

> **Key Point**
>
> There were many reasons why William gained a victory at Hastings including luck, religion, William's leadership and Harold's mistakes.

> **Key Words**
>
> housecarl
> thegn
> fyrd
> cavalry
> infantry
> pillaged
> Papal

> **Quick Test**
>
> 1. Who were the fyrd?
> 2. Why had William been given the Pope's blessing (known as Papal blessing)?
> 3. Why did the Saxon army break rank and leave the shield wall?

Anglo-Saxon Resistance and the Norman Response

You must be able to:

- Give examples of the Saxon rebellions against William after his victory at Hastings
- Explain how William dealt with rebellious Saxons.

Saxon Actions after Hastings

- The Saxons did not want to accept William as their new king.
- There were many **rebellions** with the aim of removing William from the throne.
- In 1067, Harold Godwinson's mother led forces against William but was defeated.
- From 1069 to 1070 in the north of England, the Saxon leaders Edwin and Mocar allied with Edgar Aetheling and the Danes. Their aim was to seize York and gain control of the north. William defeated the rebels and bribed the Danes to return home.
- In 1070, Hereward the Wake and Morcar attempted a final rebellion against William on the Isle of Ely (Cambridge). Allied with an army sent by the Danish king, the rebels made good ground and held off the Normans. The rebels were betrayed and the Norman soldiers defeated them.
- Hereward's rebellion in 1070 was seen as the last real challenge to William's power.

William's Actions after Hastings

- William realised that he would have to consolidate his power because the Saxons would not simply accept him as their new king.
- Even before the Battle of Hastings he had built castles. They would later become bases from which the Normans would consolidate power and control.
- He gave his Norman supporters land in order to reorganise old Anglo-Saxon earldoms and to subdue and control the Saxons.
- He dealt swiftly and severely with any threats to his power.
- William made his half-brother, Bishop Odo, Earl of Kent. He was second in command of England, along with William FitzOsbern, once William had returned to Normandy shortly after the victory in 1066.

The Harrying of the North, 1069–1070

- William wanted revenge on the north for trying to overthrow him. This was known as the **Harrying** of the North.
- The Normans set fire to large areas of the north of England.
- Crops were destroyed and animals slaughtered.
- Men, women and children were murdered.
- Survivors starved because the land and their livelihoods had been decimated.

> **Key Point**
>
> The Saxons rebelled to show William he was not accepted as the rightful king.

Drawing of Hereward the Wake fighting the Normans

> **Key Point**
>
> After he became king, in theory, William had at his disposal the whole of England.

The Feudal System

- William's supporters who had helped him win the Battle of Hastings expected a share of the spoils of war; they wanted land.
- William realised that he needed to place loyal **barons** in areas around England in order to maintain his power over the Saxons.
- William granted land to his barons but it came with conditions.
- He expected the barons to provide military service to him when needed and also to show loyalty and offer help/advice/money when required.
- All but two Saxon earls were replaced with Norman barons in the **feudal** system.
- Barons could lend land to knights in return for military service.
- Knights could lend land to the **villeins**. The villeins did not own the land but had to work on it. They also had many duties they had to complete for the lord, for example, pay taxes and provide supplies.
- William was very careful not to place his barons too close together. He feared that with access to knights, barons could work together to oust him.
- In this system, everyone knew their place and it meant that everyone was loyal to their lord.

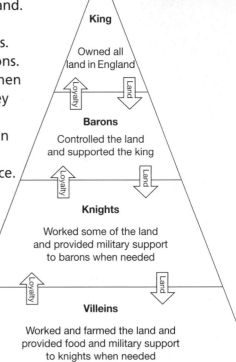

The Feudal System

The Revolt of the Earls, 1075

- The revolt of the earls could have proved difficult for William to control if the Saxon people had got behind it.
- Norman earls, Roger of Hereford and Ralph of East Anglia led the revolt. A Saxon earl, Waltheof was also involved in the planned revolt but he backed out and told William of the plan.
- This revolt was caused by William refusing to allow the marriage of Emma (the daughter of William FitzOsbern and sister of Earl Roger) to Earl Ralph of East Anglia. The pair married despite William's refusal.
- William focused his forces on defeating Ralph in Norwich. Ralph fled to Denmark to gain Danish support, leaving his wife fighting William's forces. She was defeated before Danish help arrived.
- Earl Roger started his rebellion in the west of England but was cut short because locals loyal to William would not support him.
- William punished Roger and Ralph severely. They lost all of their land and influence. Earl Waltheof was punished by being beheaded.
- This was the last serious challenge to William's reign. The Saxons had decided to support William instead of facing an unknown and unstable future without William as their king.

Key Point

William used severe methods to crush the rebellions and assert his power over the Saxons.

Quick Test

1. Which rebellion is viewed as the last real Saxon threat to William's power?
2. What did William do to the north of England as revenge for rebelling against him?
3. Briefly explain how land was divided up in the feudal system.

Key Words

rebellion
Harrying
baron
feudal
villein

Life Under Norman Control

You must be able to:

- Explain the continuities between Saxon society and Norman society in England post conquest
- Explain what changed after the Norman Conquest in England.

Society

- The feudal system ensured that everyone knew their place and was kept under William's control.
- Most Saxons had land and/or jobs of importance taken from them and given to Norman counterparts as part of William's conquest.
- Boundaries of **earldoms** were changed to reflect the new areas controlled by the barons.
- The Norman Conquest broke England's links with Denmark and Norway. There became greater links with Normandy and elsewhere in Europe.
- Women were treated worse under the Normans.
- The Saxon language began to incorporate French words.

Government

- Much of the government of England remained unchanged by William.
- William saw no need to change systems that had worked well under the rule of Edward.
- The **Curia Regis** replaced the **Witan**. William needed the Curia Regis for advice and to make important decisions. As with the Witan, the king did not have to listen to the Curia Regis but it made sense to keep their support by following their advice.
- The day-to-day running of the country was done by the **Chancellor** (this was continuity from Saxon times). William gave this position to Normans; they ensured that the king's will was carried out. The position of the Chancellor increased in importance during Norman times.
- Administrative shires, **sheriffs** and positions in local government continued much the same as during Edward's reign, except that William filled the positions with Normans.

Norman England

Key Point

Many things to do with the day-to-day running of the country remained unchanged by William and life continued as before.

Justice

- Shire courts remained to hear cases summoned by the sheriff.
- The hundred courts from Saxon times continued to hear cases and made decisions on day-to-day disputes.
- Trial by ordeal did still occur but trial by jury became more frequent.
- William allowed church courts to have their own code of laws. These would deal with clergymen accused of crimes.

- William introduced a new law – the Murdrum Law. This meant that if a Norman was murdered the nearest village would be held responsible for bringing the perpetrator to justice. If no one was caught for the crime then the village would be fined heavily.
- Canon Law was the law that the church abided to.

Taxation

- William was able to use the feudal system as a way of gaining taxes.
- Shires would pay the king taxes either in money or goods. The sheriff would be responsible for collecting the tax.
- The **geld** was a taxation system left over from Saxon times. William did not change this as it gave him another source of income. It was levied according to the hides of land held by individuals.

Towns and Villages

- The Normans destroyed some towns and villages to make way for castle building after the conquest.
- The Domesday Book records 112 **burhs**. Burhs were busy places with trade and commerce being a central focus. Livestock, fish, wool and salt were goods for which trade was important.
- Coastal burhs in the south were used as ports for international trade with Normandy.
- Compared to burhs, villages were underdeveloped. The main focus in the village was agriculture.
- The most important building in the village was the church. Surrounding the church would be wattle and daub houses and fields.
- Peasant houses would consist of one room that would be shared with animals still alive in the winter months. They would eat produce from the land and have clothes made from animal by-products such as wool and leather.
- In spring peasants would sow seeds, summer would be busy with harvesting the crops, autumn would be spent ploughing the land and in winter some of the animals would be killed for food and clothes.
- William introduced a poaching law that protected his love of hunting. Deer, boar and vegetation within the forest became protected. This was known as the Forest Laws.
- William also increased areas of forest under the Forest Laws. This had a significant impact on the people that would forage and hunt for food. There were strict punishments for people found poaching.

Key Point
William knew the importance of having loyal Normans in positions of power and so replaced Saxon people to consolidate his power.

A Norman church in Gloucestershire

Quick Test

1. What was the role of the person that helped William with the day-to-day running of the country?
2. What was the national tax that William was paid based on the hides of land owned by individuals?
3. Why did William not make huge changes to the way England was governed?

Key Words
earldom
Curia Regis
Witan
Chancellor
sheriff
geld
burh

Norman Castles and the Domesday Book

You must be able to:

- Explain the purpose of Norman castles
- Explain why the Domesday Book was created and the significance of it.

The First Norman Castles

- William had prepared for the Battle of Hastings by bringing **prefabricated** wooden castles with him on his fleet.
- William had built castles in England before the Battle of Hastings had taken place.
- The wooden castles were easy to build and could be used as a base for his initial preparations for the Battle of Hastings.
- After his victory he could use the castles to consolidate his power over the Saxons.
- William built his castles in strategic locations as he moved around England following his victory at Hastings, as well as in places where locals had rebelled.
- The castles were a visual reminder to the Saxons that the Normans were in charge.
- William used the castles as a base for his Norman barons to control the countryside up and down England as part of the feudal system. He destroyed towns and villages to build his castles if they were in the way.
- The first Norman castles were **motte and bailey** castles.

A Norman motte and bailey showing the motte (mound) with the castle keep on top and the wooden palisade (fence) surrounding the bailey castle

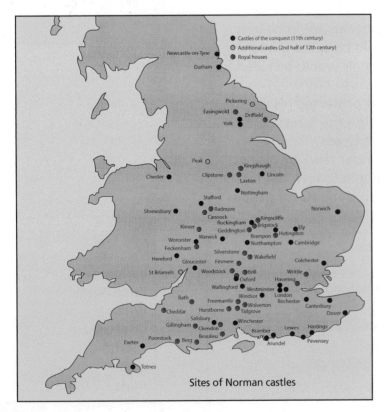

Sites of Norman castles

> ● Castles of the conquest (11th century)
> ○ Additional castles (2nd half of 12th century)
> ● Royal houses

Key Point

Castles were used for many purposes – to consolidate Norman power over the Saxons, as a base for soldiers and barons and as important administrative centres when William's conquest was complete.

Later Norman Castles

- Eventually the wooden castles were replaced with stone ones. This was because wooden castles were easy to set on fire and, on occasion, angry local Saxons did set castles alight.
- Castles became an integral part of William's domination of England. They were used as a base from which taxes were collected and barons ruled over the villeins.
- The presence of barons and knights within the castles kept the Saxons firmly obedient to the king.

Domesday Book

- The Domesday Book was a survey ordered by William to find out information about England.
- By 1085 William faced threats of invasion from Scandinavia and had been fighting costly battles in northern France.
- As a result, his **treasury** was low. He needed to discover how much tax he could claim from the population.
- It is also possible that he wanted to know England's economic and social state after the conquest and the years of unrest that followed.
- William ordered the survey in 1085.
- Commissioners travelled around England in 1086 and asked locals about the land, people, animals, buildings and resources.
- Each village was visited twice by two different sets of questioners. This ensured that the survey was accurate.
- The information was collated and written in Latin into two volumes.
- The survey illustrated the feudal system in action and the information could have been used to strengthen the position of the Normans.
- The key focus of Domesday was financial – gaining more tax; however there were other important pieces of information that would have been useful to William:
  - Detailed knowledge of the geography of England would also help William defend his kingdom against invaders.
  - Having detailed knowledge about the men in the kingdom would also have helped William gather an army to fight if and when needed.
  - Also, knowing where animals were would have been useful if he needed to feed his army whilst marching to defend England from invasion.
- William died before it had been completed.

Rochester Castle - a Norman keep

The Domesday Book

Key Point

The Domesday survey was compiled to gather information about England. William needed to know how much tax he could gather to help defend his new kingdom.

Quick Test

1. What were the first Norman castles called?
2. Why were they used?
3. What year did William order the Domesday survey?
4. What was the main reason for the Domesday survey?

Key Words

prefabricated
motte and bailey
treasury

The Norman Church and the Death of William I

You must be able to:

- Explain why the church had such power and influence in medieval society
- Explain what happened to the English throne after the death of William.

The Norman Church

- William replaced Saxon bishops and abbots with Norman counterparts to consolidate his conquest and control.
- The church was incredibly wealthy. Each person paid **tithes** to the church and worked a couple of days each year for free on the church land.
- The church had a great influence over the people (rich and poor). It was believed the only way to get to heaven was to follow the teachings of the church.
- Members of the **clergy** who were accused of a crime were dealt with by the church courts.

> ### Key Point
>
> The church had great power and influence in medieval society.

Monasteries

- **Monasteries** owned huge amounts of land and as a result were very wealthy. e.g. Canterbury.
- **The Cluniac Reforms** demanded greater religious devotion and encouraged pilgrimages as part of this.
- Monasteries were reformed along the rules of St Benedict. Monks had to follow strict instructions as to how they should conduct themselves both inside and outside the monastery. Latin would be used alongside sign language in the monasteries and in worship.

Ruins of a Norman monastery - Castle Acre Priory

The Role of the Archbishop of Canterbury

- Archbishop Stigand (Saxon Archbishop of Canterbury) was too powerful for William to unseat straightaway within his reforms.
- Lanfranc became Archbishop of Canterbury in 1070 when Stigand was finally unseated. He encouraged the replacement of English bishops with Norman counterparts.
- Lanfranc was responsible for maintaining excellent state–church relations during William's reign.
- Lanfranc manoeuvred the church in England so that it accepted authority from the Pope but remained as independent as possible.

The Investiture Controversy

- The Investiture Controversy was a period of tension between the Popes and monarchs in the 11th and 12th centuries to determine who would choose bishops and abbots.

- Usually kings would invest (choose) a new bishop who they knew would remain loyal. This would ensure that church and state worked well together.
- In 1075 Pope Gregory VII said that only the church could select any new bishops and abbots because churchmen were God's representatives on Earth.
- In January 1076 at an assembly in Worms, the German king, Henry IV Holy Roman Emperor, along with German and northern Italian bishops rejected their obedience to the Pope. Henry IV wanted to be able to choose his own bishops without interference from Rome.
- The Pope responded by **deposing** Henry IV and **excommunicating** all those involved. Henry realised that he could not risk being on such bad terms with the church and asked for forgiveness in 1077. This was not the end however as tensions continued and he was deposed and excommunicated again in 1080.
- In 1077 the Pope formally stated that monarchs could not invest bishops. This left a legacy of a power struggle between the church and monarch that remained throughout the Middle Ages.
- Bishop Odo argued with the Archbishop of Canterbury (Lanfranc) over land. There were many court battles over this issue.
- In 1082 Odo attempted to travel to Italy along with Norman barons to buy himself the role of Pope. William could not let this happen and worked with Lanfranc to imprison Odo for **sedition**.
- After William's death, William Rufus released Odo only for him to join forces with William's eldest son, Robert and try to depose him. Odo and Robert were defeated and Odo was exiled.

The Death of William I and the Succession Crisis

- In 1077 Robert and his brothers, William Rufus and Henry, had fallen out. William had not punished the younger sons for their actions toward Robert and this had angered Robert.
- Robert organised support from loyal Normans to seize Rouen Castle. Robert failed at his attempt and William ordered his arrest. Robert fled and thus tension remained between Robert and his father.
- William died from an injury sustained whilst on his horse fighting in France. He died 5 weeks after the riding accident.
- William named Robert as Duke of Normandy, William Rufus as King of England and Henry received a substantial sum of money.
- After William's death, Lanfranc organised support from the Saxons for William Rufus as the next king instead of Robert.

Statue of William I on his horse.

> **Key Point**
>
> William divided his kingdom and money between his three sons.

> **Key Words**
>
> tithe
> clergy
> monastery
> The Cluniac Reforms
> depose
> excommunicate
> sedition

> **Quick Test**
>
> 1. What percentage of annual income/goods did people have to give to the church?
> 2. What year did Lanfranc become Archbishop of Canterbury?
> 3. Who did William name as his successor to the English throne?

Norman England: Anglo-Saxon Society on the Eve of Conquest

1 Give one example of how criminal guilt was decided in Anglo-Saxon society.

2 Describe the social hierarchy in Anglo-Saxon England.

3 In which year did Edward the Confessor become King of England?

4 Study the image below of a king with his Witan. Using the source and your knowledge explain whether you agree that the Witan played a central role in the running of Anglo-Saxon England.

Write your answer on a separate piece of paper.

5 Explain the cultural features of Anglo-Saxon England.

Write your answer on a separate piece of paper.

6 Study the source below from Archbishop Wulfstan.

> The Christian king must severely punish wicked men ... He must be merciful and yet austere; that is the king's right – and that is the way to get things done in a nation.

How can this source be used to explain the change in law and order throughout the Anglo-Saxon period? Your answer should include your knowledge of the period.

Write your answer on a separate piece of paper.

Norman England: The Succession Crisis of 1066

1 Which event highlighted the superiority of King Edward over the Godwine family?

_____

2 What position did Harold Godwinson hold from 1053? _____

3 Who did Edward supposedly promise the throne to on his deathbed?

_____

4 What can we learn about Edward's death from the source below? Use details from the source and your own knowledge.

Write your answer on a separate piece of paper.

5 Give two reasons why the Witan would have supported Harold Godwinson's claim to the throne.

_____

_____

_____

6 Explain why there was a disputed succession after Edward's death.

Write your answer on a separate piece of paper.

Practice Questions

Norman England: The Rival Claimants to the Throne in 1066

1   Name the King of Norway who laid claim to the English throne after Edward's death.

_____

2   Describe the reasons why Hardrada believed he was the rightful successor to the throne.

_____

_____

_____

_____

3   What was the reason for the Pope's support of William's planned invasion.

_____

_____

4   William of Poitiers in the 1070s stated that:

> Harold … swore loyalty to the duke … he took an oath in his own free will…

Does this source prove that Harold promised to support William's claim?

Write your answer on a separate piece of paper.

5   Explain why Edgar's claim was not more of a problem to the other contenders.

_____

_____

_____

_____

6   Harold Godwinson had the strongest claim to the throne in 1066. How far do you agree?

Write your answer on a separate piece of paper.

Norman England: The Battles of Fulford and Stamford Bridge

1 When was the Battle of Fulford fought? ....

2 Why was the Battle of Fulford being fought?

....

....

....

....

3 How far do you agree that the most significant consequence of the Battle of Fulford was that the Viking army's confidence had been boosted by victory?

Write your answer on a separate piece of paper.

4 Explain why the victory at the Battle of Stamford Bridge was important for Harold Godwinson.

....

....

....

....

5 Give two turning points from the Battle of Stamford Bridge to show when the battle turned in the favour of Harold Godwinson.

....

....

....

....

6 Explain why Harold Godwinson decided to march north to meet Hardrada.

Write your answer on a separate piece of paper.

Practice Questions

Norman England: The Battle of Hastings

1 Why would having the Pope's blessing be an advantage to William's army?

Write your answer on a separate piece of paper.

2 What was the name of the hill that Harold Godwinson positioned his troops upon before the start of the battle?

....

3 Explain how William had prepared well for the battle.

Write your answer on a separate piece of paper.

4 A Norman writer stated after the battle:

> … it was only William's courage that saved us.

Does this explain why the Normans were victorious in the Battle of Hastings?

Write your answer on a separate piece of paper.

5 Below is a section of the Bayeux Tapestry showing the start of the Battle of Hastings. What features of the tapestry make it convincing? Use your own knowledge to explain your answer.

Write your answer on a separate piece of paper.

6 Describe two tactics Harold used during the Battle of Hastings.

Write your answer on a separate piece of paper.

Norman England: Anglo-Saxon Resistance and the Norman Response

1 Who did William make Earl of Kent after his successful invasion of England?

....

2 Which part of England rebelled in 1069–1070?

....

....

3 Give two features of the Harrying of the North.

....

....

....

4 Explain how the feudal system helped William control the Saxons.

....

....

....

....

....

....

5 Does the lack of a leader explain why the Saxons could not fight against Norman control after the Battle of Hastings?

Write your answer on a separate piece of paper.

6 Give a reason why William dealt so severely with the Revolt of the Earls in 1075.

....

....

....

....

Practice Questions

Norman England: Life Under Norman Control

1 Give three examples of things that William continued with, following his coronation as king of England.

_____

_____

_____

2 Describe the Murdrum Law.

_____

_____

_____

3 What effect would the Forest Law have on the Saxons?

_____

_____

_____

_____

_____

_____

4 'The coronation of William I had very little effect on ordinary Saxons'. How far do you agree?

_____

_____

_____

_____

_____

_____

5 Below is a drawing of a medieval village. What can you learn about medieval life from this source?

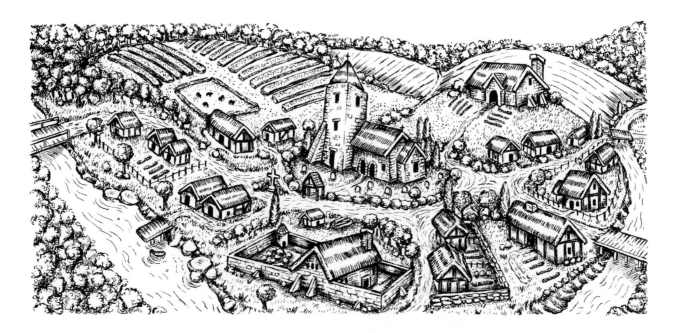

6 Give an example of a job (national or local) that William filled with Normans.

Practice Questions

Norman England: Norman Castles and the Domesday Book

1 What were the first Norman castles called?

_____

2 Give three ways in which castles were used to consolidate William's power after 1066.

_____

_____

3 Look at the image of a Norman castle. How do you know this is an example of an early Norman castle?

Write your answer on a separate piece of paper.

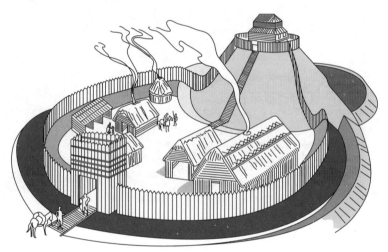

4 In what year was the Domesday survey commissioned? _____

5 Explain how the Domesday survey helped William consolidate his power over the Saxons.

Write your answer on a separate piece of paper.

6 The _Anglo-Saxon Chronicle_ states that:

> … there was no single hide … one ox nor one cow nor one pig which was there left out, and not put down in his record.

What can you infer about why William commissioned the Domesday survey from this quote?

Write your answer on a separate piece of paper.

Norman England: The Norman Church and the Death of William I

1 Give two reasons why the church was so powerful in the time of William I.

2 What was a tithe?

3 Being excommunicated in the Middle Ages was a terrible punishment. Give a reason why.

4 Explain why Lanfranc was given the role of Archbishop in 1070.

5 Describe two features of the Investiture Controversy.

Write your answer on a separate piece of paper.

6 Why was there a succession crisis after William's death in 1087?

Write your answer on a separate piece of paper.

Elizabeth I and Her Government

You must be able to:

- Explain the different features of Elizabethan government
- Outline who were the key members of Elizabeth's government
- Explain why Elizabeth I never married and what the consequences were.

England in 1558

- England was a divided country in 1558 in terms of religion with the population split between Catholics and Protestants.
- This division in religion had a significant impact on how people supported Elizabeth. Catholics saw Elizabeth as the illegitimate child of Henry VIII and Anne Boleyn. This is because many Catholics did not recognise the legitimacy of the marriage between Henry VIII and Anne Boleyn. This meant that Catholics in England believed that Elizabeth I was not the rightful Queen of England.
- Three million people lived in England and Wales, and it was a structured and hierarchical society.
- After a series of bad harvests in the mid 1550s, there was an increase in food prices and unemployment.
- England was at war with France and had lost Calais, which was its last military outpost in France. This was a blow to English prestige.
- A combination of war, rising unemployment and inflation led to Elizabeth I inheriting a country with a debt of £300,000 making England on the verge of bankruptcy.

Queen Elizabeth I

Elizabeth and Propaganda

- A significant reason for Elizabeth's popularity throughout her reign was her careful use of propaganda. She used portraits to project an image of legitimacy, wealth, success, wisdom, power and control.
- Portraits were carefully controlled and approved by Parliament. Portraits were often the only way that many people would see an image of Elizabeth as she never visited Wales or the north or south-west of England.

Key Features of Elizabeth's Government

- Elizabeth I, as Queen of England, was in control of the country and controlled the work of her government as well as having the power to command the army and navy.
- Elizabeth I was surrounded by the royal court, which was made up of nobles, officials and servants.

Houses of Parliament

- Within the royal court was the **Privy** Council, which was the chief administrative and executive political body.
- Parliament's responsibility was to pass laws and taxes. Parliament was called and dismissed at the Queen's pleasure.
- The law courts were responsible for administering law and order with a series of courts responsible for different aspects of law.
- Parliament was called thirteen times during Elizabeth's reign; as MPs' freedom to speak out against government policy grew, it increasingly became a source of opposition.

Key Ministers

- William Cecil, Lord Burghley, was Elizabeth's Secretary of State for most of her reign and was arguably her most important **minister**.
- Robert Dudley, Earl of Leicester, held a variety of government positions and had romantic designs on Elizabeth. He had a serious rivalry with Lord Burghley.
- Sir Francis Walsingham was Secretary of State with a special responsibility for foreign affairs. He built up a strong spy network that helped stop plots against Elizabeth.

Elizabeth I and the Succession Question

- As a young, inexperienced woman many people within Elizabeth's government wanted her to marry quickly and have children to establish a smooth succession after her death. This was particularly important because Elizabeth had no brothers or sisters to whom she could pass the throne.
- Elizabeth had lots of potential suitors with the most important being Robert Dudley, Earl of Leicester. This created divisions and jealousies in the royal court as well as the Privy Council.
- Elizabeth never explained why she never married. Some of the possible reasons were:
  - the potential for any husband to try to control Elizabeth and rule himself.
  - the potential to upset factions if she married someone from England.
  - the potential to upset countries if she married a foreign prince.
- Elizabeth only confirmed who she wanted to succeed her when she was on her deathbed in March 1603 – her closest relative, her cousin's son, James VI of Scotland.

> **Key Point**
>
> Elizabeth I was responsible for making sure that the country was run properly and that every part of government was doing its job.

Queen Elizabeth I being carried by her courtiers

> **Key Point**
>
> Never before had England had an unmarried monarch.

> **Quick Test**
>
> 1. When did Elizabeth I die?
> 2. Who was the Earl of Leicester?
> 3. Who was Elizabeth's Secretary of State for most of her reign?
> 4. What was the Privy Council?
> 5. How many people lived in England and Wales in 1558?

> **Key Words**
>
> Privy
> minister

 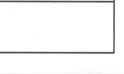

The Elizabethan Religious Settlement

You must be able to:

- Explain the main parts of the Elizabethan Religious Settlement
- Explain the reactions towards the Elizabethan Religious Settlement
- Explain the problems the Elizabethan Religious Settlement caused.

Divisions in Religion

- Elizabeth inherited a divided country in 1558. England was split over religion; the official religion switched back and forth between Catholicism and Protestantism from the 1530s onwards.
- Elizabeth was brought up a Protestant and she was supported by the House of Commons and the Privy Council.
- However, powerful elements of English society remained Catholic, notably the clergy and the House of Lords.

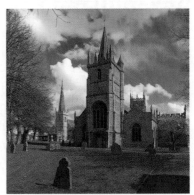

An Elizabethan Protestant church

The Creation of the Elizabethan Religious Settlement

- Elizabeth wanted to create a **moderate** Church of England acceptable to most people. In 1559, she met with Parliament to create this new moderate church.
- After four months of discussions, Elizabeth and Parliament passed two Acts – the Act of Supremacy and the Act of Uniformity – that made up the Elizabethan Religious Settlement.

> ### Key Point
>
> Elizabeth tried to find a 'middle way' between Catholics and Protestants.

Act of Supremacy

- The Act of Supremacy dealt with the nature and leadership of the Church of England.
- The Act restored the Royal Supremacy and made Elizabeth the Supreme Governor of the Church of England. This made Elizabeth Head of the Church of England without giving her the actual title. Some felt Catholics would not accept the agreement if Elizabeth had the title of Head of the Church of England.
- The Act imposed an oath on all clergy and office holders to accept Elizabeth as Supreme Governor and follow the new Prayer Book.

Act of Uniformity

- The Act of Uniformity dealt with the acts of worship in the Church of England.
- The Act introduced a new Protestant Prayer Book that had to be used in every church.

- Church services and the Bible had to be in English.
- Ornaments and decorations were allowed in church.
- The clergy were allowed to marry and had to wear **vestments**.
- **Recusants** were fined.

The Reaction Towards the Elizabethan Religious Settlement

- Elizabeth's new Archbishop of Canterbury, Matthew Parker, was a moderate Protestant and was an important figure in ensuring that the new Church of England was inclusive and was not too strict.
- As a result, most of the clergy took the oath of loyalty to the new Church with only 3% refusing to do so. However, all the Catholic bishops did resign and were replaced by Protestants.
- Recusancy fines were not strictly enforced.
- The Pope, Pius IV, did not **excommunicate** Elizabeth, which helped determine the limited Catholic reaction to the Settlement as there were no rebellions or uprisings against it.

Archbishop Matthew Parker

Problems Caused by the Elizabethan Religious Settlement

- With the mass resignation of the Catholic bishops, this left a gap of highly trained clergy as many were replaced with men who had a lack of education. This unsettled **Puritans**, the more extreme Protestants, who began to increase preaching of their vision of the church in services.
- The Elizabethan Religious Settlement was vague in terms of setting the doctrine of the new Church of England. To tackle any inconsistencies between churches, the government issued two documents – the Injunctions and the 39 Articles – which moved the doctrine closer to the Protestant views.
- After pressure from the Puritan elements of the clergy, the Advertisements were issued in 1566. These laid down fixed rules on the conduct of services and vestments and led to dissent from some in the clergy who were dismissed in the Vestments Controversy.

> **Key Point**
>
> At the beginning of her reign, Elizabeth was careful not to commit herself openly to one religion, although she was a Protestant.

> **Quick Test**
>
> 1. Name the two acts that made up the Elizabethan Religious Settlement.
> 2. In which year was the Elizabethan Religious Settlement passed?
> 3. Who opposed the Elizabethan Religious Settlement?
> 4. What measures made up the Act of Uniformity?
> 5. What was the main aim of the Elizabethan Religious Settlement?

> **Key Words**
>
> moderate
> vestments
> recusant
> excommunicate
> Puritan

Elizabeth I and Spain, 1558–1587

You must be able to:

- Explain the nature of England's relationship with Spain
- Explain why England went to war with Spain in 1585
- Describe the key events between England and Spain.

Links Between England and Spain in 1558

- The King of Spain, Philip II, was married to Elizabeth's sister and **predecessor**, Mary.
- Philip II of Spain wanted to marry Elizabeth when Mary died, but Elizabeth rejected his advances.
- England had an important trading relationship with Spain as Spain owned Antwerp – the home of the most important wool market. England's economy relied on access to Antwerp, as England produced some of the finest wool in Europe.

> **Key Point**
>
> Philip II of Spain was Elizabeth's brother-in-law.

Friendship Between Spain and England in the 1560s

- Philip II of Spain was disappointed when Elizabeth rejected his marriage proposal and when Elizabeth established a new Protestant Church. However, he still wanted to remain on good terms with England.
- Philip knew that if Elizabeth was overthrown and replaced by her heir Mary, Queen of Scots, England would become allies with France because of Mary's strong links with the French royal family. Spain and France were rivals and enemies and Spain did not want England to be allied with France.
- The Netherlands was the most valuable part of Philip II's **empire**. The easiest route from Spain to the Netherlands was through the English Channel. Remaining on good terms with Elizabeth meant that Philip II was able to continue to use the route without fear of attack from English ships.
- For Elizabeth, good terms with Spain in the early years of her reign was something she wanted because she could not afford an expensive war and she felt she had to deal with Mary, Queen Of Scots, who was a greater threat to her crown.

Phillip II of Spain

> **Key Point**
>
> The 1560s saw a solid friendship between England and Spain.

Why did War Break Out Between England and Spain in 1585?

- England's religious differences with Spain became more important and threatening. This was especially true after 1570, when the Pope excommunicated Elizabeth and ordered Catholics to overthrow her.

- In 1562 **civil war** broke out between Catholics and Protestants in France. This led to France no longer being a threat to Spain or England. Spain was no longer worried about an Anglo-French **alliance**.
- Philip II had to face a Protestant revolt in the Netherlands in 1572. He was angered with Elizabeth's secret support of the Dutch rebels by supplying them with money and weapons. Elizabeth also sheltered Dutch exiles and allowed Dutch ships to use English ports.
- Elizabeth encouraged English sailors, like Hawkins and Drake, to attack the Spanish empire in the New World. These attacks, especially by Drake, were very successful and brought Elizabeth riches. These attacks enraged Philip.
- Plots in the 1570s and 1580s, such as the Ridolfi Plot, had Spanish support. This led to the Spanish ambassador being expelled from the English court.
- In 1584 the Spanish were on the verge of victory in the Netherlands. This worried Elizabeth because Spain would then be free to threaten England. In 1585 Elizabeth signed the Treaty of Nonsuch, which agreed to send an army to the Netherlands to help the rebels to face Spain.
- By agreeing to the Treaty of Nonsuch, England and Spain were now at war.

Statue of Sir Francis Drake

Key Point

The period 1568–72 is often called the 'years of crisis' by historians who see this as a period of decline in the relationship between England and Spain.

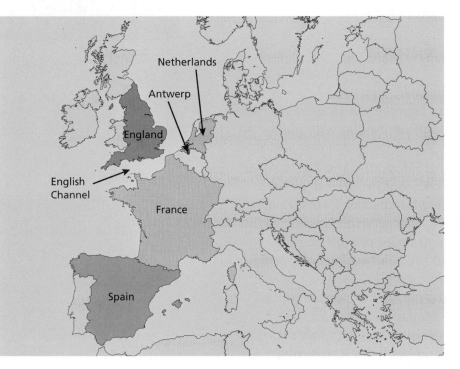

Quick Test

1. What family link connected Elizabeth and Philip II of Spain?
2. What did the Treaty of Nonsuch agree to?
3. When did England and Spain go to war?
4. Where was the most important cloth market in Europe?
5. When was Elizabeth excommunicated?

Key Words

predecessor
empire
civil war
alliance

Elizabeth I and Mary, Queen of Scots

You must be able to:

- Describe the links between Elizabeth I and Mary, Queen of Scots
- Explain the threat Mary, Queen of Scots posed to Elizabeth I
- Explain why Elizabeth I decided to have Mary, Queen of Scots executed.

The Link Between Elizabeth I and Mary, Queen of Scots

- Elizabeth I did not marry. This meant that her closest relative was her cousin Mary, Queen of Scots. Therefore Mary, Queen of Scots was the **heir** to the English throne.
- This link posed significant problems for Elizabeth I in a number of ways:
    - Mary, Queen of Scots was a Catholic. She declared that she was the rightful Queen of England as Elizabeth I was really a **bastard** because her parents' marriage was invalid.
    - Mary, Queen of Scots was a potential figurehead for any Catholic plot and **rebellion** against Elizabeth.

Mary, Queen of Scots Comes to England

- In 1565, Mary married Henry, Lord Darnley. Darnley was English and a Catholic sympathiser although unpopular with many important Scottish nobles.
- The marriage quickly collapsed in 1566 during the Rizzio Affair where Mary's secretary, David Rizzio, was murdered and a heavily pregnant Mary was roughly handled by Darnley's allies.
- Darnley was murdered in 1567 and Mary herself was suspected in the plot but her involvement was never proved.
- Three months later, Mary married the chief suspect of Darnley's murder – James Hepburn, Earl of Bothwell.
- Mary's marriage to Bothwell had a number of consequences:
    - Bothwell was hated by many Scottish nobles and the marriage led to a Protestant uprising against Mary's rule.
    - Mary was forced to **abdicate** and her baby son, James, became King.
    - Mary was imprisoned in Loch Leven Castle, but a year later in 1568 she escaped captivity and fled to England.

Mary, Queen of Scots

> **Key Point**
>
> Mary, Queen of Scots was the closest living relative of Elizabeth and as such was the rightful heir to the English throne.

> **Key Point**
>
> Mary, Queen of Scots' son, James, became the King of England after Elizabeth I died in 1603.

Mary, Queen of Scots' Imprisonment in England

- Although Elizabeth had sympathy for Mary as she was the legitimate ruler of Scotland and should be assisted to regain her position, Elizabeth's councillors did not want to assist Mary.
- Mary was placed under house arrest and moved from place to place in the centre of England to make it difficult for supporters to land in England by sea and march to free her. She was kept short of supplies such as bedding and clothes.
- This lasted nineteen years due to a combination of Catholic threats and Elizabeth's indecision on what to do.
- Between 1568 and 1587, there were a number of Catholic plots to liberate Mary and overthrow Elizabeth:
  - the Northern Rebellion of 1569 – an attempt by Catholic nobles from northern England to overthrow Elizabeth
  - the Ridolfi Plot of 1571 – hatched and planned by Roberto Ridolfi
  - the Throckmorton Plot of 1583 – revealed when Sir Francis Throckmorton was interrogated
  - the Babington Plot of 1586 – led by chief conspirator Sir Anthony Babington.

Loch Leven Castle, where Queen Mary was imprisoned

Execution of Mary, Queen of Scots

- In 1586, Francis Walsingham uncovered a plot planned by Anthony Babington, a young Catholic gentleman, that aimed to rescue Mary and murder Elizabeth.
- The evidence of this plot included a letter by Mary in which she approved of the plot. This was presented to Elizabeth by Walsingham and she agreed to put Mary on trial for treason.
- The trial took place in October 1586 and Mary was found guilty.
- After much indecision, Elizabeth signed the death warrant in February 1587, and Mary was executed at Fotheringhay Castle.
- The consequences of Mary's execution were many:
  - Elizabeth was furious, claiming she never intended the death warrant to be used. She sent a formal apology to King James VI of Scotland for the death of his mother.
  - King Philip II of Spain was furious and continued his plan to invade England with his armada.
  - There were strong protests in France but this led to nothing serious.

King James I of England / King James VI of Scotland

Quick Test

1. When did Mary escape to England?
2. Where was Mary executed?
3. What was the relationship between Elizabeth and Mary?
4. Who was Mary's second husband?
5. Who was Mary's secretary, and how did he die?

Key Words

heir
bastard
rebellion
abdicate

The Attack of the Spanish Armada, 1588

You must be able to:

- Explain why Philip II of Spain launched an attack on England
- Compare the Spanish and English forces
- Explain why the Spanish Armada failed to invade England.

Causes of the Attack of the Spanish Armada

- Long-term friction between Philip II and Elizabeth existed because Elizabeth rejected Philip II's proposal of marriage in the late 1550s.
- The differences in religion between the Catholic Philip II and the Protestant Elizabeth I became increasingly difficult.
- English assistance for the Dutch rebels against the Spanish and English privateers' attack on Spanish treasure ships were a source of fury for Philip II.
- The execution of the Catholic Mary, Queen of Scots enraged Philip II.

Philip II's Plan of Attack on England

- The Spanish **Armada** would set sail from Cadiz harbour around the Iberian Peninsula, through the English Channel and land in the Netherlands.
- The Armada would pick up a Spanish force of 30,000 Spanish troops in the Netherlands, sail across to England and land in Kent.
- The Spanish forces would march on London with 25,000 English Catholics. Once London was defeated, Elizabeth would be overthrown and replaced with a Catholic monarch.

Spanish Armada Delayed

- Philip II wanted to launch the attack in 1587 but was delayed by a number of factors:
  - Drake launched a surprise attack on Cadiz harbour, destroying much of the Spanish Armada, in 1587.
  - The Spanish **Admiral**, the Marquis de Santa Cruz, died. He was replaced with the Duke of Medina Sidonia, who did not want the job.
  - The Spanish Armada set sail in April 1588 only to be blown off course by a series of bad storms.

Comparison of the Spanish and English Forces

- The Spanish Armada totalled around 130 ships compared with 200 English ships – although much of the latter were merchant ships.

Replica of Spanish galleon

Key Point

The causes of the attempted invasion of the Spanish Armada were rooted back to the beginning of the reign of Elizabeth I.

Cannon on a Spanish galleon

- Spanish **galleons** were much larger, designed to carry treasure, while the English galleons were much smaller but very fast.
- The Spanish Admiral, the Duke of Medina Sidonia, was completely inexperienced at fighting at sea, while the English Vice Admirals, Drake and Hawkins, had extensive experience in fighting at sea.
- The Spanish used 30,000 trained men compared with the English using 14,000 sailors supported by 20,000 soldiers – many were untrained.

The Course of the Attack of the Spanish Armada

- The Spanish Armada was first spotted off the English coast on 29 July 1588. They were sailing in a crescent shape formation, which had at that point never been broken.
- This triggered a ten-day naval battle across the English Channel. Neither side gained an advantage as the Spanish never broke formation and landed at Calais while the English fended off the Spanish attack.
- On 7 August, the English launched unmanned **fireships** towards the docked Spanish ships. This caused panic and the Spanish ships fled, breaking their formation.
- The English attacked the Spanish who were now out of formation at the Battle of Gravelines. This was decisive as many Spanish ships were damaged – only one was sunk. The Spanish Armada was forced to flee up the North Sea and around the British Isles.
- Journeying around the British Isles was traumatic as the Spanish Armada had run out of food and water and did not know the area. They crashed on rocks and nearly half the ships sank and thousands of Spanish sailors were killed.

Reasons for the Failure of the Spanish Armada

- The English military leaders had more naval experience.
- The Spanish plan wasn't clear about where to land in the Netherlands and landed 30 miles away from the Spanish soldiers.
- The Spanish Armada was unlucky in running into storms and bad weather in the North Sea.
- The English ships were more suited to fighting, as they were smaller and quicker with lighter cannons compared with the Spanish ships.

Old wooden globe

Key Point

Even after the failure of the Spanish Armada, England was still at war with Spain.

Key Point

The reasons for the failure of the Spanish Armada were a mixture of bad luck and bad planning.

Quick Test

1. Which Spanish port did Drake attack in 1587?
2. Who led the Spanish Armada?
3. When did the Spanish Armada attack England?
4. Where did the fireships attack the Spanish Armada?
5. How many ships were in the Spanish Armada?

Key Words

Armada
Admiral
galleon
fireship

Threats Posed to Elizabeth I, 1558–1601

You must be able to:

- Assess the extent of the threat posed by each rebellion
- Explain the causes and consequences of each rebellion
- Know the narrative behind each rebellion.

The Northern Rebellion – 1568

- The Northern Rebellion was led by the Earls of Northumberland and Westmoreland, who were leading Catholic nobles in the north of England.
- The aim of the **rebellion** was to rescue Mary, Queen of Scots from captivity, overthrow Elizabeth I, replace Elizabeth with Mary as Queen of England and return England to Catholicism as the official religion.
- Although the rebels gathered 6000 soldiers, the rebellion was easily crushed by an army sent to the north by Elizabeth.
- The main reasons for the failure of the Northern Rebellion were:
  - the lack of support from Mary, Queen of Scots, who thought the rebellion was doomed from the start, as well as from Spain and the Papacy.
  - strategic errors from the rebels, such as having no plan to spring Mary from imprisonment.

Mary, Queen of Scots

> **Key Point**
>
> Most rebellions were inspired by religion.

The Ridolfi Plot – 1571

- Roberto Ridolfi was a Florentine nobleman and banker who had business connections in England. It appears that he headed a plot in 1571 that aimed to free Mary, Queen of Scots, marry her to the Duke of Norfolk, overthrow Elizabeth and replace her with Mary.
- Supported by Philip II of Spain, the plot intended for the Duke of Alba to lead 6000 Spanish troops to England from the Netherlands. However, Spain backed down and the troops did not materialise.
- The plot was uncovered by the Privy Council and presented to Elizabeth, pressuring her to execute Mary, which Elizabeth refused to do.

The Throckmorton Plot – 1583

- The Throckmorton Plot aimed for French Catholic forces, backed with Spanish and Papal money, to invade England, liberate Mary and start a Catholic uprising.
- The plot was revealed when Francis Throckmorton, who was the intermediary between Mary, Queen of Scots and de Mendoza, the Spanish Ambassador, was arrested and interrogated.

> **Key Point**
>
> Mary, Queen of Scots was a legal monarch and this deterred Elizabeth from taking any action against her for a significant period of time.

- The plot showed the Privy Council that an alliance between France and Spain would be directed against Protestant England and they wanted a strong response.

The Babington Plot – 1586

- A Catholic gentleman, Anthony Babington, planned to rescue Mary, Queen of Scots, murder Elizabeth I and replace her with Mary.
- Secret letters between the plotters and Mary, hidden in beer barrels, were intercepted by Francis Walsingham, who presented them as evidence to Elizabeth.
- Babington was arrested and confessed, implicating Mary, who was put on trial and subsequently executed.

The Earl of Essex Rebellion – 1601

- The Earl of Essex was becoming increasingly disgruntled with how he thought he was being treated by Elizabeth I.
- In debt and with his major business interest – a monopoly on sweet wines – taken away from him, he decided to lead a rebellion against Elizabeth with 300 rebels in London.
- After arresting members of the Privy Council who had been sent to arrest him, Essex and his supporters marched on the centre of London. However, the rebellion quickly crumbled and after 12 hours Essex was arrested and soon executed for **treason**.

The Rise of the Puritans

- Puritans were strict Protestants who wanted to 'purify' the church of Catholic influences. They were called during Elizabeth's reign 'the hotter sort of Protestants'.
- Puritans campaigned for more Protestant changes throughout Elizabeth's reign as Puritan numbers were growing and the movement was becoming more popular.
- Their main form of opposition was as an organised and vocal group in Parliament, tackling Elizabeth on **vestments** and using the Prayer Book.
- Puritans never threatened to rise up and overthrow Elizabeth or invite foreign invaders to support them.

Earl of Essex

Key Words

rebellion
treason
vestments

Elizabethan Society

You must be able to:

- Explain why poverty increased and what the government tried to do about it
- Explain the nature of family life in the Elizabethan era
- Explain why the gentry class began to rise during Elizabeth I's reign
- Explain why there were growing educational opportunities.

Poverty during the Reign of Elizabeth I

- The population of England and Wales rose by over a million during the reign of Elizabeth I. There was not enough food, nor jobs to go around, so more people became poor.
- The reign of Elizabeth I was one of rising **inflation**, which meant prices went up. Wages did not keep up, which meant more people struggled to survive.
- There were a number of bad harvests in the mid sixteenth century that meant less food was produced. Food prices rose and more people found it difficult to afford to eat.
- Changes in farming, from growing crops to keeping sheep, led to rising unemployment in farming – a key industry in Elizabethan England.
- The European cloth trade collapsed, meaning many workers lost their jobs.

Government Action Against Poverty

- Growing poverty, particularly the increased number of **vagabonds** roaming the streets, became a major concern.
- Many felt that poverty brought increased disease and crime.
- Although Parliament and the Privy Council discussed the impact of poverty, it was never a high priority for Elizabeth compared with religion and foreign policy. Therefore the problem of growing poverty was passed on to local government to deal with.
- Local governments had an inconsistent approach to dealing with poverty.
- Impressed with the work in Ipswich, Norwich and London and with food prices continuing to rise, Parliament passed laws in 1572 and 1576 to provide some poor relief and to punish vagabonds.
- Increased poor relief was passed with the Elizabethan Poor Law of 1601, which lasted for over 200 years.

Elizabethan Family Life

- Elizabethan family life had a traditional structure, with an emphasis on married life, with three being the average number of children within a family. Infant mortality was very high with 134 children out of every 1000 dying before reaching adulthood.

Key Point

Poverty was a growing problem in Elizabethan England, and one that was never successfully tackled.

A 16th century watermill

- Illegitimacy rates were very low with fewer than 3% of children being born outside wedlock.
- The average age of a person getting married was 26 years old.
- Strong family bonds often existed within the wider family with grandparents often living with their children and family. This was mainly because there was no state help for the elderly.

Growth of the Gentry and Merchant Classes

- The sale of land made available from the Dissolution of the Monasteries in the 1530s and 40s created a new generation of landowners, many being **merchants** or from the **gentry** class.
- This land was rented out to farmers and enclosed, making profits for the gentry and merchants. Rising food prices helped these new landowners make lots of money.
- The gentry and merchants invested in overseas voyages and new trading companies that became very successful.
- New farming techniques, such as drainage and fertilisation, helped landowners increase crop yields and profits.
- The opportunity to hold government posts increased, both at a local and national level.

The Merchant Adventurers Hall, York – an Elizabethan building

Education

- The combined influence of the Renaissance, the Protestant Reformation and the printing press led to reading and writing being desirable skills. This led to a growing demand for education.
- What type of education was available depended upon status. The poor went to petty schools, which taught basic skills in English and Maths. The rich went to grammar schools, which taught skills such as reading Latin, and prepared students to go to university – a growing element of the education system.
- Most of the rich were educated at home by tutors and then sent their children to university. The newer universities that developed in the Elizabethan era often offered a wider curriculum and included such subjects as medicine.

> **Key Point**
>
> The rise of the gentry was an important factor in future political developments under the Stuarts.

Persecution of Witches

- Most people were frightened of women that they believed to be witches. They believed witches could use evil magic.
- Witches were blamed for causing bad harvests, injuries and death.
- More alleged witches than Catholics were executed during Elizabeth's reign.

> **Key Point**
>
> Educational opportunities widened during the Elizabethan era.

> **Quick Test**
>
> 1. Which subjects did rich children study?
> 2. Who did petty schools aim to educate?
> 3. What was the average age of someone getting married?
> 4. Why did food prices rise?

> **Key Words**
>
> inflation
> vagabond
> merchants
> gentry

Elizabethan Culture

You must be able to:

- Explain the impact of the Elizabethan theatre
- Describe the lifestyles of the rich and poor.

Key Features of the Elizabethan Theatre

- Theatres were built during the Elizabethan period to try to control wandering groups of actors, who were seen as a threat to law and order.
- The design of Elizabethan theatres was based on 'inn yards' where people sat under cover to watch plays, and Roman theatres that were popular with people who had a **Renaissance** education.
- The theatre had a single stage that was surrounded by the groundlings, which was a standing area and was the cheapest to enter. This was all surrounded by the galleries, which were covered, seated areas and cost extra to enter.

Elizabethan theatre

Reasons for the Increase of Theatres in Elizabethan England

- Many groups of actors were sponsored by influential nobles, such as the Earl of Leicester.
- Elizabeth I enjoyed plays and invited companies to perform at Court.
- Performances and plays in inn yards became very popular.
- In 1576, James Burbage built the first theatre in Britain since the Romans and this was very popular, so many copied his idea.
- The theatre was a cheap form of entertainment and there were other attractions on offer, such as food and a place to be seen and make business contacts.
- There was an increase in high quality playwrights, such as William Shakespeare, who produced very popular plays.

> **Key Point**
>
> The theatre was the most popular entertainment of the Elizabethan era, where actors and playwrights became celebrities.

Opposition to the Theatres

- Despite the growing popularity of theatres, there was significant opposition to them. The key reasons were:
  - theatres attracted large crowds that could be a source of social disorder. This was a particular problem because theatres were built outside the city walls and outside the control of the city authorities.

- Puritans thought theatres were the work of the Devil and that they produced vulgar plays which encouraged sinful behaviour.

Entertainment for the Rich

- The most popular form of art for the rich was the miniature. The rich collected miniatures as a sign of wealth as well as looking fashionable.
- Miniatures were extremely beautiful works of art showing a portrait of an important person.
- The most popular form of music for the rich was religious music, although there was a growth in secular music, particularly featuring male voice choirs.
- Popular literature at the time often included a political commentary on contemporary events and had a humanist or classical style.
- There was a boom in architecture as courtiers built bigger and better homes for Elizabeth to visit. The key features of such homes were that they were built with symmetry and were grand in size.
- Looking fashionable was an important part of Elizabethan society. Key fashions of the Elizabethan era for men were wearing clothes that would show off their legs, such as hose, and to emphasise the torso with flashed doublets. For women, rich jewellery, often in the form of miniatures, was important and worn with long flowing robes made out of silk.

Entertainment for the Poor

- The majority of the population was poor and wanted pastimes to escape the difficulties of daily life. The poor lived in cramped, dirty conditions where disease was rife and in homes that were badly made and often unstable with few rooms.
- Alehouses and drinking beer were very popular and often the best way to get a meal if you were poor. At alehouses you could buy tobacco, gamble at cards, dice or cock fighting and watch a play in the yard.
- Blood sports, such as bear baiting and cock fighting, were popular and often involved gambling as the poor were encouraged by the prospect of making quick and easy money.
- There was a growth in printing cheap books, giving more access to works of literature for the poor.

> ### Quick Test
> 1. What was a blood sport?
> 2. What could you buy at an alehouse?
> 3. What was a miniature?
> 4. Where were theatres usually built?
> 5. Who built the first Elizabethan theatre?

> **Key Point**
>
> Pastimes for the poor often happened outside their houses while for the rich they often happened at home.

Elizabethan literature

Elizabethan man smoking a long-stemmed pipe

16th century fashion

> **Key Word**
>
> Renaissance

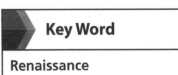

Elizabeth I and the Wider World

You must be able to:

- Explain why there was a growing trend to explore the New World
- Give examples of English explorations of the wider world
- Explain the consequences of the Elizabethan voyages.

Exploration of the Wider World During Elizabeth I's Rule

- The cloth trade, England's principal trade, collapsed in Europe during the 1550s. English merchants had to look for alternative markets in which to sell their goods. This led to greater interest in trading overseas.
- Richard Hakluyt's book – *The Principal Navigations, Voyages and Discoveries of the English Nation* – encouraged English sailors to make exploration voyages. This book was extremely influential.
- Wider developments also encouraged exploration, such as:
  - inventions to assist travel, such as the compass
  - increasing willingness of monarchs and merchants to **sponsor** voyages
  - the development of faster, lighter ships, such as caravels.

A Caravel

Trade and the Wider World

- Under Elizabeth I, trade links within Europe increased.
  - The Eastland Company was established in 1579 to import goods from the Baltic.
  - More luxury goods, such as silks and spices, were imported from the Mediterranean region.
  - The East India Company was established in 1583, opening a trade route to India.
- Trade to the New World required a licence from Spain that was rarely granted to English merchants. This led to English privateers attacking Spanish trade routes, which was quietly encouraged by Elizabeth I.

Key Elizabethan Explorers

- John Hawkins traded in African slaves who he sold in America, returning to England with gold, silver and animal skins.
- After a brutal assault from the Spanish at San Juan de Ulua, he retired from seafaring and became an adviser to the navy.
- Walter Raleigh obtained a royal **patent** to establish a **colony** in America in 1584.

Sir Walter Raleigh

- Raleigh established a colony that he called Virginia, named after Elizabeth I – 'the Virgin Queen'. The area was believed to contain an inexhaustible supply of wine, oil, sugar and flax.
- The colony did not prosper mainly because of a divided crew, bad weather and a poor choice about where to land in North America. Although the Virginia voyages are credited with introducing tobacco to England.

Sir Francis Drake's World Voyage, 1577–80

- Drake's world voyage, financed by the royal court, was motivated by attacking Spanish interests in the New World and was kept secret until it set off.
- Between December 1577 and April 1578, Drake's fleet headed for the west coast of Africa and crossed the Atlantic Ocean.
- After unsuccessfully trading in Brazil, Drake's fleet headed for the Pacific Ocean in September 1578. After hitting terrible storms, Drake's ship, *The Golden Hind*, was the sole survivor of the fleet and headed north up the west coast of South America.
- Drake attacked a series of Spanish settlements, capturing a significant amount of gold, silver and luxury goods.
- In April 1579, Drake decided to head home by going across the Pacific and around Asia and Africa, avoiding attacks from the Spanish in the New World.
- Drake reached England to a hero's welcome in September 1580.

The Main Achievements of the Elizabethan Voyages

- The main achievements of the Elizabethan voyages were:
  - Wealth – investors, such as merchants and the royal court, became very wealthy.
  - Overseas trade – new trade routes opened up during the reign of Elizabeth I and were managed by successful companies, such as The East India Company.
  - Power – England became a great sea power in the world.
  - The navy – England developed a very strong navy, which used cutting-edge technology.

Replica of *The Golden Hind*, captained by Sir Francis Drake

> **Key Point**
>
> Drake's world voyage was a significant cause of war with Spain in the 1580s.

> **Key Point**
>
> Elizabethan voyages brought great glory to England and helped to increase its status.

Quick Test

1. Who wrote *The Principal Navigations, Voyages and Discoveries of the English Nation*?
2. In which year did Drake return from his world voyage?
3. Who financed the Virginia missions?
4. What was the name of the ship in which Drake travelled the world?
5. Where did the Eastland Company import goods from?

> **Key Words**
>
> sponsor
> patent
> colony

Review Questions

Norman England: Anglo-Saxon Society on the Eve of Conquest

1 Describe the role of the Witan in Anglo-Saxon England.

....

....

....

....

....

2 Which three groups of people created the Anglo-Saxon peoples?

....

3 What was the role of an earldom in Anglo-Saxon England?

Write your answer on a separate piece of paper.

4 Explain the consequences of the Anglo-Saxon kings' conversion to Christianity on England.
Write your answer on a separate piece of paper.

5 John Blair states:

> ... there was more to early Anglo-Saxon society than warfare, savage loyalties and ostentatious splendour...

How far do you agree with this interpretation?

Write your answer on a separate piece of paper.

6 Was the land as important to people by the end of the Anglo-Saxon period as it had been at the beginning? Use the image and your own knowledge to make a judgement.

Write your answer on a separate piece of paper.

Norman England: The Succession Crisis of 1066

1 In what year did Edward the Confessor become king of England? ....

2 Why did Duke William of Normandy think that Harold Godwinson would support his claim to the throne once King Edward died?

....

....

....

....

....

3 In what year did Harold make his oath to William? ....

4 Explain why the House of Godwin was so powerful by 1066.

Write your answer on a separate piece of paper.

5 The most significant reason to explain why there was a succession crisis in 1066 was that Edward had not fathered any children during his life.

How far do you agree? Explain your answer.

Write your answer on a separate piece of paper.

6 Why did Edward promise the throne to William?

....

....

....

....

....

Review Questions

Norman England: The Rival Claimants to the Throne in 1066

1 What was the family connection between Edward and Harold Godwinson?

....

2 Why did William believe he was the rightful successor to the English throne?

Write your answer on a separate piece of paper.

3 The following image from the Bayeux Tapestry depicts Harold being crowned king. What can we learn about this event from the source?

Write your answer on a separate piece of paper.

4 Give two reasons why it was important for Harold's claim to the throne that the Witan supported him.

Write your answer on a separate piece of paper.

5 Harald Hardrada's claim to the English throne was significantly improved thanks to Tostig's support. How for do you agree? Explain your answer.

Write your answer on a separate piece of paper.

6 Where did Harold's official coronation ceremony take place?

....

Norman England: The Battles of Fulford and Stamford Bridge

1 Who led the Viking forces during the Battle of Fulford?

....

2 Describe the features of the Battle of Fulford.

Write your answer on a separate piece of paper.

3 What were the consequences of defeat for the Saxons at the Battle of Fulford?

....

....

....

....

....

....

....

4 Describe the features of the Battle of Stamford Bridge.

Write your answer on a separate piece of paper.

5 Harold Godwinson was lucky to gain victory at Stamford Bridge.

How far do you agree? Explain your answer.

Write your answer on a separate piece of paper.

6 How was Hardrada killed in the Battle of Stamford Bridge?

....

Review Questions

Norman England: The Battle of Hastings

1. On what date did the Battle of Hastings take place? ....

2. Describe the types of soldiers Harold had in his army before the battle.

....

....

....

....

3. Below is an image from the Bayeux Tapestry. It shows William preparing for the invasion of England. What makes this source convincing?

   Write your answer on a separate piece of paper.

4. Describe the events that occurred during the Battle of Hastings.

   Write your answer on a separate piece of paper.

5. Harold was unlucky to lose the Battle of Hastings. How far do you agree with this statement?

   Write your answer on a separate piece of paper.

6. What date was William crowned King of England?

....

Norman England: Anglo-Saxon Resistance and the Norman Response

1 Why do you think the Saxons would not accept William as their king after his victory at Hastings?

....

....

2 Why did William reorganise the Saxon earldoms?

Write your answer on a separate piece of paper.

3 Give two features of the Revolt of the Earls in 1075.

....

....

....

....

4 What was the social structure in England as a result of the feudal system?

....

....

....

5 William's greatest challenge to his reign was the rebellions in the north. How far do you agree?

Write your answer on a separate piece of paper.

6 Study the below source, written by Durham Priory monk Simeon of Durham shortly after the Harrying of the North.

> It was horrific to behold human corpses decaying in the houses, the streets and the roads, swarming with worms. For no-one was left to bury them in the earth, all being cut off either by the sword or by famine ... There was no village inhabited between York and Durham – they became lurking places to wild beasts and robbers.

What makes this source convincing?

Write your answer on a separate piece of paper.

Review Questions

Norman England: Life Under Norman Control

1 Describe two features of the Forest Law.

2 Why did William introduce the Murdrum Law?

3 Below is a drawing of a medieval town. Is this a realistic portrait of medieval life?

Write your answer on a separate piece of paper.

4 William's reign changed very little in England. How far do you agree? Explain your answer.

Write your answer on a separate piece of paper.

5 What did William replace the Witan with?

6 Explain the role of the Chancellor.

Norman England: Norman Castles and the Domesday Book

1 How did William use castles to help him prepare for the Battle of Hastings?

Write your answer on a separate piece of paper.

2 Why did barons use castles?

3 Describe two features of early Norman castles.

4 'Building castles was the most important factor in ensuring William controlled the English'.

How far do you agree with this statement? Explain your answer.

Write your answer on a separate piece of paper.

5 Explain why William commissioned the Domesday Book.

6 Study the below source, taken from the *Anglo-Saxon Chronicle*.

> After this, the King had much thought and very deep discussion with his council about this country – how it was occupied or with what sort of people. Then he sent his men all over England into every shire and had them find out how many hundred hides there were in the shire, or what land and cattle the King himself had in the country, or what dues he ought to have in twelve months from the shire.

How was the information collected for inclusion in the Domesday Book? Use the source and your own knowledge to explain your answer.

Write your answer on a separate piece of paper.

Review Questions

Norman England: The Norman Church and the Death of William I

1 Describe a feature of the Cluniac Reforms.

....

....

2 Why did people follow the teachings of the church in medieval society?

....

....

....

....

....

3 'Bishop Odo was hungry for power during William's reign and after he died.'

Give an example to support this statement.

....

....

....

....

....

4 In what year did the Pope state that monarchs could not invest new bishops? ....

5 How did William divide his inheritance between his sons before he died?

....

....

....

6 How far do you agree that William was right to move away from the tradition of the first-born son inheriting everything?

Write your answer on a separate piece of paper.

Elizabethan England: Elizabeth I and Her Government

1 What problems did Elizabeth I face when she became Queen in 1558?

2 How did Elizabeth I use propaganda to show she was a legitimate Queen of England?

3 Why was the succession a problem for Elizabeth I and her ministers?

4 Why was Lord Burghley a significant figure in Elizabeth's government?

5 How important was Parliament in the structure of the Elizabethan government?

Write your answer on a separate piece of paper.

6 'England was a backwater in Europe in 1558.'

How far do you agree with this statement?

Write your answer on a separate piece of paper.

Practice Questions

Elizabethan England: The Elizabethan Religious Settlement

1 How was England divided by religion in 1558?

_____

_____

_____

2 What did the Elizabethan Religious Settlement agree to?

_____

_____

_____

3 What was the reaction towards the Elizabethan Religious Settlement?

_____

_____

_____

4 What problems did the Elizabethan Religious Settlement create?

_____

_____

_____

5 What were the aims of the Elizabethan Religious Settlement?

_____

_____

_____

6 How far was the Elizabethan Religious Settlement a compromise?

Write your answer on a separate piece of paper.

Elizabethan England: Elizabeth I and Spain, 1558–1587

1   Why did Elizabeth and Spain enjoy good relations in the 1560s?

....

....

....

....

2   Why was the period 1568 to 1572 the 'years of crisis' between England and Spain?

....

....

....

....

3   What impact did the Netherlands have on the relationship between England and Spain?

....

....

....

....

4   What role did Sir Francis Drake play in the relationship between England and Spain?

....

....

....

5   Why did England and Spain go to war in 1585?

Write your answer on a separate piece of paper.

6   What links did Elizabeth have with Philip II of Spain before she became Queen?

....

....

....

....

Practice Questions

Elizabethan England: Elizabeth I and Mary, Queen of Scots

1 Explain the reasons why Mary was forced to abdicate as Queen of Scotland.

2 Why did Mary's presence in England after 1568 pose a problem for Elizabeth?

3 Explain the impact of Mary's execution.

Write your answer on a separate piece of paper.

4 Describe how Mary, Queen of Scots was treated in England between 1568 and 1586.

5 Why was Mary's marriage to Bothwell a disaster?

6 Explain why Mary, Queen of Scots was executed in 1587.

Elizabethan England: The Attack of the Spanish Armada, 1588

1 Why did Philip II launch his attack on England with his Armada?

2 What were the key features of the Spanish Armada?

3 Why was Spain's plan to attack England flawed?

4 What happened to the Spanish Armada when it reached the North Sea?

5 Why did Philip II fail to attack England in 1587?

Write your answer on a separate piece of paper.

6 Which was the most important turning point in the defeat of the Spanish Armada – the Battle of Gravelines or the Battle across the English Channel?

Explain your answer.

Write your answer on a separate piece of paper.

Practice Questions

Elizabethan England: Threats Posed to Elizabeth I, 1558–1601

1 Why did the Northern Rebellion fail?

2 Why did the Earl of Essex rebel in 1601?

3 How far were the Puritans a threat to Elizabeth?

4 Outline the role played by Sir Francis Walsingham in defending England against the plots against Elizabeth I.

5 What were the consequences of the Babington Plot?

6 'Out of all the plots against Elizabeth I, The Northern Rebellion was the greatest threat.' How far do you agree with this view? Explain your answer.

Write your answer on a separate piece of paper.

Elizabethan England: Elizabethan Society

1. What were the key causes of poverty in Elizabethan society?

....

....

2. What actions did the Elizabethan government take against poverty?

....

....

....

3. Why did the gentry and merchant classes thrive during the Elizabethan period?

....

....

....

4. What were the key features of Elizabethan family life?

....

....

....

5. What were the key developments in Elizabethan education?

....

....

....

....

6. 'The collapse of the European cloth market in the 1550s was the most important reason for growing poverty in Elizabethan England.'

   How far do you agree? Explain your answer.

   Write your answer on a separate piece of paper.

Practice Questions

Elizabethan England: Elizabethan Culture

1 Why were theatres so popular in Elizabethan England?

2 To what extent was there opposition towards the theatre?

3 What entertainment did the rich enjoy in Elizabethan England?

4 How similar were pastimes for the rich and for the poor?

Write your answer on a separate piece of paper.

5 To what extent did entertainment for the poor change during the Elizabethan period?

6 What were the key features of the Elizabethan theatre?

Elizabethan England: Elizabeth I and the Wider World

1 Why was there greater interest in exploring during the Elizabethan era?

_____

_____

_____

2 Why did trade links develop under Elizabeth?

_____

_____

_____

3 What was the impact of Drake's world voyage?

_____

_____

_____

4 Why did Raleigh's Virginia project fail?

_____

_____

5 What role did John Hawkins play in exploration?

_____

_____

_____

6 What was the most important achievement of the Elizabethan voyages?

Write your answer on a separate piece of paper.

Medieval Medicine (Middle Ages) 1

You must be able to:

- Explain beliefs about the cause of disease and illness in the Middle Ages
- Explain the preventions and treatments used in the Middle Ages
- Analyse the main factors that led to regression in understanding about health in the Middle Ages.

Ideas About Cause of Disease

- During the Greek period, **Hippocrates** devised the **Theory of the Four Humours** – that the body was made up of four main elements – and in order to remain healthy these four humours should stay balanced.
- The four humours consisted of: black bile, blood (red bile), yellow bile and phlegm.
- During the Roman period, **Galen** developed Hippocrates' ideas, so alongside advocating the four humours, Galen devised the **Theory of Opposites**.
- The theory stated, for example, that if a person felt cold, they should eat something hot to improve their health.
- It is widely argued that the influence of the church in the Middle Ages caused **regression** in medicine.
- Because the Christian church grew in this period, the main belief was that illness was caused by God and indeed it was widely believed that if you had sinned, you would be punished through ill health.
- Very little research went into the cause of illness; in fact, it was considered a crime to dismiss or question Galen's ideas!

Hippocrates

Medieval Doctors, Training, and Cures

- There were few trained physicians and doctors in the Middle Ages; the few physicians there were charged high fees and were available to only the extremely wealthy.
- By the 12th century doctors had to prove they had studied for a number of years before they could practise; however, all training was controlled by the church and so revolved around Galen's ideas.
- There was no science as we know it today; instead alchemy (a mixture of philosophy, superstition and medieval 'science') was prevalent.
- Women would look after their families when ill and medicines would take the form of herbal remedies such as honey or poppy juice.
- People would also visit barber surgeons who would bloodlet and amputate limbs. They had no qualifications, just sharp tools!
- Finally, people would visit **apothecaries** for herbal medicines.

Galen

Key Point

Some Roman ideas remained after they left, mainly from Hippocrates (Greek) and Galen (Roman) and these were only really understood by medical students.

Treatments

- The majority of treatments did not work. They included:
  - herbal remedies such as honey or poppy juice
  - praying
  - **bloodletting**, commonly through placing leeches on the skin, which would suck the blood from the patient
  - amputation
  - superstitions, such as using the positions of the planets to determine diagnosis.

Hospitals

- At the beginning of the Middle Ages, there were very few hospitals. Monasteries and convents cared for the sick.
- The Christian Church felt it was their duty to look after people in England and therefore more hospitals were created by them (although they were small and not at all as we would imagine a hospital today).
- The key idea for the existence of hospitals was 'care not cure'.
- They were run by monks and nuns and were really places of rest for the old or poor rather than people who were actually ill.
- People who were actually ill, especially those with contagious diseases such as leprosy, were banned from hospitals!
- Separate hospitals opened for leprosy suffers, called 'lepor houses'.
- Some of the most famous hospitals include St Bartholomew's in London and St Leonard's in York.
- These hospitals focused on providing healthy food, rest and prayer to patients; the nuns would create herbal remedies for their patients and there would be no science in their treatments.
- Women were not permitted to attend university in the Middle Ages so the treatments they gave to patients would be those passed down from within their family.
- For pilgrims during the Crusades, the **Knights Hospitillars** set up a hospital in Jerusalem too. This provided care for the injured, poor and sick crusaders.

Arab Medicine

- While there were few Muslims in Britain at this point, Islamic beliefs in the field of medicine had a big impact elsewhere.
- Because Muslims also believed in Galen and Hippocrates' work, books written by Muslims influenced the way medicine was used in Britain and the rest of the Western world.
- The Koran taught Muslims that it was wrong to oppose Galen.

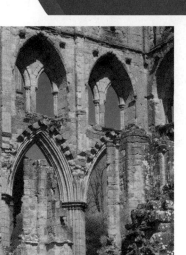

Ruins of medieval monastery

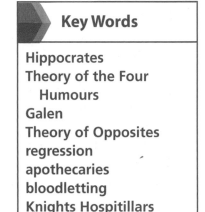

Key Point

The Church controlled nearly all aspects of medicine. As people thought God caused illness, no research went in to finding the cause of disease. Therefore understanding regressed.

Key Words

Hippocrates
Theory of the Four Humours
Galen
Theory of Opposites
regression
apothecaries
bloodletting
Knights Hospitillars

Quick Test

1. Name the four types of humour.
2. Give one reason why medicine and health regressed in the Middle Ages.
3. Give one limitation of hospitals.

Medieval Medicine (Middle Ages) 2

You must be able to:

- Explain the reasons why public health was so poor in the Middle Ages
- Explain the preventions and treatments used for the Black Death
- Analyse the main factors that led to such a high death rate from the Black Death.

Public Health

- **Public health** was poor in the Middle Ages due to three main reasons: beliefs in the causes of illness, living conditions, and the lack of any remaining Roman public health systems.
- People in the Middle Ages were very religious and because of this, they believed little could be done about ill health as God controlled this.
- While many people realised that they were living in dirty conditions, and 'bad air' could be a contributing factor, it remained the belief of most that God still held ultimate power.
- When the Romans left England, they took their knowledge, materials and money with them.
- Slaves had built the **aqueducts** and sewers that had kept England clean while the Romans were in power. The Roman army kept towns hygienic to create a more productive population to support their Empire.
- Once the Romans left, there was no money to maintain the aqueducts and sewage systems, so they went to ruin.
- Because so many people lived in poverty, living conditions became extremely poor.
- Famine was rife as there was not enough clean, healthy food for the population.
- People would leave their waste in the streets where others would walk and animals roamed towns and cities – the diseases from these animals easily spread to people.
- Because people didn't understand how germs spread (until the Industrial Revolution), many did not worry that they were eating infected meat or leaving sewage near water taps.
- Finally, war caused diseases as wounds would become quickly infected due to the dirty living conditions.

Case Study: The Black Death

- In 1348, one-third of Britain's population died due to the Black Death.
- This was caused by fleas on rats that arrived from ships.
- There were two types of plague: **bubonic** and **pneumonic**, with the latter always being fatal.

> **Key Point**
>
> When the Romans left Britain with their army, aqueducts and public health systems such as sewers were no longer maintained.

Roman aqueduct, Bath

> **Key Point**
>
> Public health in the Middle Ages was extremely poor. Because people believed that God caused illness, little to no research went in to cleanliness or how to stay healthy.

Medieval Beliefs About the Causes of the Black Death

- Medieval beliefs about causes of the Black Death included:
  - Religious: punishment for disobeying God/sinning.
  - **Miasma**: bad air (smells in the air from rubbish in the streets).
  - Planets: people believed that if planets such as Mars and Jupiter were too close together, this would cause the Plague.
  - Strangers: Jews, women believed to be witches or anyone considered an 'outsider' was met with suspicion.

Avoiding the Black Death

- **Flagellants** would whip themselves in order to receive forgiveness from God.
- People carried sweet smelling herbs to avoid the bad air; it was believed if you couldn't smell it, it wouldn't make you ill.
- People would pray to God to ask for forgiveness for their sins. They believed if they repented, God would have mercy on them and make them well.
- Staying indoors and lighting fires: it was believed that if you lit a fire you would kill the 'bad air'.
- Clearing up street rubbish: although people didn't understand how germs were spread yet, many believed that the dirt from street rubbish was not good for people's health, as it was a contributing factor to the 'bad air'.

> **Key Point**
>
> Food waste, sewage, animals and people all lived in close proximity to each other and drinking water was collected from rivers, which were often near toilets and sewage.

Symptoms

- Symptoms of the bubonic plague would include:
  - **buboes**
  - high fever
  - headaches
  - vomiting, diarrhoea and stomach cramps
  - shaking
  - seizures
- The pneumonic plague would also cause lung infections. This type of plague was rarer but far more deadly.

Illustration of people suffering from bubonic plague

Treatments

- Medieval treatments included praying to God.
- Superstitions such as having lucky charms, were widely believed to treat illness.
- Cutting open buboes and holding bread against buboes were also tried as possible treatments.

> **Quick Test**
>
> 1. Give two reasons why public health was so poor during the Middle Ages.
> 2. Give three Medieval beliefs about the cause of the Black Death.
> 3. Give three ways Medieval people believed you could avoid the Black Death.
> 4. Give three symptoms of the Black Death.

> **Key Words**
>
> **public health**
> **aqueducts**
> **bubonic**
> **pneumonic**
> **miasma**
> **flagellants**
> **buboes**

Renaissance Medicine (1400s–1600s) 1

You must be able to:

- Explain why understanding about the body progressed in the Renaissance period
- Explain the importance that science and technology played in people's understanding about the body
- Analyse the reasons why people's health did not improve in this period.

Challenging Galen

- The two most influential individuals that challenged Galen during the **Renaissance** period were **Andreas Vesalius** and **William Harvey**.

Andreas Vesalius

- The most influential text during the Renaissance period was that written by Andreas Vesalius.
- After stealing and dissecting bodies of criminals in the middle of the night, the Italian Professor of Surgery at Padua realised that Galen had made several mistakes.
- He published his findings in his very famous book, *The Fabric of the Human Body* in 1543.
- Most importantly, Vesalius found that Galen had been wrong about the jaw bone: there was only one bone, not two. Galen had dissected dogs rather than humans and didn't realise that they have a different type of anatomy.
- Additionally, Vesalius realised that there were no invisible holes in the **septum** as Galen had previously stated, so blood did not flow into the heart through these.

William Harvey

- After Vesalius' work, people slowly started to doubt other beliefs they had held.
- In 1628, a London doctor named William Harvey published a book called *An Anatomical Account of the Motion of the Heart and Blood in Animals.*
- Harvey had worked with influential men such as **Fabricius**, who had proved that veins had valves, and Harvey went on to discover that blood was carried around the body in veins.
- Harvey also made another important discovery: how blood flowed through the body.
- Due to improvements in technology, water pumps were created and it is very possible that Harvey's observations of these water pumps being used led to his discovery that the heart could be acting as a pump for the blood in the body too.
- It's important to remember though that people still did not understand everything about the way blood works.

Key Point

During the Renaissance period, exciting discoveries were made, such as the realisation that the world was round and not flat! Discoveries such as these made people question other long-standing beliefs such as those held by Galen.

Andreas Vesalius

Key Point

While Galen and Hippocrates' ideas started being challenged in the Renaissance period, it still took a long time for people to support the new discoveries and believe what they had assumed was fact for so long, was actually wrong.

Ambroise Paré and Surgery

- Ambroise Paré, a barber-surgeon with the French army during the 16th century, helped change people's ideas about surgery.
- On one occasion during 1536, the cautery oil he used to **cauterise** wounds ran out. Instead, he used a much less painful process that included rose oil and egg yolks and found that this allowed the wounds to heal better.
- Paré also found that catgut ligatures could be used to tie arteries when limbs were amputated; again, this was less painful than cauterisation.
- Due to these discoveries, Paré published *Apology and Treatise* in 1575, teaching surgeons how to better treat their patients.

The Influence of Technology

- The discovery and creation of microscopes allowed people to discover capillaries that transport blood to veins from the arteries.
- The printing press allowed ideas to spread very quickly. Before the creation of the printing press, books were written by hand (usually by monks) and therefore few books were written and circulated widely.
- Because technology improved, some people were able to spend more time enjoying the cultural side of life. This meant people spent more time observing and drawing.
- More detailed images of animals and the human body were published meaning people's understanding of **anatomy** increased further.
- People such as **John Hunter**, a Scottish surgeon, stressed the importance of observation.

Changing Ideas

- During the Renaissance period, the influence of the Church declined because new Churches such as the Church of England, created by Henry VIII, were established and took away authority from the previously powerful Catholic Church. The Church of England became very powerful.
- In 1660 **The Royal Society** was created, where educated men met to discuss scientific thinking and ideas. It was set up by King Charles II and books were published through it that contained new ideas, experiments and discoveries.

William Harvey

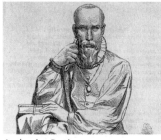
Ambroise Paré

> **Key Point**
>
> While the printing press allowed ideas to spread quickly, many did not accept them as they were so different to what they'd previously learnt.

> **Key Point**
>
> People's understanding about anatomy increased, but understanding of health, and causes of illness did not.

> **Key Words**
>
> Renaissance
> Andreas Vesalius
> William Harvey
> septum
> Fabricius
> cauterise
> anatomy
> John Hunter
> The Royal Society

Quick Test

1. What influential book did Andreas Vesalius write?
2. Give two ways in which Vesalius disagreed with Galen.
3. What influential book did William Harvey write?
4. What important discovery did William Harvey make?
5. Give one reason why the printing press was so important in allowing understanding to progress.

Renaissance Medicine (1400s–1600s) 2

You must be able to:

- Describe which of the Medieval beliefs continued into the Renaissance and why they did
- Explain the limitations of the discoveries made during the Renaissance
- Analyse the reasons why people's health did not improve during the Renaissance.

Public Health

- There were still many problems with public health in the Renaissance period; in fact, it actually got worse because towns and cities were increasing in size.
- People still left rubbish and sewage in the streets, still drank dirty water and let animals roam around towns.
- Infectious diseases continued in the Renaissance period. The Sweating Sickness was a contagious disease prevalent between 1485 and 1551. It could kill people within three hours and symptoms included headaches, fever, shortness of breath and sweating. In 1529, it killed over 1000 in four weeks.
- The most deadly disease during this period though was the **Plague**.
- The Plague had never totally gone away, but it appeared again more prominently in 1665.
- Because people still did not understand the causes of disease, **quack methods** were popular in trying to keep people healthy.

Treating a sufferer of the Plague

Preventions

- There were a number of ways in which people thought they could prevent disease:
  - Burning cats and dogs: people believed that animals may be causing the diseases to spread.
  - Banning large crowds of people in places such as theatres: people believed that the Plague could spread more quickly in large crowds.
  - People prayed to God, fasted and whipped themselves: people still believed that the Plague was a punishment from God for their sins.
  - Houses would be boarded up if someone within the household had the Plague and the other members of the household would not be allowed to leave, even if they had not contracted the disease.
- Many of the above preventions remained largely the same as they did in The Middle Ages. This was because people still did not understand what caused disease.

Hospitals

- As many hospitals in the Middle Ages had been run by the Church after the **dissolution of the monasteries**, many of those hospitals were closed down.

> **Key Point**
>
> It is important to remember that there was lots of continuity (lack of understanding of the causes of disease) as well as progress (the study of anatomy) during the Renaissance period.

> **Key Point**
>
> Because people's understanding of the cause of disease did not improve, treatments largely remained the same and public health was just as poor as in the Middle Ages.

- However new hospitals were also created, and these relied less on the Church; instead being paid for by local people and councils.

Hospitals: The Positives

- The size of individual hospitals increased: for example, St Bartholomew's. This meant more people could be treated than before.
- In Edinburgh and London, some hospitals started to admit patients with infectious diseases.
- Simple surgeries were carried out.
- The majority of physicians and doctors in hospitals had been trained at university.
- Thomas Sydenham introduced the idea of observing patients more carefully and increasing and improving bedside practice.

Hospitals: The Negatives

- The majority of hospitals still cared rather than cured; patients were given food, water and warmth.
- Poor people would go to hospitals alongside the old, but those with money would pay for a doctor to visit their home.
- Nurses still continued to use herbal remedies and many of the women working in the hospitals had no medical training.

Government

- The government did not believe it was their role to intervene in people's health.
- Because it was believed that God caused illness, people felt that it was a waste of their money to spend it on improving health.
- However, because public health was worsening, some measures were passed and the government did try to tackle some problems, but these were largely unsuccessful:
  - some towns had public toilets installed but many people still left their sewage in the streets
  - some towns had public baths installed but there were very few of these
  - laws were passed by individual towns that stated streets needed to be kept clean
  - people who did not keep streets clean were fined.

Outside St. Bartholomew's Hospital, London.

> ### Quick Test
>
> 1. Give two reasons why public health was so poor during the Renaissance.
> 2. Give three ways people believed you could avoid the Plague during the Renaissance.
> 3. Give two positives of Renaissance hospitals.
> 4. Give two limitations of Renaissance hospitals.
> 5. Give two policies that the government implemented to try to improve public health in the Renaissance period.

> ### Key Words
>
> Plague
> quack methods
> dissolution of the monasteries

Industrial Medicine (1700s–1900) 1

You must be able to:

- Explain why public health was so poor towards the beginning of the Industrial Revolution
- Explain why public health and treatment improved towards the end of the Industrial Revolution
- Analyse the government's role in improving public health during the Industrial period.

Public Health

- Due to an increase in population as people moved to the city, public health deteriorated.
- People lived in more cramped conditions than ever before as cheap, **back-to-back housing** was commissioned by the government to give homes to all those who were newly employed by the freshly created factories.
- The key public health issues at the time of the Industrial Revolution were:
  - an increase in the number of people in small spaces
  - cheap, poor quality, damp housing created
  - poor, unclean drinking water
  - poor working conditions in factories such as cotton factory workers developing breathing problems
  - lack of availability of fresh food in towns and cities.

Housing for workers of industry

Workers at a textile factory in England in the 19th century

Solutions and Limitations

- Very little effective action took place until the 1800s.
- In 1842, Edwin Chadwick published a report on the Sanitary Conditions of the Labouring Population.
- His report highlighted the poor conditions that working-class people lived in and his suggestions were put into action in the **Public Health Act of 1848**.
- This act set up the General Board of Health with the aim of improving sanitary conditions. It suggested:
  - sewers should be improved
  - rubbish should be removed from the streets
  - drinking water should be clean
  - medical officers should monitor the cleanliness of towns.
- These were only advisory policies, not enforcement policies; that is, towns did not legally have to do the above.
- Many people did not like Chadwick's conclusions as it meant the more wealthy people would have to pay higher taxes to pay for the changes.
- The government and public believed in a **'laissez-faire'** style approach to government involvement in people's health.
- It was not just Chadwick who played an important role in improving Public Health. John Snow's observations led to one of the greatest discoveries of the Industrial Revolution; however, due to traditional attitudes, people still did not enforce change.

Key Point

During the Industrial Revolution, problems with public health increased along with the size of towns and their populations. Back-to-back housing created cramped living conditions and there was still not enough fresh drinking water.

John Snow and Cholera

- Snow believed **cholera** spread through water rather than air.
- He jotted down the area where deaths from cholera took place during the 1854 epidemic and found that all the victims were using the same water pump in Broad Street. The handle to the water pump was removed and no more people died of cholera.
- Even though there was now proof, people's attitudes did not change quickly enough and there was no public health act in the 1850s, leading to further outbreaks of cholera in 1865.

Further Government Involvement

- In 1875, the **Second Public Health Act**, known as the 'Great Clear Up' came into force. This had a much bigger impact as it:
  - forced councils to appoint **medical health officers** to each town, to clear up streets and to create sewer systems and provide clean drinking water
  - improved people's living conditions
  - improved people's health
  - increased **life expectancy**.

Treatments

- By the end of the Industrial Revolution, people's understanding of science had improved.
- This had an impact on the types of treatment people received in hospitals.
- However, once again, the speed of change should not be exaggerated. Progress was made in terms of:
  - pharmacies became more popular
  - companies such as Beechams invested money into researching **patent** medicines
  - pills were increasingly used, especially after the creation of pill machines in 1840 by **William Brockeden**
  - there was a decrease in the use of herbal remedies.
- The progress made in terms of how understanding of science led to more effective treatments had limitations however:
  - people still used herbal remedies
  - the impact of the new understanding of disease on people's health was very slow until the 1900s
  - some patent medicines did not work and there was little government control over these initially.

Key Point

Diseases such as cholera, typhoid and smallpox were rife and consequently there was an increase in the need for scientific research as there was increasing pressure to find cures.

Key Point

While people were still wary of new ideas, attitudes started to change, alongside the amount of government involvement in people's health.

A 19th century hospital

Key Words

back-to-back housing
Public Health Act (1848)
laissez-faire
cholera
Second Public Health Act (1875)
medical health officer
life expectancy
patent
William Brockedon

Quick Test

1. Give two reasons why public health was so poor at the beginning of the Industrial Revolution.
2. Give two diseases that were common during the period.
3. Give three suggestions made by the Public Health Act of 1848.
4. Give three laws made by the second Public Health Act.

Industrial Medicine (1700s–1900) 2

You must be able to:

- analyse how successful the breakthroughs in health were during the Industrial period
- explain how treatments improved in the Industrial period.

Edward Jenner and Smallpox

- In 1796 Edward Jenner **inoculated** people with **cowpox** and found they did not contract **smallpox** (he had previously noticed that cowmaids never contracted smallpox).
- In 1840 the government paid for people to receive these **vaccinations** against smallpox. In 1853 it became compulsory.
- In 1979 smallpox was finally wiped out around the world.
- Yet people were slow to change their attitudes: some people believed that giving a human an animal's disease would cause them to grow animal features!
- People were still very religious and they believed inoculations and vaccinations were going against God's wishes.
- The Royal Society initially refused to publish Jenner's ideas, although eventually published them in 1798.

Edward Jenner vaccinating a young boy against smallpox.

Pasteur – Developments in Bacteria

- The majority of diseases could not be vaccinated against, especially those caused by germs.
- In 1861 Louis Pasteur developed the **Germ Theory** and later Robert Koch discovered which specific germs caused disease.
- Pasteur discovered **microbes** after experiments on sour milk; he published his theory in 1861 and after more experiments, scientists agreed with his theory and for the first time ever, people understood what caused disease.
- Koch was also doing similar experiments; through staining a microbe that caused TB under a microscope, other microbes such as cholera and plague could be identified.
- Pasteur used Koch's advances to improve people's health by creating vaccinations such as the one against anthrax.
- Emil von Behring used Koch and Pasteur's work to discover the way in which antibodies worked. In 1890, Behring developed a cure for diphtheria.
- Other scientists also used Koch and Pasteur's work to stop illnesses such as typhoid and tetanus.

Louis Pasteur

Hospitals – Progress and Limitations

- At the start of the Industrial Revolution, the focus of hospitals remained 'care not cure' and most were unclean and disorganised.
- New hospitals created during this period were set up by charities and councils; this meant they relied less on the Church.

Key Point

Science and technology aligned with other factors to improve health during the Industrial Revolution, such as changing attitudes, teamwork, the role of the individual and government action.

- **Cottage hospitals** were established in 1869 and these focussed on care *and* cure.
- There was an improvement in hygiene after the publication of Pasteur's Germ Theory.
- Ignaz Semmelweis demonstrated the importance of cleaniness through the reduction of deaths that occurred in his labour ward when doctors' and nurses' hands were washed in chlorinated lime water.

Florence Nightingale and Mary Seacole

- Florence Nightingale noted poor hygiene when working as a nurse during the **Crimean War**. She pressurised the government to ensure hospitals were clean and well organised and wrote *Notes on Nursing* in 1859, and *Notes on Hospitals* in 1863, improving hospitals, conditions and nursing.
- However, Nightingale was not a 'hands on' nurse and didn't support Pasteur's Germ Theory.
- Mary Seacole, a Jamaican, also nursed wounded soldiers during the Crimean War. Although she received less support than Nightingale, partly due to her race, she set up the 'British Hotel' where she nursed sick and convalescent soldiers.

Florence Nightingale treating patients during the Crimean War

Progress in Surgery

- Various factors brought about progress in surgery.
- James Simpson accidentally discovered **chloroform** in 1847 after giving it to his friends during a dinner party. Soon afterwards, chloroform was being used by women in labour all over Europe; even Queen Victoria used it during the birth of her eighth child.
- Increasing use of **anaesthetics** during operations decreased panic among patients and meant more people would undergo surgery.
- **Antiseptics** were used during surgery. Joseph Lister discovered carbolic acid in 1865 and realised that if carbolic acid was used during surgical procedures, infection would decrease.
- There was a further move from antiseptic to **aseptic** surgery. Koch realised that although carbolic acid reduced infection, hot steam and **sterilisation** of instruments wiped out germs completely.
- Once anaesthetics were used, but before antiseptics were discovered, more people died during surgery as surgeons took longer (as their patients were no longer in pain).
- The increase in deaths was due to an increase in blood loss and infection. This was known as the **black period of surgery**.

> **Key Point**
>
> Individuals like Florence Nightingale helped speed up progress, but her influence only had an impact due to changes in attitudes to science and government involvement.

> **Key Words**
>
> **inoculated**
> **cowpox**
> **smallpox**
> **vaccinations**
> **Germ Theory**
> **microbes**
> **cottage hospitals**
> **Crimean War**
> **chloroform**
> **anaesthetics**
> **antiseptics**
> **aseptic**
> **sterilisation**
> **black period of surgery**

> **Quick Test**
>
> 1. Give two successes of Edward Jenner's discovery.
> 2. What was 'the black period of surgery'?
> 3. What was Pasteur's main discovery?

Modern Medicine (1900s–Present) 1

You must be able to:

- Explain the impact of the discovery and understanding of DNA
- Explain the impact of scientific treatments such as magic bullets and penicillin
- Analyse the successes and limitations of science in twentieth century healthcare.

The Impact of World War One

- World War One (1914–1918) quickened the developments and improvements in surgery due to the wide range of wounds caused by new techniques in warfare.
- Plastic surgery developed due to the **skin grafting** techniques devised by **Harold Gilles** in his plastic surgery unit.
- Marie Curie had discovered the element radium which was used in X-rays. During World War One she created smaller, mobile X-ray machines, driving them to the front line herself and holding training courses for doctors to explain the new techniques.
- Transplant surgery and **prosthetic limbs** improved due to a much greater and more sudden need for them.

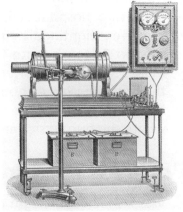

An early portable X-ray machine

Blood Transfusions

- Although blood transfusions had (largely unsuccessfully) been carried out since the 1600s, it wasn't until 1901 that Karl Landsteiner's discovery of blood groups made transfusions much more successful.
- There was still the problem of clotting, however, and it wasn't until the outbreak of war that solutions were found.
- More blood was needed quickly so in 1915 Richard Lewisohn added sodium citrate to blood to stop clotting.
- The first blood depot was created in 1917 before the Battle of Cambrai. Blood needed to be stored and so Richard Weil introduced the use of refrigerators in 1915.
- In addition Francis Rous and James Turner discovered that blood could be kept fresh by adding citrate glucose in 1916.

DNA

- Although DNA was discovered in the nineteenth century, people did not generally understand its significance.
- In 1953 Francis Crick and James Watson discovered that DNA was in all human cells, which led to further understanding of **genetics**.
- Understanding of DNA meant that people could now grasp genetic diseases, not just those caused by germs.
- Others who were important in the understanding of DNA:
  - Maurice Wilkins devised X-ray crystallography to allow Crick and Watson to develop their experiments and research further

- Rosalind Franklin was the first person to discover the double helix structure of DNA.
- The new understanding of DNA and genetics allowed further developments to occur such as stem cell research, understanding of Down's Syndrome, and understanding of conditions and illnesses such as diabetes, Parkinson's and Alzheimer's.

Scientific Treatments

- Because of the focus on science in the twentieth century, treatments such as herbal remedies and those involving superstition decreased dramatically.
- The focus was on pills, medicines and other scientific treatments.
- New diseases such as Spanish Influenza, which killed 80 million worldwide (1918–1920) prompted further scientific focus.
- The two key developments in treatment in the first half of the century were **magic bullets** and **penicillin**.

Magic Bullets

- Magic bullets are drugs that kill bacteria.
- Paul Ehrlich in 1909 discovered **Salvarsan 606**, which cured syphilis.
- However, Salvarsan 606 was also dangerous as it could kill patients.
- Gerhard Domagk developed **Prontosil** in the 1930s after testing it on mice and then his daughter.
- The key ingredient in both magic bullets was **sulphonamide**.

Penicillin

- In 1928 the first **antibiotic**, known as penicillin, was discovered by Alexander Fleming, but it did not have an immediate impact.
- Fleming had been experimenting with bacteria and realised that mould growing in a Petri dish was actually killing the bacteria. Due to lack of funds, Fleming couldn't continue his work.
- In the 1930s, Howard Florey and Ernst Chain developed research on penicillin, testing it on humans.
- During that decade and the early 1940s Britain did not have the time and space needed to grow the mould required for penicillin due to being involved in World War Two.
- The USA had previously refused to fund this, but after joining the war in 1941 it offered the funding for the antibiotics.
- Antibiotics were expensive, therefore without the creation of the **NHS**, many people wouldn't have been able to afford them.

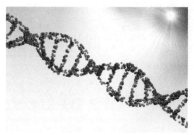
DNA double helix

Penicillin mould in a laboratory flask

> ### Key Point
>
> Because of the increasing evidence and funding that supported scientific discoveries, science and technology dominated medical progression, as religion had done centuries earlier.

> ### Key Words
>
> skin grafting
> Harold Gilles
> prosthetic limbs
> genetics
> magic bullet
> penicillin
> Salvarsan 606
> Prontosil
> sulphonamide
> antibiotics
> NHS

> ### Quick Test
>
> 1. Give examples of medical developments that occurred due to the outbreak of World War One.
> 2. Name two types of magic bullets discovered during the twentieth century.
> 3. How were antibiotics made available to the mass population?

Modern Medicine (1900s–Present) 2

You must be able to:

- Explain why the government became involved in people's health in the twentieth century
- Explain the impact government involvement such as the Liberal reforms and the NHS had on the public's health
- Evaluate the successes and limitations of government involvement in people's health.

The Role of Government

- The role the government played in improving people's health dramatically increased during the twentieth century.
- While many people believed the government should still take a laissez-faire approach, the studies of Charles Booth and Seebohm Rowntree argued differently.
- Between 1889 and 1903, Charles Booth studied the poor in London.
- In 1901 Rowntree carried out a study in York entitled *Poverty: A Study of Town Life*.
- Both Rowntree and Booth found that illness and poverty were not the fault of the poor. They found that lack of money for food and quality housing was to blame.

A poor family in the early twentieth century

The Liberal Reforms

- With the Liberal landslide general election victory of 1906, the Liberal government, headed by Lloyd George, implemented a set of **reforms** that some people believe to be the beginning of the **welfare state**. Others, however, believe the welfare state really didn't begin until the creation of the NHS in 1948.
- The Liberal reforms had a huge impact on the lives of people in Britain; however, there were also limitations.

Successes of the Reforms

- 1906 saw the introduction of school meals for poor children. This had a positive impact on the health of the poorest children. In 1907, this was extended to all children.
- In 1907 health visitors began to monitor young children and their mothers to check general health and wellbeing.
- In 1908 the Old Age Pensions Act was introduced. This gave financial support to the elderly, which improved their health due to them having a better standard of living.
- The 1911 National Insurance Act gave workers some sick pay, support was provided for the unemployed and medical treatment to those in work.

Limitations of the Reforms

- While the School Meals Act improved children's health during term time, this dramatically decreased during school holidays.
- As the National Insurance Act was only given to (some) workers, the majority of women were not covered.

> **Key Point**
>
> During the **Boer War** of 1899–1902, nine out of ten British men were declared unfit to fight. This concerned the British government as they realised that the poor health of the population was risking Britain's security.

> **Key Point**
>
> Not all workers were covered under the National Insurance Act. Some workers, such as farmers and servants were not covered.

The Creation of the NHS

- Due to the impact of World War Two, the health of British citizens became highlighted once again.
- The **evacuation** of children emphasized the varied level of public health in Britain. Many children from cities were unclean, had head lice, and couldn't read, which led to lower skilled jobs and poorer standards of living in the long term.
- In 1944 William Beveridge wrote a report that stated there were 'Five Evils' in Britain that the government needed to tackle, including disease and **squalor**.
- In light of this, in 1948, Health Minister Aneurin Bevan set up the National Health Service. The role of the **NHS** was to provide free healthcare to everyone, from 'cradle to grave'.

Successes of the NHS

- Free access to doctors, and free prescriptions.
- Creation of family doctors and health care centres.
- Free to call ambulances.

Criticisms of the NHS

- While the majority of people were in support of the NHS, there were still some reservations.
- Some people did not want to pay extra taxes to fund the NHS.
- Doctors felt they were being too controlled by the government.
- Some people still believed in the laissez-faire approach.
- Charities and councils felt they were no longer needed for healthcare.

Modern-day NHS

The Cost of the NHS

- The NHS is becoming very expensive and incurring lots of debt.
- Measures have been taken to privatise some areas of the NHS in order to reduce the amount of money lost.
- Lots of people are against the privatisation of the NHS as this will mean people will need to pay for more treatments.
- People who can afford it can choose to go private. Some people believe this is creating a 'two-tier' system of care, with the more wealthy receiving better treatment.

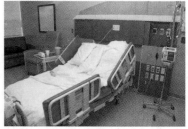

A modern-day private hospital room

Key Words

Boer War
reforms
welfare state
evacuation
squalor
NHS

Quick Test

1. Name two acts introduced by the Liberals.
2. Give two limitations of reforms implemented by the Liberals.
3. Name two of the five evils highlighted by the Beveridge Report.
4. Give two reasons why the NHS was created.

Modern Medicine (1900s–Present) 3

You must be able to:

- Explain and give examples of the improvements made in medicine and treatment
- Explain the ways in which the government is increasingly becoming involved in people's lifestyles
- Evaluate the successes and limitations of scientific development.

Developments in Medicine

- In 1967 Christiaan Barnard performed the first heart transplant and while the patient only lived for 18 days, this was a major breakthrough.
- Currently, 75% of heart transplant patients now live for three years.
- In the 1970s and 80s, the first **MRI scans** were completed.
- MRI scans use strong radio waves and magnetic fields to show detailed images of the inside of the body.
- An MRI scan can examine most areas of the body including the brain, spinal cord and blood vessels.
- Through MRI scans, conditions such as sports injuries and tumours can be diagnosed.
- During the 1970s and 80s the first **ultrasounds** were used. These use high-frequency sound waves to show parts of the inside of the body and can be used to monitor unborn babies.
- Lasers are used to remove diseased tissue.
- Radiation therapy is used to control or kill cancer cells.
- Keyhole surgery allows surgeons to access parts of the body without having to make large cuts.

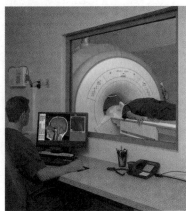
Monitoring an MRI scan

> **Key Point**
>
> Science and technology are rapidly advancing every day. Some of the most recent improvements such as MRI scanning have had the greatest impact.

Developments in Cancer Medicine

- Recently, there has been an increase in the number of treatments used for cancer.
- Previously, surgery and **radiotherapy** were used to fight the growth of tumours; however, now treatments such as **chemotherapy**, **radiation** and **endocrine** therapy are used.
- For lung cancer especially, the government has introduced a range of initiatives such as 'No Smoking' campaigns to make people aware of how to reduce the risk of cancer.
- Additionally, charities such as The British Lung Foundation have been established to help fight cancer further.

Viral Diseases in the Twentieth Century

- One example of a relatively new disease is **AIDS**, which was first reported in 1981.
- At the start of the epidemic, AIDS was feared and there was no treatment. The majority of times it was fatal. There is still no cure.
- Once **HIV** was discovered, effective antiretroviral drugs were

> **Key Point**
>
> More than ever before, people feel that the government should take an increasing role in trying to improve people's heath through initiatives such as healthy living campaigns.

developed, which now means that people with HIV can lead healthy lives.

- By 2000, over 30 million people had been infected with AIDS – the majority being in Africa – and to date, no magic bullets or vaccines have been developed for AIDS.
- Because of an improvement in antibiotics, some viral diseases such as **Ebola** have emerged.
- An Ebola epidemic broke out in Africa in 2014.
- Ebola is resistant to antibiotics, meaning it is more difficult to treat.
- So far, Ebola has killed over 10,000 people worldwide.

The Role of the Government

- The government's role in public health is still important.
- Examples such as anti-smoking campaigns to reduce cancers such as lung cancer and campaigns to reduce alcohol consumption to reduce liver disease show how the government is trying to improve people's health.
- Other health campaigns created by the government include:
  - **Change4Life**: a healthy eating and living campaign that focuses on reducing alcohol and sugar consumption and promoting the 'five a day' consumption of fruit and vegetables. Change4Life also promotes the importance of exercise in our lifestyles today, contributing £3 million towards Change4Life sports clubs.
  - Flu campaigns: explaining what to do if a person contracts flu.
  - National anti-drugs campaigns: explaining the negative impact of illegal drugs.

Limitations of Scientific Developments

- In the 1960s, **thalidomide** caused babies to be born with disfigurements such as a lack of limbs.
- Some people disagree with scientific involvement for moral and religious reasons; for example, that science such as embryo research is interfering too much in God's plan.
- In some instances, there has been a move to alternative medicines such as herbal remedies, **acupuncture** and meditation to improve health.

Revise

A suspected Ebola patient being taken to hospital

Key Point

Science was the key focus of twentieth and twenty-first century medicine and while it has had a positive effect in many areas, some problems have occurred. In some instances, this has led to a move back towards the popularity of herbal remedies.

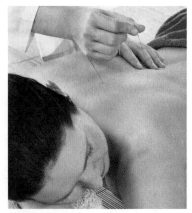

Acupuncture

Key Words

MRI scan
ultrasound
radiotherapy
chemotherapy
radiation
endocrine
AIDS
HIV
Ebola
Change4Life
thalidomide
acupuncture

Quick Test

1. Give two new ways in which cancer can now be treated.
2. Name two developments that occurred between the 1960s and the 1980s.
3. Name two diseases that have emerged during the twentieth century.
4. Name two campaigns that the government has introduced to improve health.
5. Give two limitations of scientific development.

Review Questions

Elizabethan England: Elizabeth I and Her Government

1 What functions did Parliament play in Elizabeth's government?

2 Was England a divided country in 1558?

3 How did portraits help to show Elizabeth as a powerful figure?

4 Why did Elizabeth never marry?

Write your answer on a separate piece of paper.

5 What role did Robert Dudley, Earl of Leicester, play in Elizabeth's government?

6 Who was the most significant minister under Elizabeth I?

Explain your answer.

Write your answer on a separate piece of paper.

Elizabethan England: The Elizabethan Religious Settlement

1 How did the Protestants react to the Elizabethan Religious Settlement?

2 What did the Act of Uniformity aim to establish?

3 What did the Act of Supremacy aim to establish?

4 What was the role of Matthew Parker in establishing the Elizabethan Religious Settlement?

5 Why did the Catholics largely accept the Elizabethan Religious Settlement?

6 What was the impact of the Elizabethan Religious Settlement on the clergy?

Write your answer on a separate piece of paper.

Review Questions

Elizabethan England: Elizabeth I and Spain, 1558–1587

1 Why did friendship with England in the 1560s suit Philip II of Spain?

2 What role did Hawkins and Drake play in the relations between England and Spain?

3 How did plots against Elizabeth impact upon relations with Spain?

Write your answer on a separate piece of paper.

4 Why was Philip II disappointed with Elizabeth in the 1560s?

5 Why was Antwerp important in England's relationship with Spain?

6 Why was an anti-French alliance with Spain less important in the 1560s?

Write your answer on a separate piece of paper.

Review

Elizabethan England: Elizabeth I and Mary, Queen of Scots

1 Why was Mary's marriage to Lord Darnley a disaster?

....

....

2 What was the link between Elizabeth and Mary, and how did this cause problems for Elizabeth?

Write your answer on a separate piece of paper.

3 Why did Mary flee to England in 1568?

....

....

....

4 What consequences did Mary's marriage to Bothwell have?

....

....

....

....

5 What role did Sir Francis Walsingham play in Mary's downfall?

Write your answer on a separate piece of paper.

6 Explain the role of Mary's husbands in her downfall in Scotland.

Write your answer on a separate piece of paper.

Review Questions

Elizabethan England: The Attack of the Spanish Armada, 1588

1 Why did the Spanish Armada fail to invade England?

2 What was the impact of the death of Admiral Santa Cruz?

3 What was the outcome of the fight across the English Channel?

4 What was Drake's role in the defeat of the Spanish Armada?

5 'The Spanish Armada was defeated more by bad luck than English skill.'

How far do you agree? Explain your answer.

Write your answer on a separate piece of paper.

6 Who had the most effective navy – England or Spain?

Write your answer on a separate piece of paper.

Elizabethan England: Threats Posed to Elizabeth I, 1558–1601

1 What happened during the Northern Rebellion?

Write your answer on a separate piece of paper.

2 How much of a threat was the Ridolfi Plot?

3 How did the Puritans oppose Elizabeth?

4 What did the Throckmorton Plot show to the Privy Council?

5 What were the aims of the Babington Plot?

6 Which was the greater threat – the Ridolfi Plot or the Throckmorton Plot?

Write your answer on a separate piece of paper.

Review Questions

Elizabethan England: Elizabethan Society

1 What was the role of local government in dealing with poverty?

2 How did education provision improve in the Elizabethan period?

3 Why were more people accused of being witches in this time period?

4 What factors allowed for the rise of the gentry and merchants?

5 How did farming help the gentry and merchants become wealthy?

6 Why did unemployment rise in the Elizabethan period?

Elizabethan England: Elizabethan Culture

1 What entertainment did theatres offer?

_____

_____

2 Why did Puritans oppose the theatre?

_____

_____

_____

3 Why was literature increasingly popular in Elizabethan England?

_____

_____

_____

4 Why was fashion popular in Elizabethan England?

_____

_____

5 What did the poor look for in entertainment?

_____

_____

_____

6 What were the key features of entertainment for the poor?

_____

_____

_____

Review Questions

Elizabethan England: Elizabeth I and the Wider World

1 What impact did exploration have on England's relationship with Spain?

2 Why did Sir Francis Drake want to make a world voyage?

3 Why did Elizabeth I want to expand trade with the wider world?

4 What were the main consequences of Elizabethan voyages?

5 Why was exploration seen as a glorious part of Elizabeth I's reign?

6 Who was the most successful Elizabethan explorer?

Write your answer on a separate piece of paper.

Health and Medicine: Medieval Medicine (Middle Ages) 1

1 Explain Hippocrates' idea of 'the four humours'.

2 State whether medicine and public health regressed or progressed between the Roman and Medieval period.

3 Explain Galen's Theory of Opposites.

4 Write a clear and organised summary of treatments in the Medieval period.

5 Why did hospitals have limited impact when it came to improving people's health? Explain your answer.

6 'There was little progress in medicine in Britain during the Medieval period because of religion.' How far do you agree? Explain your answer.

Write your answer on a separate piece of paper.

Practice Questions

Health and Medicine: Medieval Medicine (Middle Ages) 2

1. Give one reason why 'cures' for the Black Death did not work.

2. Give one example of a herbal remedy for the Black Death.

3. Explain how religious people would try to avoid the Black Death.

4. Write a clear and organised summary to show why public health was so poor in the Middle Ages.

   Write your answer on a separate piece of paper.

5. What correct ideas did people have about avoiding illness in the Middle Ages?

6. 'In the Middle Ages, the Black Death was so deadly because of the strength of people's religious beliefs.'

   How far do you agree? Explain your answer.

   Write your answer on a separate piece of paper.

Health and Medicine: Renaissance Medicine (1400s–1600s) 1

1 Why did people start to question Galen during the Renaissance period?

_____

_____

_____

_____

_____

2 Describe Fabricius' discovery.

_____

3 Give two examples of Vesalius' discoveries that disproved Galen in the Renaissance period.

_____

_____

4 Describe why the importance placed on religion started to reduce during the Renaissance period.

_____

_____

_____

_____

5 Describe why Vesalius' and Harvey's discoveries did not improve people's health during the Renaissance period.

_____

_____

6 'The progress made in understanding the body during the Renaissance period was due to the reduction of importance of religion.'

How far do you agree? Explain your answer.

Write your answer on a separate piece of paper.

Health and Medicine: Renaissance Medicine (1400s–1600s) 2

1 Give one example of a quack method used to try to keep the Plague away.

2 Give two examples of techniques used to try to prevent the Plague.

3 Give three examples of how the government tried to improve public health.

4 Describe what public health was like during the Renaissance period.

5 Explain why the government was not successful in tackling Britain's poor public health during the Renaissance.

6 'Training and treatment in hospitals during the Renaissance period improved.'

How far do you agree? Explain your answer.

Write your answer on a separate piece of paper.

Health and Medicine: Industrial Medicine (1700s–1900) 1

1 Give three reasons why public health worsened during the first part of the Industrial Revolution.

2 Give one example of how technology improved treatments during the Industrial Revolution.

3 Give two reasons why Chadwick's report did not improve public health.

4 Give two examples of how treatment changed during the Industrial Revolution.

5 Explain John Snow's discovery and its impact.

6 'The Public Health Acts had a limited effect on improving conditions during the Industrial Period.'

How far do you agree? Explain your answer.

Write your answer on a separate piece of paper.

Practice Questions

Health and Medicine: Industrial Medicine (1700s–1900) 2

1 Explain the importance of Jenner's discoveries.

_____

_____

_____

_____

_____

_____

2 Describe the importance of cottage hospitals.

_____

_____

3 Explain the importance of Joseph Lister's discovery.

_____

_____

_____

_____

4 Explain the importance of Koch's discoveries.

Write your answer on a separate piece of paper.

5 Describe the changes that took place in hospitals during the Industrial Revolution.

Write your answer on a separate piece of paper.

6 'Florence Nightingale's work was the main reason for the improvements in nursing and hospitals.'

How far do you agree? Explain your answer.

Write your answer on a separate piece of paper.

Health and Medicine: Modern Medicine (1900s–Present) 1

1 Explain why the understanding of DNA allowed medicine and health to progress during the twentieth century.

_____

_____

_____

_____

2 Describe Crick and Watson's contribution to science and medicine during the twentieth century.

Write your answer on a separate piece of paper.

3 Describe two ways in which World War One helped medicine to progress.

_____

_____

_____

_____

4 Explain the importance of magic bullets in improving people's health in the twentieth century.

_____

_____

_____

_____

5 Describe how the outbreak of World War One allowed blood transfusions to progress.

Write your answer on a separate piece of paper.

6 'Government intervention was the main factor that allowed penicillin to improve people's health.'

How far do you agree? Explain your answer.

Write your answer on a separate piece of paper.

Practice Questions

Health and Medicine: Modern Medicine (1900s–Present) 2

1 Describe Charles Booth's and Seebohm Rowntree's discoveries about poverty.

2 Give an example of a Liberal reform that improved people's health.

3 Give two reasons why the NHS was set up.

4 Explain why the Liberals implemented their reforms.

5 'The Liberal reforms improved people's health in Britain.'

How far do you agree? Explain your answer.

Write your answer on a separate piece of paper.

6 'The NHS has been wholly positive.'

How far do you agree? Explain your answer.

Write your answer on a separate piece of paper.

Health and Medicine: Modern Medicine (1900s–Present) 3

1 Name one major medical development of the twentieth century.

2 Explain the importance of MRI scanning.

3 Explain two limitations of scientific development.

4 Write a clear and organised summary of the developments made in cancer treatment and prevention.

5 How successful have scientific developments been in the twentieth century?

Write your answer on a separate piece of paper.

6 'The main reason for an improvement in people's health during the twentieth century is due to the role of the government.'

How far do you agree? Explain your answer.

Write your answer on a separate piece of paper.

1000–1500: Crime

You must be able to:

- Understand the aims of Saxon laws
- Understand how the Normans enforced law and order
- Describe the nature of crime in Medieval England.

Saxon Laws

- During Saxon times, England was divided into seven different kingdoms, each ruled by a warrior king. Each kingdom had its own laws made up by the ruler.
- Each kingdom had its own laws and so did the many kingdoms that made up Scotland and Wales.
- A king's most important tasks were to defend his country from attacks and to make sure his laws were obeyed. Laws were made by kings after consulting nobles and bishops.
- The king's laws had two main aims: to protect landowners' property from damage or theft; to protect people from violence.
- These laws covered all aspects of criminal behaviour, including theft, violence and murder.
- The laws allowed a person or relative to claim a fine known as the **wergild** if a crime was committed against them. The level of compensation depended on the seriousness of the crime and was paid by the criminal. Very serious crimes such as treason carried the death penalty. Repeat offenders were also savagely dealt with.
- Some kings in Saxon England allowed victims of crime to legally hunt down the criminals and punish them. These were known as **blood feuds**; however, these revenge attacks often led to more violence.

Illustration of a Saxon knight

The Norman Conquest

- Following the Norman Conquest, William the Conqueror brutally punished anybody in England who rebelled against the Normans.
- William was determined that the English would obey his laws, and was prepared to use brutal methods if necessary, including burning villages and destroying crops and animals. Any survivors died of starvation.
- Castles were built across the country to terrorise the English. They were filled with knights and barons who were given unlimited power to run the region.
- William believed that any crime committed was a threat against his rule and he used the death penalty for serious crimes.
- William introduced the Forest Laws which banned people from cutting down trees for fuel or building. People in the forests were forbidden from owning a dog or a bow and arrow. If caught and found guilty of this crime, the punishment was to be blinded.

> **Key Point**
>
> The Normans kept many Saxon laws but added new ones such as the Forest Laws.

> **Key Point**
>
> All land was owned by the king.

- The Normans enforced laws more harshly than the Saxons to prevent or punish rebellions.

The Middle Ages

- Most crime during the Middle Ages was small-scale, including theft of money, food and belongings. These were usually of low value.
- The people who made the laws were those with the power and wealth. Crimes that threatened this power and wealth were considered serious, and could be punished by death.
- Violent crimes such as murder were rare and accounted for a small minority of cases, although it is difficult to know what the true crime rate actually was during the Medieval period, due to a lack of reliable evidence.
- Theft of livestock, goods and property were the most common types of crime.
- Three quarters of crimes were committed by people known to the victim, many of whom were respectable villagers. There were few professional criminals.
- Poverty and famine were common for peasants in the Middle Ages. A growing population meant more people looking for work, and wages were low. A series of bad harvests pushed up food prices.

Outlaws

- Gangs of **outlaws** who roamed the country were feared. They stole from anyone, frequently stealing food, clothing and pots and pans.
- Outlaws would often keep the money they stole, rather than distributing it to the poor.
- Churches were favourite targets for gangs of outlaws, because they contained valuable ornaments made of silver and gold. They also contained money that had been given for the care of the poor.
- Outlaws would threaten their victims with arson, and extort money or goods in return for not burning homes down. Outlaws regularly used violence, including threatening victims with a knife, or simply killing the victim before robbing them.
- Approximately 10% of murder victims were killed during robberies.
- Many gangs were able to evade capture and were often protected from capture by local people or wealthy friends.

> **Key Point**
>
> Most crime in the Middle Ages was petty theft of money, food and belongings. Violent crimes were a small minority of crimes.

Bows in a forest

> **Quick Test**
>
> 1. Who made the laws in Saxon times?
> 2. What percentage of murder victims were killed during robberies?
> 3. What type of structure did William the Conqueror build across the country?

> **Key Words**
>
> wergild
> blood feud
> outlaw

1000–1500: Punishment

You must be able to:

- Understand the aims of medieval punishment
- Understand the different methods of trial by ordeal
- Describe the role of the church.

Medieval Punishments

- Serious crimes carried the death penalty; these included treason against the king, **arson** and betraying their lord.
- Punishments for reoffenders included mutilation, such as having their nose, hand or foot cut off, or their eyes put out.
- A person who did not attend court was known as an outlaw. An outlaw no longer had the protection of the law and could be killed by anyone as punishment.

Medieval Law Enforcement

- In the Medieval period there was no police force; people relied on friends or family to help catch criminals.
- **Tithing** was an alternative way of keeping law and order.
- All men over the age of twelve had to belong to a group of ten men known as a tithing. The function of a tithing was for each man to be responsible for group behaviour.
- If a member of the tithing broke the law, the other members had to bring him to court or pay the compensation fine to the victim.
- The **hue and cry** was a larger scale version of the tithings, and was based on loyalty to the village.
- If a victim of crime raised the hue and cry by calling out for help, the entire village had to join in the hunt to find the criminal. Saxons were used to protecting each other in this manner.
- Parish constables were first appointed in 1250. They were usually leading villagers who tried to keep the peace in their spare time. They were not paid, and only held the job for a year.

> **Key Point**
>
> There was no police force. Tithings and the hue and cry were the main methods of catching criminals.

Trials

- Trials took place in front of juries of local people.
- **Trials by ordeal** took advantage of people's belief in God and were a way of allowing God to decide someone's guilt. It was believed that God helped innocent people and punished the guilty.
- Trial by ordeal could involve trial by any of the following methods.
  - Trial by hot iron was usually taken by women and involved having to carry a piece of red-hot iron for three metres.

How quickly the wound healed would determine her guilt or innocence.

- – Trial by hot water was usually taken by men and involved having to place the hand into boiling water to retrieve an object. How quickly the wound healed would determine his guilt or innocence.
- – Trial by blessed bread was taken by priests. The priest had to pray that he would be choked by the bread if he lied, and he then had to eat the bread. If the priest choked, he was guilty.
- – Trial by cold water was usually taken by men. The accused was tied up and lowered into a river. If he sank he was innocent; if he floated he was guilty.
- Trial by ordeal was abolished in 1215. From the 1100s royal judges travelled the country dealing with serious cases.

Punishments

- County courts were held by Justices of the Peace (JPs) who were leading landowners. Each manor had a weekly court run by a local lord.
- Capital punishment was the most common punishment in royal courts and was used for many offences, including theft.
- Hanging and other punishments were carried out in public to scare possible offenders.
- Fines were the most common punishments in manor courts. Prisons were only used for people who were awaiting trial.
- The **stocks**, **pillory** and whipping were also used for minor crimes.

The Church

- The Church increased its influence after the Norman invasion. The Church believed that punishment should aim to reform the criminal.
- Immoral actions such as sex outside marriage became crimes. Church courts were set up to deal with these, and for anyone not following church rites.
- All clergy could be tried in a church court and proved their right to this by reading a passage from the Bible.
- Church courts could not impose the death penalty, so people learnt a passage of the Bible off by heart to claim 'benefit of the clergy'.
- Nobody could be arrested if they were in a church – known as the right of **sanctuary**. If they confessed to the crime they would be allowed to leave the country.

Pillory

Medieval stocks

Key Point

Anyone who could read a verse from the Bible could claim 'benefit of the clergy' and be tried in a church court.

Key Words

arson
tithing
hue and cry
trial by ordeal
stocks
pillory
sanctuary

Quick Test

1. What was a person who did not attend court called?
2. How old did you have to be to join a tithing?
3. In what year was trial by ordeal abolished?

1500–1700: Crime

You must be able to:

- Understand why crime increased after 1500
- Understand the problems caused by begging and vagrancy
- Describe why treason was a serious crime after 1500.

Factors Affecting Crime Rates

- British society from 1500–1750 saw many changes, including an increase in crimes – both traditional kinds and new kinds created by new laws, known as **the Bloody Code**.
- The number of people committing crimes rose because of two main reasons:
  - prices and unemployment were high
  - taxes were increased during wars.
- A strong government meant lower crime rates as criminals were more likely to be punished.

Why Did Crime Increase?

- An increase in population and decline of feudalism meant more people moved to urban areas and therefore towns became larger. This led to more street criminals and thieves – known as 'footpads'.
- Increased unemployment meant that more people moved around looking for work. This led to more people begging, which became a crime in the sixteenth century – Elizabeth I passed laws against begging.
- Trade between towns grew and roads improved between 1700 and 1750. This led to a new type of thief, the highwayman, who robbed travellers on the roads.
- The end of feudalism led to a reduction in common land because the owners fenced it off. This led to an increase in **poaching** as landowners restricted who could hunt on their land.
- Changes in people's beliefs and the religion of the monarch led to more people committing **heresy** during the sixteenth century.
- Trade restrictions and tax increases helped create the new crime of smuggling: people imported or exported illegal goods and made large profits.

> **Key Point**
>
> Crime increased as the population in urban areas began to grow larger.

The grave of notorious highwayman, Dick Turpin

> **Key Point**
>
> Laws were passed against new crimes such as begging, heresy and highway robbery.

Begging and Vagrancy

- Begging was a new crime. Laws can change because of pressure from new rulers or ordinary people. These new laws sometimes create new crimes. Begging is an example of a new crime in this period.
- Rulers who felt they were under threat would punish crimes very harshly to deter other criminals.
- Increasing unemployment and no system to help those in need meant that there were higher numbers of beggars in the late fifteenth and sixteenth centuries.
- Beggars were seen as a threat to society and laws were passed to prevent begging. Beggars were hated and feared and people resented having to pay out money to support them.
- The Vagabonds and Beggars Act (1494) meant that beggars were put in stocks for three days and nights, then sent back to where they were born, or most well known.
- In 1531 beggars were classed as either deserving or sturdy.
    - Deserving beggars were those who were sick or injured. They were given a badge to identify them and were allowed to beg.
    - Sturdy beggars were considered lazy, and therefore punished.
- The **Vagrancy** Act, 1547 stated that beggars should be forced to work, and could be whipped and branded. The Act was repealed because it became impossible to enforce.

Metal chain collar for criminals

Treason

- **Treason** was showing disobedience or disloyalty to the monarch. This was a serious crime and one that became more common after 1485.
- Treason increased during this period due to the changing religions of the ruling monarchs. It was expected that the population would follow the same religion as the monarch. There were many arguments during this period about whether the country should be ruled by a Catholic or Protestant monarch.
- Punishment of treason involved public hanging, drawing and then quartering. This was a brutal and horrific death, and was used to deter others from committing treason.
- Nobles who committed treason were usually beheaded.

Gallows

Key Words

the Bloody Code
poaching
heresy
vagrancy
treason

Quick Test

1. Who passed laws against begging in the 16th century?
2. What year was the Vagabond and Beggars Act introduced?
3. What did deserving beggars wear to identify them?

1500–1700: Punishment

You must be able to:

- Understand why the Bloody Code was introduced
- Understand policing methods
- Describe how cases were tried between 1500 and 1700.

The Bloody Code

- As towns grew bigger, more crimes occurred. This worried those who made the laws. As a result, they increased the number of crimes carrying the death penalty, as they thought that would reduce crime.
- Typical punishments included flogging, hanging and execution.
- Punishments were usually physical and the public would watch the spectacle. This would shame the criminal and also deter others from committing crimes.
- Between 1688 and 1823 the number of crimes punishable by death rose from 50 to more than 200. This period became known as the Bloody Code.
- Stealing a rabbit or damaging a tree became hanging offences. The aim was to frighten people so they wouldn't commit crimes.
- However, it did not work. Fewer people were hanged in the eighteenth century compared to the seventeenth because juries found people 'not guilty' to avoid giving them the death penalty.
- New punishments were introduced. Local judges began to build Houses of Correction – these were essentially the first prisons. Beggars were sent to them from 1576.
- **Transportation** began to be introduced during the late seventeenth century. Petty criminals or political criminals could be sent as labourers to English colonies.

The Tower of London

> **Key Point**
>
> Savage and terrifying punishments such as hanging, drawing and quartering were used to deter people from committing crimes.

Policing

- There was no national system for catching criminals. Methods used to catch criminals included:
  - Watchmen, or 'charlies', were paid to patrol London. The nickname came about because they were set up in 1663 during the reign of Charles II.
  - Unpaid parish officials called **constables** arrested beggars and petty criminals.
  - Thief takers were paid by the victim of a crime to catch the criminal and bring them to justice.
- Jonathon Wild was a famous example of a thief taker. He claimed to have had over 60 thieves hanged, and returned stolen goods for rewards. However, he was actually a criminal who ran a successful gang of thieves.

> **Key Point**
>
> There was no national system of policing, and catching criminals with watchmen and constables remained inefficient.

- He caught thieves who were either rivals or gang members who wouldn't obey him.
- Wild was hanged in 1725.

Trials and Juries

- Minor cases were heard locally by one or two Justices of the Peace. More serious crimes were heard by groups of JPs with local men serving on a jury.
- The most serious crimes were heard by royal judges who were the only ones able to pass a death sentence.
- Punishments would vary depending on the class and gender of the criminal.
- Commoners were treated differently to nobles, women were treated differently to men, and priests were treated differently to ordinary people.

Torture rack

Gunpowder Plot

- Guy Fawkes and the Gunpowder Plot is a famous example of committing treason.
- On 5 November 1605, a number of Catholics planned to kill King James I at the opening of Parliament. They were angry that Catholic worship was illegal and wanted a Catholic monarch to rule England.
- Guy Fawkes was an explosives expert and he had prepared 36 barrels of gunpowder in a cellar underneath Parliament.
- However, the plotters were betrayed and Guy Fawkes was caught in the cellar of the Houses of Parliament guarding the barrels of gunpowder. After three days of horrific torture on the rack, he revealed the names of the plotters and they were arrested, found guilty of treason and sentenced to death by being hung, drawn and quartered.

Parliament

Quick Test

1. Who ordered Houses of Correction to be built?
2. In what year was Jonathon Wild hanged?
3. How many barrels of gunpowder were in the Gunpowder plot?

Key Words

transportation
constables

1700–1900: Crime

You must be able to:

- Understand the impact of industrialisation on crime after 1700
- Understand the reasons why the crime rate increased
- Describe why smuggling was difficult to prevent.

Changes in Society

- The movement of the population from the countryside to the towns had increased dramatically after 1750. Crime continued to increase, but by 1850 had begun to fall. The most common crime was petty theft.
- The development of cheap illustrated newspapers meant that crime could now be reported all over Britain and consequently many people were more aware and afraid of crime.

Industrialisation and the Impact on Crime

- **Urbanisation** meant factories developed in towns and cities. The population increased and huge slums developed.
- The government brought in new laws to control people as crimes against property increased.
- There was an increase in street theft, burglary and drunk and disorderly behaviour. **Smuggling** of illegal goods also increased.
- There was also an increase in prostitution, rioting, public disorder and protest – particularly in the poorest areas of towns and cities.
- Landowners and factory owners were concerned about unrest from workers. They believed that a revolution would take place. Most protesters were ordinary working people who were scared of extreme poverty.
- Chartists protested at conditions for workers and the right to vote, and the Luddites were against machines removing traditional craft jobs.
- In 1715 the Riot Act made it a **capital offence** for more than 12 people to meet up together. This law was used to prevent protests against hardships e.g. shortage of food and cuts in wages.

Luddites breaking down a factory door

> **Key Point**
>
> The government was concerned about the threat of riots and protests by working class people who were being treated very harshly.

Reasons for the Increase of Crime

- It was harder to keep track of the movement of people in large, over-crowded towns and cities and this also made it easier for criminals to avoid being caught.
- Professional criminals in urban areas increased in number, and because they would hide out in dens, overcrowded areas of slum housing and extreme poverty known as 'rookeries', or within gangs of thieves, it was difficult to catch them.
- Extreme poverty meant that people were forced to steal to survive and this made the poor resentful of the wealth of the rich.

Crimes Against Authority

- The number of charges for treason decreased, but the French Revolution of 1789 had made the government and upper classes fearful that revolution could also happen in Britain.
- Many people wanted reforms, for example the right to vote or the right to strike, and were prepared to protest to be heard.
- In 1833, six workers from Tolpuddle, Dorset met to discuss plans by landowners to reduce their wages. The men formed a trade union and swore a secret oath on the Bible. Local landowners heard about this, and the men were arrested and charged. They were sentenced to 7 years transportation to Australia.
- Public outcry at the harshness of the sentence meant that Parliament decided they had been unfairly convicted and returned them from Australia in 1836.
- The government treated protestors very harshly but in the late nineteenth century Parliament agreed to improve working conditions.

Crimes Against the Person

- Violent crimes decreased during this period, even though it did not appear to be the case at the time.
- In the 1850s, there was widespread concern about **garroters**, criminals who used chloroform or would part-strangle people and rob them.
- The Whitechapel murders in 1888 committed by 'Jack the Ripper' horrified people, due to the violence and brutality suffered by the victims. The case was widely reported in newspapers, causing widespread fear and panic.

Smuggling

- Smuggling increased during the period 1740–1850 because the tax on imported goods was so high. Smugglers made large profits by bringing goods into the country illegally and selling them on cheaply.
- However, many people thought the smugglers were heroes and that the government was being unreasonable.
- Customs officers tried to stop smuggling and catch and prosecute the smugglers. However, they found this very difficult because there was a large area of the coast to protect.
- Others involved in smuggling included the traders, the buyers, those who hid the smuggled items and people who gave smugglers alibis to protect them.
- Smuggling decreased after 1850 as taxes on imported goods were cut.

Whitechapel, London, where Jack the Ripper committed his crimes

> **Key Point**
>
> Smuggling increased and proved difficult to prevent as many smugglers were seen as heroes and made huge profits.

> **Quick Test**
>
> 1. What type of media developed at this time?
> 2. What were criminals who strangled their victims called?
> 3. What year did the Whitechapel murders take place?

> **Key Words**
>
> urbanisation
> smuggling
> capital offence
> garroters

1700–1900: Punishment

You must be able to:

- Explain the development of the police force
- Understand why transportation ended
- Describe how prisons were reformed.

Bow Street Runners

- During the 18th century, watchmen patrolled the cities on foot at night. Parish constables dealt with petty crime and soldiers dealt with riots and large protests.
- The Bow Street Runners were set up in 1750 by John and Henry Fielding. The Bow Street Runners were paid by magistrates to catch criminals; they were given equipment including handcuffs, a pistol and a stick. The aim was to increase the number of criminals captured and sent to court.
- In 1763 they set up a Bow Street horse patrol to stop highwaymen entering or leaving London. This only lasted 18 months; crime in London was increasing and there weren't enough patrols.
- Robert Peel, the Home Secretary (1822–1828), set up a day patrol of the Bow Street Runners. He also reduced the number of death penalty offences, which ended the Bloody Code.

Pistol

Introduction of the Police

- In 1829, Parliament passed the Metropolitan Police Act. This established the first police force in London. Approximately 3200 men were recruited to police a seven-mile circle around London. In 1856, it became compulsory for all counties to have a police force.
- Recruits were carefully selected and were well trained. It was a full time, well paid job. Officers wore a uniform.
- In 1842, a detective department was set up. The police force now tried to solve crimes, as well as patrolling the streets to prevent crime. Patrols focused on areas where the crime rate was high.
- The police were not popular to begin with and were criticised for being drunk. The public felt that the police restricted their freedom. However, over time, they began to be trusted.

Punishment

- **Petty crime** was increasing and execution was too harsh, so an alternative was needed.
- Authorities were concerned with getting rid of criminals in the 17th and 18th centuries. They transported banished people to other places in the empire, mainly America and the Caribbean. These people were used as forced labour and helped Britain's interests overseas.

> ### Key Point
>
> The number of death penalty crimes was reduced so the Bloody Code was abolished; only murder and treason were punishable by execution.

> ### Key Point
>
> A professional police force was introduced to catch criminals in London. By 1856, it was compulsory across the country to have a police force.

- Transportation to Australia was used from 1787 as an alternative to hanging. It acted as a **deterrent**, removed criminals from British society and provided free labour. As many as 160,000 people were transported between 1787 and 1868.
- Transportation was **abolished** in 1868 because Australia no longer required forced labourers. It was becoming too expensive and not a strong enough deterrent; the government had built more prisons – this was cheaper than transportation.

Prisons

- The death penalty became less acceptable so criminals were imprisoned instead. This removed them from society and acted as a deterrent.
- Each prison was run by a gaoler, who each had their own set of rules and regulations for their prisoners. Often, better conditions were only available if the prisoner paid the gaoler.
- Prison systems tried to reform prisoners so they wouldn't re-offend, rather than solely using harsh punishment.
- The 'Separate' and 'Silent' systems isolated prisoners to encourage self-reflection and remorse. But these systems were expensive to run so some prisons continued to use hard labour.

Hangman's noose and gallows in a Victorian jail

Prison Reformers

- John Howard was one of many **prison reformers** who visited prisons and was shocked by the conditions there.
- In his 1777 report *The State of the Prisons in England and Wales*, he suggested measures to improve health and sanitation, including separation of prisoners, and better warders, inspections and diet.
- In 1785, Sir George Paul was allowed to build a new gaol in Gloucester that included individual cells, separation of prisoners, medical care and exercise facilities.
- Elizabeth Fry visited Newgate prison in 1813 and was horrified by the conditions: women crammed together and exploited by male prison warders. She set up education classes to reform female prisoners. She worked to get better food and clothes and treated prisoners with respect and kindness. Fry wanted women to be able to live useful lives once they were freed.
- Robert Peel set up the 1823 Gaol Act to pay gaolers, and provided basic education to prisoners. Prison inspections were to take place and visits by doctors and chaplains were arranged. Women gaolers were provided for women prisoners.
- By the 1830s, prisoners were given clean, separate cells and more work to do. A new prison building programme was also introduced.

Robert Peel, Home Secretary

Quick Test

1. Who set up the Bow Street Runners?
2. How many men were recruited into the police force?
3. What was John Howard's report called?

Key Words

petty crime
deterrent
abolished
prison reformers

1900–Present: Crime

You must be able to:

- Describe why new methods of crime have developed
- Understand why crime rates have risen since 1950
- Describe new examples of crime that have emerged.

Crime Rates

- As British society developed during the twentieth century, criminals found new and different methods of committing crimes.
- Britain has developed into a multi-cultural society, and become more prosperous. Britain has also become far more reliant on technology. Rates of recorded crime gradually fell between 1850 and the 1940s. Since the 1950s, however, crime rates have begun to rise, possibly due to the public having less respect for others and for authority.
- It is also likely to be caused by the fact that far more actions are now classed as crimes.
- Victims of crime are now more likely to report it – particularly due to insurance claims. Also, methods of recording crime have improved.
- There was an increasing trend towards violent crime and **anti-social behaviour** during the twentieth century. Figures suggest that crimes involving sex and violence accounted for 5% of all crime; however, in recent years it has increased to 6%.
- The government continues to make new laws to deal with issues it is concerned about; and public opinion can pressure the government to create new laws. Changing attitudes and opinions may also play a large part in the introduction of new laws.

Burglary

> **Key Point**
>
> Crime rates rose during the twentieth century; however, there is an increased recording and reporting of crime too.

Older Crimes

- Common crimes committed since 1900 include: driving offences and car theft, vandalism and burglary, assault and mugging, and petty theft.
- An increase in anti-social behaviour, such as creating a disturbance, graffiti and being drunk and disorderly, has also occurred.
- Theft has always been a common crime; however, in the twentieth century computers and improvements in transport created new ways for criminals to steal, such as computer hacking or car crime.
- Crimes such as smuggling tobacco or alcohol to make huge profits have happened for years. Drug smuggling rose during the twentieth century and is now a serious crime. It has become lucrative for criminals and is also linked to other major types of crime.

Car theft

New Crimes

- Since the mid twentieth century, new crimes have emerged, such as sex discrimination, computer hacking, traffic crime and race crime.
- Car theft is one of the biggest categories of crime, particularly amongst teenage boys.
- Motor crime covers a range of offences such as drunk driving to traffic offences. In 1996, there were nearly 1.3 million car crimes.
- **People trafficking**, or 'selling' people for prostitution and forced labour has been occurring for centuries; restrictions on immigration have led to a rise in this particular crime. In recent years, criminal gangs have targeted this trade and made vast sums of money.
- Cyber-crime, such as stealing money or defrauding people by gaining their details or 'phishing', is a new version of fraud, and one of the fastest growing crimes in Britain.
- Hooliganism increased during the later part of the twentieth century. Football became a major source of this crime. Matches were less a source of entertainment and more a chance to get involved in fighting and inflict pain on others.
- Terrorism is not a new crime, but modern weapons, transport and communication mean that more ordinary people are at risk. Most commonly, this had been the threat of bombings by the IRA or more recently Al Qaeda or ISIS.
- The number of attacks has been relatively small, but the threat to public order and safety has made terrorism a huge concern.
- The Race Relations Act of 1965 made it illegal to **discriminate** on the grounds of colour, race or ethnic origin in businesses and workplaces and to stir up racial hatred. In 1976, the Commission for Racial Equality was set up. Most victims of race crime are members of ethnic minority groups. Cases such as the murder of Stephen Lawrence in 1993 have been important in highlighting this particular type of crime, and ensured that racism is treated as a serious offence.
- Many of these 'new crimes' are similar in methods and motives to crimes committed in previous centuries. However, because of media reporting, people can be given the impression that crime is rising and the general public is at risk.

Cyber crime

Racism

Quick Test

1. What has Britain become more reliant on during this period?
2. How many car crimes took place in 1996?
3. In what year was the Race Relations Act introduced?

Key Words

anti-social behaviour
people trafficking
discriminate

1900–Present: Punishment

You must be able to:

- Understand how policing has developed in the twentieth century
- Understand why the death penalty was controversial
- Describe the changes in the nature of punishment.

Technology Improvements

- Since the beginning of the twentieth century, policing has dramatically improved and has been supported by the impact of technology on preventing, discovering and prosecuting crimes.
- Improvements in technology include radios, CCTV and computers for detecting and recording crimes. Improvements in science include fingerprinting, DNA evidence, and transport development such as cars, motorbikes and helicopters.

Changes in Policing

- The police now work with forces and agencies in the UK and worldwide.
- Motorised transport means that the police can reach crimes and crime scenes faster, although it has led to a reduction of police officers 'on the beat'.
- The modern police force represents Britain's multicultural society and includes female officers and officers from different ethnic groups. The first women joined the police force in 1920 and the first female Chief Constable was appointed in 1996.
- In 1982 Neighbourhood Watch schemes were set up in the UK to help prevent and detect crime in local neighbourhoods.
- Police regularly engage with the community through social media.
- In 2002 Police Community Support Officers (PCSOs) were introduced as another measure in crime prevention and in an attempt to improve the image of the police force.

Specialist Police Units

- There are a number of specialist police units:
- CID (Criminal Investigation Department) – detectives investigating serious crimes. Forensic science and the use of DNA have been important in this area.
- Special Branch – aims to prevent all forms of terrorism.
- NCA (National Crime Agency) – detects and prevents serious organised crime, including drug and people trafficking.
- Traffic Department – deals with issues relating to road use.
- Police Central e-crime Unit (PCeU) – deals with cyber crime.

Capital Punishment

- Capital punishment was last used for murder in 1964 and abolished in 1965. Controversial cases led people to question it:

CCTV has changed police supervision of difficult areas

Police

- 1950 – Timothy Evans was hanged for murdering his wife and baby. Evidence later proved that he was innocent.
- 1953 – Derek Bentley was hanged for murdering a policeman, even though he hadn't fired the gun. He was posthumously pardoned in 1998.
- 1955 – Ruth Ellis was hanged for murdering her boyfriend, despite having been subjected to violent abuse for years.

New Punishments

- New punishments are aimed more at rehabilitating criminals, as **reform** and paying back society are now considered important.
- **Community sentences** involve working on community projects for a required number of hours.
- Treatment programmes are given out for criminals with drug or alcohol problems.
- ASBOs (Anti-Social Behaviour Orders) require people to conform to a set of rules.
- Electronic tagging is used to ensure that offenders remain indoors during specified times.
- Restorative justice involves the offender and victim meeting to discuss why the crime was committed.

> **Key Point**
>
> Ideas about the nature of punishment have changed as reform and rehabilitation of criminals is seen as increasingly important.

Prison

- Prisons try to reduce re-offending rates through education and giving prisoners work that teaches them new skills. However, they have mixed success rates and the public do not always support what can be portrayed as 'easy' or 'cushy' prisons.
- The use of prisons continued to increase after 1900. Different prisons (for example 'open' or high security) are used to house different types of criminals.
- Since 1907, prisoners have been released on **probation** – they have to report to probation officers, and are put back into prison if they break the conditions.
- In 1948, hard labour and corporal punishment in prisons was abolished.
- Borstals were set up for young people in the early 1900s and used work and education to try to reduce youth re-offending rates. In 1982, they were replaced by Youth Detention Centres, with fixed term sentences and a tougher regime, called a 'short, sharp, shock'. But re-offending rates remained as high.
- There has been a rise in female prisoners – although only approximately 6% of the total prison population is female.

Strangeways Prison, Manchester

> **Quick Test**
>
> 1. In what year did women first join the police force?
> 2. What does PCSO stand for?
> 3. In what year was hard labour abolished in prisons?

> **Key Words**
>
> reform
> community sentences
> probation

Case Studies

You must be able to:

- Understand how and why witchcraft was harshly punished in the sixteenth and seventeenth centuries
- Understand the roles and treatment of conscientious objectors during the First and Second World Wars.

Witchcraft – Case Study, 1500–1700

- Witchcraft had been a crime since medieval times, but in the sixteenth and seventeenth centuries it was regarded as a more serious crime and was harshly punished.
- There were a number of reasons for the increase:
  - Religion – many people believed that the devil was doing evil acts on a regular basis.
  - War – conflicts led people to become more suspicious of each other.
  - Authority – King James strongly believed in witchcraft and had written a book about witchcraft called *Demonology*. Many other important members of authority also believed in witches and witchcraft.
  - **Prejudice** – most of the people who were accused of being a witch were old, poor, single and uneducated women. They were often vulnerable and isolated from their own community.
  - Changing attitudes – people were worried they might be 'cursed' by a poor person they had refused to help and looked for scapegoats on whom they could blame their bad luck.

Evidence of Witchcraft

- People accused of witchcraft were tested to find evidence of their guilt. The following signs were used to convict people:
  - If a person had unusual marks on their body like spots, freckles and pimples, these were used as examples of guilt.
  - Witness accounts and statements suggesting the person had committed evil deeds, or a **confession** after torture from the accused.
  - If they did not bleed when pricked with a needle or knife.
  - If they floated when they were thrown into water they were regarded as guilty – this was known as the swimming test.
- People found guilty of major witchcraft were usually hung.
- Witchcraft prosecution began to decline after the Civil War as there was increased political stability and people became less suspicious of others.
- Some still believed in the devil but the increase of education and scientific understanding helped provide **rational** explanations for events that had previously been blamed on witches.

A 17th century witches' monument

Key Point

A variety of tests were carried out to gain evidence to prove people were witches.

17th century gallows

- Witchcraft laws were finally abolished in 1736.
- Matthew Hopkins was the Witchfinder General. He accused women of witchcraft and often used torture to get them to confess. The accused women were hanged. Hopkins earned money for each witch that was executed.

Conscientious Objectors – Case Study, Twentieth Century

- During the First World War, the government introduced a law known as **conscription** that said that all men aged between 18 and 41 could be made to join the armed forces. This was introduced from 1916.
- Over 15,000 men refused to fight on religious or **moral** grounds. They were conscientious objectors (COs). They felt it was not right to be involved in a conflict where humans were killing each other.
- Military tribunals made up of officers and professionals were set up to decide if their claims were genuine.
- Only 400 were given total **exemption** from taking part in the war.
- However, many COs agreed to do other war-related work such as working in hospitals, or driving injured soldiers around.
- Over 1000 men refused to take part in the war at all. These men were put on trial by special courts called tribunals, and if they were found guilty, they were sent to prison, and had their voting rights taken away – 71 men died in prison as a result of poor treatment.
- During the Second World War, the government was more lenient towards COs. Prison was only used as a last resort.
- Conscription was re-introduced from April 1939 for men and December 1941 for women.
- Over 45,000 people were given complete or partial exemption. Those with partial exemption were given non-combat roles, such as working on farms or in factories. These were still important roles to help Britain win the war, but the COs avoided any direct conflict.
- However, much of the public still resented the COs and they were often abused in the street, beaten up or sacked from their jobs.

Key Point

Witchcraft prosecution began to decline after the Civil War.

New British Army recruits being inspected by King George

Key Point

During the Second World War conscientious objectors were only sent to prison as a last resort.

Key Words

prejudice
confession
rational
conscription
moral
exemption

Quick Test

1. Who was the Witchfinder General?
2. In what year was witchcraft abolished?
3. How many men refused to fight in the First World War?
4. What year was conscription introduced in the First World War?

Review Questions

Health and Medicine: Medieval Medicine (Middle Ages) 1

1 Explain why hospitals did not improve people's health in the Middle Ages.

2 Explain how Arab medicine had an impact on beliefs about health in Britain.

3 Name the theory that was devised by Galen.

4 Explain Hippocrates' beliefs.

5 How important was the role of women in medicine and treatment in the Middle Ages?

6 'Health was so poor in the Middle Ages because of people's reluctance to move away from Galen's and Hippocrates' beliefs.'

How far do you agree? Explain your answer.

Write your answer on a separate piece of paper.

Health and Medicine: Medieval Medicine (Middle Ages) 2

1 Give one reason why the Roman removal from Britain caused regression.

2 Give one reason why medicine did not progress in the Middle Ages.

3 Who were flagellants and what did they do?

4 Write a clear and organised summary of the importance of religion in medicine in the Middle Ages. Support your summary with detailed examples.

5 Write a clear and organised summary of the types of remedies people tried to cure the Black Death.

Write your answer on a separate piece of paper.

6 'Public health was so poor in the Middle Ages because of people's lack of scientific knowledge.'

How far do you agree? Explain your answer.

Write your answer on a separate piece of paper.

Review Questions

Health and Medicine: Renaissance Medicine (1400s–1600s) 1

1 Give one reason why people were slow to accept Vesalius' discoveries.

2 Explain why Vesalius' and Harvey's discoveries did not improve people's health.

3 Explain the importance of technology to the progress of medical understanding in Britain.

4 Write a clear and organised summary of the reasons for the change in people's ideas during the Renaissance period.

Write your answer on a separate piece of paper.

5 How important was the role of religion in medicine and treatment in the Renaissance period?

Write your answer on a separate piece of paper.

6 'The work of Vesalius was the most important reason for the progress in medical understanding in the Renaissance period.'

How far do you agree? Explain your answer.

Write your answer on a separate piece of paper.

Health and Medicine: Renaissance Medicine (1400s–1600s) 2

1 Give one reason why 'cures' for the Plague did not work.

2 Give one example of how people tried to prevent the Plague.

3 Explain how the government tried to improve public health in the Renaissance period.

4 Write a clear and organised summary of the problems of hospitals in the Renaissance period.

5 What improvements were there in hospitals during the Renaissance period?

Write your answer on a separate piece of paper.

6 'In the Renaissance period, there were improvements in people's understanding about public health.'

How far do you agree? Explain your answer.

Write your answer on a separate piece of paper.

Review Questions

Health and Medicine: Industrial Medicine (1700s–1900) 1

1 Explain why public health worsened during the Industrial Revolution.

2 Explain why the first Public Health Act of 1848 did not improve people's health.

3 Explain the importance of the second Public Health Act of 1875.

4 Write a clear and organised summary of the improvements in treatments during the Industrial Revolution.

Write your answer on a separate piece of paper.

5 How important was John Snow's discovery in improving public health?

Write your answer on a separate piece of paper.

6 'Health was so poor in the Industrial Revolution because of the increase of people in towns and cities.'

How far do you agree? Explain your answer.

Write your answer on a separate piece of paper.

Health and Medicine: Industrial Medicine (1700s–1900) 2

1 Give one reason why Florence Nightingale's impact could be seen as limited.

....

....

2 Explain how Edward Jenner improved health during the Industrial Revolution.

....

....

....

....

....

3 Explain the importance of Pasteur's discovery.

Write your answer on a separate piece of paper.

4 Write a clear and organised summary of the progress made in surgery during the Industrial period.

Write your answer on a separate piece of paper.

5 How important was the role of Florence Nightingale in improving health care in the Industrial Revolution?

Write your answer on a separate piece of paper.

6 'Health improved in the Industrial period because of Koch's discovery.'

How far do you agree? Explain your answer.

Write your answer on a separate piece of paper.

Review Questions

Health and Medicine: Modern Medicine (1900s–Present) 1

1 Why was Fleming unable to continue his work?

2 Explain how Florey and Chain enabled medicine to progress.

3 Explain the importance of magic bullets as treatment.

4 Write a clear and organised summary of the development of understanding of DNA.

Write your answer on a separate piece of paper.

5 How important was the role of the US in enabling antibiotics to be produced?

Write your answer on a separate piece of paper.

6 'The outbreak of World War One was the most important factor in allowing health to improve in the twentieth century.'

How far do you agree? Explain your answer.

Write your answer on a separate piece of paper.

Health and Medicine: Modern Medicine (1900s–Present) 2

1 Give one success of the NHS.

_____

2 Explain why the NHS was set up.

_____

_____

_____

3 Explain the importance of the Liberal reforms.

_____

_____

_____

_____

_____

_____

_____

4 Write a clear and organised summary of the problems faced by the NHS.

Write your answer on a separate piece of paper.

5 How important was the Boer War in allowing the Liberals to create their reforms?

Write your answer on a separate piece of paper.

6 'William Beveridge's report in 1944 was the main reason the NHS was set up.'

How far do you agree? Explain your answer.

Write your answer on a separate piece of paper.

Review Questions

Health and Medicine: Modern Medicine (1900s–Present) 3

1 Give an example of a virus that emerged during the twentieth century.

_____

2 Describe a treatment now used to fight cancer.

_____

_____

_____

3 Name two scans that were developed during the twentieth century.

_____

4 Write a clear and organised summary of the new diseases that emerged in the twentieth century.

Write your answer on a separate piece of paper.

5 Explain how government campaigns have improved people's health in recent years.

_____

_____

_____

_____

_____

_____

6 'Scientific developments in the twentieth century were wholly positive.'

How far do you agree? Explain your answer.

Write your answer on a separate piece of paper.

1000–1500: Crime

1 How did William ensure his laws were obeyed?

_____

_____

2 What were the aims of a Saxon king's laws?

_____

_____

3 How was a wergild administered?

_____

_____

4 Why were gangs of outlaws feared?

_____

_____

_____

5 How was crime punished during Saxon times?

_____

_____

_____

_____

6 Why did ordinary people hate the Forest Laws introduced by William?

Write your answer on a separate piece of paper.

Practice Questions

1000–1500: Punishment

1 What was the most common punishment given in a Manor Court?

....

2 What methods of punishment were used in the Medieval period?

....

....

....

3 Which four courts could people be tried in?

....

....

4 Explain why trial by ordeal was carried out.

....

....

....

5 Explain how law and order was enforced in this period.

....

....

....

....

6 Why was the church an important feature of Medieval crime and punishment?

Write your answer on a separate piece of paper.

1500–1700: Crime

1 Why did heresy increase during the sixteenth century?

2 Why was the punishment for treason so brutal?

3 Explain why highway robbery became more common.

4 Describe three reasons why crime increased during this period.

5 What happened to beggars with the introduction of the Vagrancy Act?

6 Explain why the crime of poaching increased.

Write your answer on a separate piece of paper.

Practice Questions

1500–1700: Punishment

1 Why were royal judges important?

....

....

2 Why did the plotters attempt to kill King James?

....

....

3 Why is this period known as the Bloody Code?

....

....

....

4 Describe three methods of policing that were used during this period.

....

....

....

....

5 Why did the Bloody Code fail to end smuggling?

Write your answer on a separate piece of paper.

6 'Policing did not improve during this period.'

How far do you agree? Explain your answer.

Write your answer on a separate piece of paper.

1700–1900: Crime

1 What was the most common crime committed during this period?

2 Where did slums develop?

3 Name two groups who were affected by worker unrest.

4 How did the development of the media influence opinion on crime?

5 Which types of crime increased during this period?

6 Explain why there was an increase in crime.

Practice Questions

1700–1900: Punishment

1 How did Robert Peel end the Bloody Code?

2 Give two reasons why the police were not popular to begin with.

3 What were the main features of the Metropolitan Police force?

4 Why did attitudes to punishment change?

5 Explain three attempts used by Elizabeth Fry to reform prisons for women.

Write your answer on a separate piece of paper.

6 Why did the crime rate fall after 1850?

Write your answer on a separate piece of paper.

1900–Present: Crime

1 Describe three ways in which Britain developed during the twentieth century.

_____

_____

_____

2 Why have crime rates risen since 1950?

_____

_____

_____

3 Why are new laws introduced by the government?

_____

_____

4 Give three examples of how terrorism has developed in the late twentieth and early twenty-first centuries.

_____

_____

5 Give three examples of anti-social behaviour.

_____

_____

6 Give examples of new crimes that have emerged in recent years.

_____

_____

Practice Questions

1900–Present: Punishment

1 What improvements in technology during the last century have helped the police?

....

....

....

2 Give three examples of new punishments.

....

....

3 Why did Youth Detention Centres replace borstals?

Write your answer on a separate piece of paper.

4 What is the purpose of prison in the twenty-first century?

....

....

....

....

....

5 Describe three examples that demonstrate how the use of capital punishment became more controversial.

Write your answer on a separate piece of paper.

6 How successful has the use of prisons been in this period?

Write your answer on a separate piece of paper.

Case Studies

1 Why were most of those accused of witchcraft old women?

_____

_____

_____

_____

2 Give three examples of supposed signs or evidence of witchcraft.

_____

_____

3 'Matthew Hopkins was just a conman.'

How far do you agree? Explain your answer.

Write your answer on a separate piece of paper.

4 Give two reasons why conscientious objectors refused to fight.

_____

_____

_____

5 Why were conscientious objectors treated harshly during the First World War?

_____

_____

_____

6 How were conscientious objectors treated during the Second World War?

_____

_____

Review Questions

1000–1500: Crime

1 Why is it difficult to know the true crime rate from the Medieval period?

2 Which crimes were considered serious in the Medieval period?

3 Why were churches targeted by outlaws?

4 How did outlaw gangs manage to evade capture?

5 Why were Norman laws so harsh?

6 Give three reasons why life was difficult for peasants.

1000–1500: Punishment

1 Give two reasons why punishments took place in public.

2 Give two ways that criminals were hunted in the Medieval period.

3 Describe how trial by hot water proved guilt or innocence.

4 Explain the difference between a royal court and a church court.

Write your answer on a separate piece of paper.

5 Describe the key features of a parish constable's job.

6 Would you describe Medieval punishment as harsh or lenient?

Write your answer on a separate piece of paper.

Review Questions

1500–1700: Crime

1 What was the punishment for nobles who committed treason?

2 How could a strong government affect crime rates?

3 Describe the two different types of beggars.

4 Give two factors that affected crime rates during this period.

5 Why was there an increase in the number of street criminals and thieves?

6 Why did begging increase during this period?

1500–1700: Punishment

1 Name three types of punishment used in this period.

2 What was transportation?

3 Why did religious protests increase? Give an example of one.

4 How was Guy Fawkes punished?

5 Was Jonathon Wild a hero or villain? Explain your answer.

Write your answer on a separate piece of paper.

6 'The Bloody Code was a failure.'

How far do you agree? Explain your answer.

Write your answer on a separate piece of paper.

Review Questions

1700–1900: Crime

1 Which two groups protested for the right to vote and for better working conditions?

2 How was the Riot Act used?

3 How did media developments affect crime reporting?

4 Which crimes increased in poorer districts of towns and cities?

5 Why were the Tolpuddle Martyrs arrested?

6 Why did the Jack the Ripper case become notorious?

1700–1900: Punishment

1 Which three countries could people be transported to?

2 Describe how Sir George Paul improved prisons.

3 How did the Gaol Act try to improve prisons?

4 Why did reforms in punishment take place?

5 How did policing develop during this period?

Write your answer on a separate piece of paper.

6 Give two similarities and two differences between the Bow Street Runners and the Metropolitan Police.

Write your answer on a separate piece of paper.

Review Questions

1900–Present: Crime

1 Give three examples of common crimes committed since 1900.

2 Explain how fraud has evolved in the twentieth and twenty-first centuries.

3 Give two reasons for the increase in people trafficking.

4 Give two examples of cyber crime.

5 Why was the Race Relations Act of 1965 important?

6 Give two examples of old crimes that have now become new crimes in this period.

Write your answer on a separate piece of paper.

1900–Present: Punishment

1 What does NCA stand for and what is their aim?

....

....

....

....

2 Give a limitation of the development of motorised transport for the police.

....

3 Give two examples of scientific developments in police investigation.

....

....

....

4 Explain three examples of alternative punishment.

Write your answer on a separate piece of paper.

5 Give three examples of specialist police units.

....

....

....

....

....

6 'Improved technology is the most important development in recent years for policing.'

How far do you agree? Explain your answer.

Write your answer on a separate piece of paper.

Review Questions

Case Studies

1 Why did some people confess to witchcraft?

2 How did rational explanations affect witchcraft accusations?

3 Why did witchcraft become a crime that was harshly punished?

4 Give three examples of work that a conscientious objector may have to do.

5 Give examples of two punishments for conscientious objectors.

....

....

....

6 'Conscientious objectors were treated too harshly.'

How far do you agree? Explain your answer.

....

....

....

....

....

....

....

....

....

....

....

....

....

....

Mixed Questions

Norman England

Where space is not provided, write your answers on separate pieces of paper.

1 In what year did Edward marry Edith (Godwine's daughter)?

2 Give two reasons why William had a strong claim to the English throne in 1066.

3 In Anglo-Saxon England, what was a thegn?

4 Why did the Saxon forces get defeated at the Battle of Fulford?

5 Explain how castles helped William control England.

6 'William only commissioned the Domesday Book in order to get more tax from the Saxons.'

How far do you agree with this statement?

Explain your answer.

7 Name two types of soldiers that William had in his army during the Battle of Hastings.

8 'Harald Hardrada lost the Battle of Stamford Bridge because he was no match for the Saxon army.'

How far do you agree?

Explain your answer.

9 What date did William land at Pevensey Bay?

10 What did Robert inherit from his father after his death?

11 Explain why there was a crisis in 1066 when Edward died.

12 In what year did the Norman earls, Roger and Ralph, try to stage a revolt?

13 In Anglo-Saxon England, what three groups of people usually became thralls?

14 Explain how society changed under Norman rule.

15 'There was more continuity than change in Norman England.'

How far do you agree with this statement?

Explain your answer.

16 'Edgar the Aetheling had the greatest claim to the throne in 1066.'

How far do you agree?

Explain your answer.

17 Give two reasons why Edward promised William the throne in 1051.

18 Who supported Robert's claim for the English throne?

19 Describe the tactic that William used to break the Saxon shield wall at the Battle of Hastings.

20 'The Saxons did little to hinder William's progress as king of England.'

How far do you agree?

Give reasons for your answer.

Refer to at least one Saxon rebellion in your answer.

Mixed Questions

Elizabethan England

Where space is not provided, write your answers on separate pieces of paper.

1 What links did England and Spain have in 1558?

2 'Elizabeth's government did little to help the poor.'

How far do you agree?

Explain your answer.

3 'Making trade links was the most important reason why exploration boomed under Elizabeth.'

How far do you agree with this view?

Explain your answer.

4 What was agreed in the Elizabethan Religious Settlement?

5 What were the main consequences of the Throckmorton Plot?

6 What was the threat posed by Mary, Queen of Scots to Elizabeth I?

7 Why was England's financial position difficult in 1558?

8 'Religious differences were the most important reason why the Spanish Armada attacked England.'

How far do you agree?

Explain your answer.

9 Was opposition to theatres in Elizabethan England strong?

10 How did Elizabeth show her people that she was Queen during her reign?

11 Why did Elizabeth I never marry?

12 Why did people challenge the Elizabethan Religious Settlement?

13 Did Elizabethan people become better off?

14 What was the most important achievement of the Elizabethan voyages?

15 Was Francis Drake a hero or a villain?

16 Why was the succession a problem during the reign of Elizabeth I?

17 How was the reign of Elizabeth I a 'golden era'?

18 What difficulties did being a female ruler present to Elizabeth I?

19 Why did the Spanish Armada fail?

20 Which rebellion or plot posed the greatest threat to Elizabeth I?

Mixed Questions

Health and Medicine

Where space is not provided, write your answers on separate pieces of paper.

1 Explain why treatments in the Medieval period did not work.

....

....

....

2 Give one symptom of the Sweating Sickness.

....

3 Which Public Health Act had the greater impact on public health?

....

4 'The progress made in the understanding of the body during the Renaissance period was due to the role of science and technology'.

How far do you agree?

Explain your answer.

5 Give one example of how treatments were used during the Industrial Revolution.

....

6 Give the names of the individuals responsible for the development of DNA.

....

....

7 'The work of Harvey was the most important reason for the progress in medical understanding in the Renaissance period.'

How far do you agree?

Explain your answer.

8 Give one example of a prevention method used to try to stop the Plague.

9 Describe why public health was poor during the Renaissance period.

10 Describe the successes and limitations of hospitals during the Renaissance period.

11 Give two reasons why public health declined after the Romans left Britain.

12 Describe Chadwick's contribution to health in the Industrial period.

13 Give one reason why public health was so poor during the Industrial Revolution.

14 What new type of hospital was created in the Industrial period?

15 Explain Galen's beliefs.

16 Describe Florence Nightingale's contribution to medicine and treatment.

17 Give one reason why people were slow to accept Harvey's discoveries.

18 Describe two ways in which World War Two helped medicine to progress.

19 How important was Booth and Rowntree's work in allowing the Liberals to create their reforms?

20 'There was little progress in medicine in Britain during the Medieval period because of a lack of scientific knowledge'.

How far do you agree?

Explain your answer.

Mixed Questions

Crime and Punishment

Where space is not provided, write your answers on separate pieces of paper.

1 Name two influential prison reformers.

2 Why did begging become a crime?

3 Name two new crimes of the twentieth century.

4 What method of torture was used on Guy Fawkes?

5 Describe one of the main aims of king's laws in Saxon England.

6 Give three reasons why the Bow Street horse patrol was a failure.

7 What new law did William introduce after becoming king in 1066?

8 Which two factors affected the crime rate between 1500 and 1700?

9 Explain how present-day prisons attempt to reduce re-offending rates.

10 What was the punishment for nobles who committed treason?

11 What nickname was given to watchmen in the seventeenth century?

12 Who made the laws in Saxon England?

13 Explain why witchcraft prosecution began to decline.

14 Why are victims of crime now more likely to report it?

15 How did the wergild work?

16 Give examples of two groups of people involved in smuggling.

17 Describe one of the problems associated with blood feuds.

18 In what two ways could beggars be classified?

19 'The introduction of prisons was an immediate success.'

How far do you agree?

Explain your answer.

20 'The Bloody Code was a success.'

How far do you agree?

Explain your answer.

Answers

Please note that the answers given here are not intended to be full or model answers. They are intended to offer guidance on the kind of points you would be expected to include in your answer.

Pages 4-21 Revise Questions

Page 5 Quick Test: Anglo-Saxon Society on the Eve of Conquest
1. Roman Catholic (Christian church)
2. Iron or water
3. Sons of kings or rich thegns and monks

Page 7 Quick Test: The Succession Crisis of 1066
1. 1051
2. That Harold should be the next king
3. Edward had no children. He had allegedly promised the kingdom to two different people.
4. 5 January 1066

Page 9 Quick Test: The Rival Claimants to the Throne in 1066
1. Edgar the Aetheling
2. Distant cousins
3. King Magnus of Norway

Page 11 Quick Test: The Battles of Fulford and Stamford Bridge
1. Earl Morcar of Northumbria and Earl Edwin of Mercia
2. The way to York lay open for Hardrada; the people of York were forced to accept Hardrada as their king and agreed to help and support his claim to the English throne against Harold Godwinson; the victory would have boosted the Vikings' confidence
3. 25 September 1066
4. Hardrada was killed; the Viking conquest of England was defeated; Harold Godwinson remained king

Page 13 Quick Test: The Battle of Hastings
1. Peasant/amateur soldiers from Harold's army
2. Harold went back on his oath to support William's claim to the English crown
3. They had seen the Normans retreating and possibly wanted to claim their spoils of war

Page 15 Quick Test: Anglo-Saxon Resistance and the Norman Response
1. Hereward's rebellion in 1070
2. Burnt land and crops, killed people and animals. This is known as the Harrying of the North.
3. The king is the head of the feudal system. He divides land up and gives it to his barons in return for loyalty and military service. The barons give land to the knights in return for promising to fight when needed. The knights lend land to villeins who have to work on the land for free and pay taxes to the knights.

Page 17 Quick Test: Life Under Norman Control
1. Chancellor
2. Geld
3. William saw no point in changing things for the sake of it. If things worked well he wanted to keep them. He also wanted to be viewed as Edward's legitimate heir and so continued things from his reign.

Page 19 Quick Test: Norman Castles and the Domesday Book
1. Motte and bailey castles
2. To show the power of the Normans; to put down Saxon rebellions; as a base for Norman barons, soldiers and resources; to administer Norman rule
3. 1085
4. To gain tax

Page 21 Quick Test: The Norman Church and the Death of William I
1. 10% (a title = 10%)
2. 1070
3. William Rufus

Pages 22-31 Practice Questions

Page 22: Anglo-Saxon Society on the Eve of Conquest
1. Trial by ordeal – iron, water; Trial by hundred court (Any one)
2. From the top – kings, earls, thegns, ceorls and thralls
3. 1042
4. The source shows the king and the Witan in discussion; the king seems to be listening to the advice given by the Witan; all men are drawn on the same level – could show the importance of the Witan; the king could ignore the advice given by the Witan but a successful king needed to have loyal supporters – earls could have revolted against a king; the king had the ultimate power but the Witan included some churchmen; religion was very important and so the king would have wanted to remain on good terms with the Witan.
5. The majority of people's lives revolved around the land; ceorls paid food rent to the thegn; each ceorl worked a hide of the thegn's land; as the Anglo-Saxon period developed, some ceorls had specialised jobs such as shoemakers, bakers and merchants; girls would learn skills centred on the home, boys would learn skills to feed and look after their families.
6. Rather than punishing people severely on the say-so of the king, courts were becoming more important; the accused would be able to have their say and make a plea/oath. This would be taken seriously; kings would be viewed more favourably if they ruled fairly and with clear laws; the source supports this because punishments were harsh if you were proven to be guilty but also it was fair (or should have been) to everybody.

Page 23: The Succession Crisis of 1066
1. The Northumbrian Crisis in 1065 where Edward supported the removal of Tostig.
2. Earl of Wessex
3. Harold Godwinson
4. We can learn that Edward had people surrounding him as he lay dying; one man is close to his head; there appears to be a member of the clergy in attendance; the man at his head might be Harold Godwinson; the image might support Harold's claim that he was promised the throne by Edward.
5. He was an Englishman; he had proved he was a good ruler because he had helped Edward in the years before his death; he had been loyal and was a strong soldier who would fight for his country; his position as Earl of Wessex made him one of the most powerful men in England. (Any two)
6. Edward had no children so there was no direct heir to the throne; Edward had promised the kingdom to both William and Harold; the Witan supported Harold; William argued that Harold had promised to support his claim and so the Pope supported William's claim (Harold was seen as a usurper (to use something without the right) because he broke his promise and seized the crown).

Page 24: The Rival Claimants to the Throne in 1066
1. Harald Hardrada
2. Harthacnut (King of England and Norway) had no heir and promised the throne to King Magnus. Edward had seized the throne from Magnus in 1042. Hardrada was Magnus' son and therefore believed that he was the rightful heir.
3. Harold Godwinson had broken his oath to support William's claim and so the Pope gave his blessing to William.
4. It proves that people believed Harold had made an oath; it proves that the oath was made without pressure; it could be inferred that Harold had been in Normandy for the reason of making an oath and possibly sent by Edward; it does not prove the statement because the writer was Norman and so could be

158 GCSE History Revision Guide

saying there had been an oath made without pressure to justify the Norman invasion and conquest.

5. Edgar was a child; he was out of England and struggled to get a force together to match Godwinson's power; the Witan supported Harold's claim and Edgar would have found it difficult to gain the crown without fighting Harold Godwinson for it.

6. Harold was the only Englishman contesting the throne; he was Earl of Wessex and Edward had left much of the governing of England to him in his final years, meaning that Harold had experience and the support of the royal court; the Witan supported Harold's claim; arguably Edward had promised the kingdom to Harold as he lay on his deathbed.
   You should also refer to at least one other contender to show why Harold's claim may be disputed. For example, William of Normandy also had a strong claim; Edward had allegedly promised William the throne in 1051 and this claim was supported by Godwinson; Godwinson was a usurper and had wrongly seized the throne away from William; William and Edward had a strong relationship and Edward had spent much of his youth in Normandy.
   You should then reach a conclusion – how far do you agree? Completely, partly or not at all. (Example: Godwinson did/partly/did not have the strongest claim to the throne because… ')

Page 25: The Battles of Fulford and Stamford Bridge

1. 20 September 1066

2. Hardrada sailed from Norway to the north of England; when he landed he wanted to capture York; his army needed to fight Saxon earls who were defending the route inland towards York; the Saxon earls, Morcar and Edwin, led the defending forces.

3. It was a significant consequence of the battle because the Viking army would have had their morale increased by seeing the slaughter of the Saxons; the Vikings would have believed in their ability to defeat Harold Godwinson when the two sides met again at Stamford Bridge; the mental advantage the Vikings had would have been important because as they prepared for the next battle they would have been confident that the Saxons could be defeated once more; this might have also had a negative impact on the Saxon army after hearing about the Saxon defeat at Fulford; however, another significant consequence was that the way to York was open for the Vikings after the victory. This meant Hardrada was able to capture York and start to secure his influence over the north; the people of York were forced to accept Hardrada as their king and agree to support him against Godwinson; this was hugely important because it meant Harold Godwinson had to fight Harald soon to ensure that Harald's control over the north was not consolidated; a conclusion that focuses on 'how far you agree'.

4. His forces had defeated Hardrada; he remained king of England; the north could return to peace following the Viking invasion; he only had to defend his crown from the threat from William of Normandy.

5. Godwinson's forces had surprised the Viking army by arriving sooner than expected; some of the Vikings were not fully prepared and were missing their chainmail and armour; the Viking warrior blocking the bridge was killed; then Hardrada was killed.

6. Godwinson realised if Hardrada was left in the north he would be able to conquer large parts and create an almost separate Viking-controlled country from which to launch his attack on the English throne; Godwinson knew that the Vikings had defeated the earls in the north at Fulford and had captured York. This was a strategic advantage for Hardrada, and Godwinson needed to act; Godwinson knew that William of Normandy would invade to try and claim the throne. He didn't want the prospect of having a battle in the north and south at the same time. This would have weakened his army and caused further problems; Harold wanted to defeat Hardrada and make the north secure before William had a chance to invade in the south.

Page 26: The Battle of Hastings

1. Religion was very important to people in the Middle Ages – belief that God was on your side would have raised confidence (God would help secure victory to your army); soldiers would also believe that the battle being fought was a holy crusade against the usurper Godwinson if the Pope's blessing was on the campaign.

2. Senlac Hill

3. His army had brought with them from Normandy everything they would need for the conquest – weapons, variety of soldiers; William's men outnumbered the Saxon army; all of William's men were professional soldiers who had been well trained.

4. William led his men by example – he fought alongside them in the main battle. This showed his men that he was courageous and believed in the cause. His men would have been encouraged by his display on the battlefield; during the battle a rumour had spread that William had been killed, his men had started to retreat; that he had not died re-energised his men and they fought with extra conviction; however, the victory cannot all be down to William alone. When his men retreated the Saxon army broke ranks and chased the Normans down the hill. This was a turning point in the battle because it meant that the Saxon defensive line had been broken; William's tactic of feigning retreat again, which caused the shield wall to be broken, played a huge part in the victory.

5. It shows the Saxon army on top of Senlac Hill; it shows the shield wall used by the Saxons; it shows some weapons used in the battle – spears, clubs, swords, shields; it shows Norman knights on horseback in their full armour; it shows the carnage of the battle – men and horses cut to pieces, charging cavalry; it shows the Saxons maintaining their defence on the hill at the start of the battle with the Normans unable to break through the lines.

6. Harold placed his men at the top of Senlac Hill; this was a good tactic because it meant his men had height advantage and could see the Norman army; the road to London went across Senlac Hill so he blocked William's access to the city; Harold ensured his men remained firm behind their shield wall; Harold packed his men tightly behind the shields so that no area was a weakness.

Page 27: Anglo-Saxon Resistance and the Norman Response

1. Bishop Odo

2. The north (tried to ally with the Danes).

3. Land was set alight; crops were destroyed; villages were destroyed; men, women and children were murdered; animals were slaughtered; survivors starved because of the damage to the land and crops, and the death of the animals. (Any two)

4. Land was given to loyal Normans who could keep an eye on the Saxons; barons had knights at their disposal to put down any rebellions by the Saxons; the Saxons were tenants on the land and knew that their lords were the Normans who were in charge of the land; all but two Saxon earls were replaced with Norman barons.

5. Saxon earls who did try to rebel, such as Edwin and Morcar, were defeated and this meant the Saxons were unable to unite their forces against the Normans. This was an important factor in explaining why the Saxons were ineffective against the Normans because rebellions that did occur were sporadic and generally singular events; there are other reasons to explain why the Saxons could not be effective in their rebellions. The Normans had built castles in which to control and maintain obedience to the new rulers. The Saxons did not have the resources to fight against Norman barons and all of their assets; the feudal system also kept the Saxons firmly in their place and unable to properly fight back; the Harrying of the North could be used as an example of why the Saxons thought better of attempting rebellion after 1070. The north was a harsh example of what William was capable of.

6. Roger and Ralph were Normans who were supposed to be loyal towards William; if the Saxons had joined with the rebellion then William would have found it very difficult to stop; William needed to set an example of what would happen if earls tried to go against him; William had consolidated his power over the Saxons and so this was the final piece to finish his complete conquest of England – to ensure complete loyalty from his barons.

Page 28-29: Life Under Norman Control

1. Earls helped William control and run the country; the Chancellor helped with the day-to-day running of the country; administrative sheriffs; local government roles; shire courts; the hundred courts; the geld taxation system. (Any three)

2. If a Norman was murdered, the nearest village would be held responsible for bringing the guilty person to justice; if no one was caught for the crime then the village would be heavily fined.

3. The law stated that people could not hunt or scavenge for food in the forests created by William; there were heavy fines for people who were caught poaching; due to the hard lives faced by ordinary people, poaching was a way of getting more food – this

new law meant they risked a fine if they were caught; money and food were now a lot tighter/scarce.

4. Little effect – Most villagers continued to work on the land and focus on feeding their family and getting on with their lives; taxes in money and goods were still paid to the lord and the church. Did have an effect – Castles became part of the village landscape; Saxon earls were replaced with Norman barons; the Forest Laws meant harsh punishments. Conclusion to explain how far you agree.

5. Medieval life centred around agriculture (many fields); village life was simple – houses, forest for wood; the church was central to the village – the biggest building; you could infer that people would stay in their village because travel would be slow and difficult and everything people needed was close by.

6. Administrative roles in local government; sheriffs; earls

Page 30: Norman Castles and the Domesday Book

1. Motte and bailey castles.

2. Castles were built in strategic locations to force the Saxons into submission; castles were used to stop rebellions by the Saxons; barons were placed in castles to keep watch over the Saxons; the Saxons could not fight against the might of the castle and all of its resources; the castles were a constant reminder to the Saxons that the Normans were firmly in control. (Any three)

3. There is a motte (mound of earth) with a castle keep on the top; the Normans built the castle keep to act as the last line of defence in the event of an attack; the steep climb up to the keep is a convincing feature of early Norman castles; there is a wooden palisade (fence) around the castle; there are houses and huts inside the bailey where the Normans would keep resources and food; there is a gateway so the Normans knew who was coming into and leaving the castle; it is a wooden castle; the early Norman castles were built of wood.

4. 1085

5. William knew detailed information about how much tax the Saxons could afford to pay; the tax that William received could be used to build castles to further defend his position as king; William knew exact information about where people lived and could use this information to place his barons strategically around England to stop any rebellions; the Saxons felt that the questioning by the Normans meant that the Normans knew everything about them and there was nothing they could do to oppose their Norman rulers.

6. William wanted to know about the land and animals in England; he may have wanted to know this information because he was not English and had conquered England in 1066; having this information would have allowed him to have greater control over his kingdom; by knowing detailed information about the land and animals William would be able to tax people correctly depending on what they owned and how much the land was worth; knowing where animals were would have been useful if he needed to feed his army on the march, defending England from invasion.

Page 31: The Norman Church and the Death of William I

1. Everybody believed in God and went to church; people believed that in order to get to heaven they had to follow the teachings of the church; the church owned lots of land; the church had their own courts in which to try clergy – this meant they were separate from the king's court and its influence; the church was controlled by the Pope, not the king. (Any two)

2. A tax (10%) that was paid to the church in either money or goods.

3. Excommunicated meant a person was banned from the church – this meant that they would go straight to hell when they died; the clergy were God's representatives on Earth; they had the power to decide whether God would forgive a person for a sin they had committed; being excommunicated meant that a person would not be able to seek God's forgiveness. (Any one)

4. William wanted to continue his replacement of Saxon clergy with Norman counterparts; Archbishop Stigand had been too powerful to remove straight away in 1066; having a loyal Norman as Archbishop of Canterbury would help develop the relationship between the church and state.

5. It was a period of tension between the church and state in the 11th and 12th centuries; the main issue was whether kings or the church could invest (choose) bishops; in 1075 Pope Gregory VII said kings could not invest bishops; this angered King Henry

IV Holy Roman Emperor because he wanted to choose his own bishops. He rejected the Pope and said he wouldn't accept his authority; the Pope responded by deposing Henry and excommunicating all the people involved; Henry apologised to the Pope and he was reinstated; the Pope deposed Henry again in 1080 following further tensions; the Pope formally stated that monarchs could not invest bishops in 1077.

6. William had decided to go against Norman tradition by splitting his kingdom between his sons; William did not leave all of the kingdom to Robert (his eldest son); William gave William Rufus the throne in England; this decision had annoyed Robert who felt he was the rightful king of England following the death of his father; Robert joined forces with Bishop Odo to claim the English throne; Archbishop Lanfranc secured Saxon support for William Rufus' claim to the English throne.

Pages 32-49 Revise Questions

Page 33 Quick Test: Elizabeth I and Her Government

1. March 1603

2. Robert Dudley; he held a variety of government positions.

3. William Cecil, Lord Burghley

4. The chief administrative and executive political body.

5. Three million people

Page 35 Quick Test: The Elizabethan Religious Settlement

1. The Act of Supremacy and the Act of Uniformity

2. 1559

3. All of the Catholic bishops (they resigned and were replaced by Protestants.)

4. The Act of Uniformity dealt with the acts of worship in the Church of England; the Act introduced a new Protestant Prayer Book that had to be used in every church; church services and the Bible had to be in English; ornaments and decorations were allowed in church; the clergy were allowed to marry and had to wear vestments; recusants were fined.

5. England was split over religion; the official religion switched back and forth between Catholicism and Protestantism from the 1530s onwards; Elizabeth wanted to create a moderate Church of England, acceptable to most people.

Page 37 Quick Test: Elizabeth I and Spain, 1558–1587

1. Philip II of Spain was Elizabeth's brother-in-law – he was married to Elizabeth's sister and predecessor, Mary.

2. Elizabeth agreed to send an army to the Netherlands to help the rebels to face Spain – by agreeing to the Treaty of Nonsuch, England and Spain were now at war.

3. 1585

4. Antwerp

5. 1570

Page 39 Quick Test: Elizabeth I and Mary, Queen of Scots

1. 1568

2. Fotheringhay Castle

3. They were cousins.

4. James Hepburn, Earl of Bothwell.

5. David Rizzio; he was murdered by Mary's first husband, Lord Darnley, and his allies.

Page 41 Quick Test: The Attack of the Spanish Armada, 1588

1. Cadiz harbour

2. The Duke of Medina Sidonia, who was inexperienced at fighting at sea.

3. The Spanish Armada was first spotted off the English coast on 29 July, 1588.

4. The Armada docked at Calais, and on 7 August the English launched fireships towards them.

5. About 130 ships

Page 43 Quick Test: Threats Posed to Elizabeth I, 1558–1601

1. 1568

2. Strict Protestants who wanted to 'purify' the church of Catholic influences.

3. A Catholic who planned to rescue Mary, Queen of Scots, murder Elizabeth I and replace her with Mary.

4. A Florentine nobleman and banker who had business connections in England; he headed a plot in 1571 that aimed to free Mary, Queen of Scots, marry her to the Duke of Norfolk, overthrow Elizabeth and replace her with Mary.

5. 1583

Page 45 Quick Test: Elizabethan Society
1. Subjects such as Latin, which prepared them for university.
2. The poor; they were taught basic skills in English and Maths.
3. 26
4. There were a number of bad harvests in the mid-sixteenth century that meant less food was produced.

Page 47 Quick Test: Elizabethan Culture
1. Making animals fight for entertainment, as in bear baiting and cock fighting.
2. A cheap meal, as well as beer
3. An extremely beautiful work of art showing a portrait of an important person.
4. Outside the city walls (and outside the control of the city authorities).
5. James Burbage built the first theatre in Britain since the Romans, in 1576.

Page 49 Quick Test: Elizabeth I and the Wider World
1. Richard Hakluyt
2. 1580
3. Walter Raleigh
4. *The Golden Hind*
5. The Baltic

Pages 50-58 Review Questions

Page 50: Anglo-Saxon Society on the Eve of Conquest
1. It was a council consisting of bishops, earls and thegns; it met wherever the king chose; it discussed matters with the king and offered advice; it dealt with issues surrounding the succession of a new monarch; the king could ignore the Witan but it was not in his best interests to do so.
2. Angles, Saxons, Jutes
3. An area of land was divided into an earldom to help the king run and control the country; each area was looked after by an earl; each earl was responsible for providing justice and maintaining law and order.
4. The conversion to Christianity began in AD597 when Pope Gregory I sent missionaries to spread Christianity to England; people in England believed in one God rather than the many gods of the Pagan beliefs; the Saxons stopped believing in superstitions such as charms and magic and started to listen to the Christian church under the guidance from Rome; during the second half of the 10th Century many independent church leaders were replaced with monks from the Christian church. This created deep divisions in England because some people did not like being told what to do by the monks who worked for the Pope.
5. Agree – Anglo-Saxon society was not all war and fighting, for ordinary people their lives revolved around the land and the agricultural calendar; their lives were tough, they did not have 'ostentatious splendour'; people had grown to integrate and live in harmony with each other and the different tribes that had settled in the land; Anglo-Saxon England finished with laws and systems of government that would be carried on into the Norman era, proving that society was not continuous tension and fighting between the ruling families.
   Disagree – Anglo-Saxon society had many conflicts which resulted in wars between ruling families; England was under threat from enemies invading the coast and this led to rulers having to fight to keep control of their lands and protect their borders; people were rewarded for their loyalty with land and goods.
   Conclusion to explain how far you agree.
6. In the image there is a plough being pulled by oxen; there is a man leading the oxen and there are seeds being sown by another farmer; it could be inferred that the land was very important to Saxon people because this was how they would feed their family and farm the animals from which other living necessities would be gained – clothes, wool; Anglo-Saxon England was very rural and so agriculture would have played a big part in most people's lives. In different seasons people would have had different jobs to do based on the land and animals; by the end of the Anglo-Saxon period, burhs had developed (towns). In the towns other trades were more important – bakers, merchants, iron mongers; in the burhs trade developed from the rise in skilled tradesmen;

burhs on the coast developed into ports for trade with Europe; You should make a judgement based on your opinion in order to answer the question in the conclusion.

Page 51: The Succession Crisis of 1066
1. 1042
2. Edward had sent Harold to Normandy to reaffirm the promise of the kingdom of England to William once he had died. Harold made an oath to support William's claim to the throne. (Although some sources suggest that Harold was forced into making this oath and therefore he did not have to honour it when the time came.)
3. 1064
4. Harold's father, Godwine had worked hard and proved himself to be a loyal statesman. This cemented the family's links with the rulers of England pre-1066; Harold became Earl of Wessex in 1053; this made him one of the most powerful men in England; he ran Wessex well and was respected; Harold's brothers (excluding Tostig) were powerful and respected, they were earls and this meant that the family's influence was wide reaching; Harold had fought for King Edward and stopped a Welsh rebellion. He was a loyal servant to Edward.
5. Agree – because if Edward had a child then the line of succession would have been maintained and there shouldn't have been any issues about who would be the next monarch; kings usually put great importance on having a child in order to have an heir; it was the norm that the crown would pass to the child of the king.
   Disagree – there were other reasons why there was a succession crisis: Edward did not help the situation by allegedly promising the throne to two different men; England was a prize that was available after Edward died; it is no surprise that there were many people that wanted to claim it.
   Conclusion to explain how for you agree.
6. Edward had spent time in Normandy as a young man; William had helped Edward when he had returned to England to be king by sending soldiers to help him; Edward and William were cousins.

Page 52: The Rival Claimants to the Throne in 1066
1. They were brothers-in-law. Edward was married to Harold's sister Edith.
2. Edward had promised him the throne in 1051; Edward and William had a close relationship following the time that Edward spent in Normandy; William had sent soldiers to help Edward following his return to England; Harold Godwinson had promised to support William's claim.
3. Harold had an official ceremony to become King of England; there was a religious man (probably the Archbishop) who conducted the ceremony; the people who are in attendance look happy with the decision that Harold was to be crowned; it could be inferred that the Witan are the group of people in the right hand of the picture. It is known that the Witan did support Harold's claim.
4. The Witan were a group consisting of important earls and bishops; they had influence and power within England; they helped the king run the country and so it was important that they supported the choice of the new king; the Witan could depose a king if they felt he was not right for England, so by having their support Harold clearly had a strong claim.
5. Agree – Tostig was the brother of Harold Godwinson; for him to support an invasion against his own brother showed that Harold was not respected by everyone in England.
   Disagree – Tostig wanted revenge on Harold because he had supported the rebels in the Northumbrian crisis.
   Conclusion to explain how for you agree.
6. Westminster Abbey

Page 53: The Battles of Fulford and Stamford Bridge
1. Harald Hardrada
2. The earls in the north moved to defend York from Hardrada's invasion; Earls Morcar and Edwin led the Saxon defensive forces; the Saxons tried to defend York by being based south of the city; the Saxons placed themselves on a narrow strip of land with marsh ground and a river to the side; the battle started well for the Saxons, they held off the Vikings and pushed them into the marshland; as more Viking troops arrived the Saxon forces were pushed backwards; due to Hardrada having the

higher ground the Viking army could see that the Saxons were being pushed towards a natural pit; the Saxons became trapped and were slaughtered by the Vikings; the path to York lay open for Hardrada.

3. The Saxon army was significantly depleted after the battle, many had been killed and lots had been injured; York was easily captured by Hardrada; the people of York had to accept Hardrada as their king; the people of York had to promise to support Hardrada against Harold Godwinson.

4. Harold's army had marched quicker than Hardrada expected. The Saxons surprised the Vikings; the Vikings were not well prepared; the Viking army was split on two sides of a bridge; the bulk of the Viking army held off the Saxons by creating a shield wall and legend states a mighty Viking warrior was stationed on the bridge; the Saxons killed the warrior on the bridge and surged over to the other side; the Vikings were defeated when Hardrada was killed by an arrow that hit him in the neck.

5. Agree – the Vikings were surprised by the Saxon army after assuming that it would take them a long time to march north; this was lucky for Harold because it meant they were not well prepared; some Vikings had left their armour on the boat, Harold could not have planned this.
Disagree – Harold had marched his troops quickly to meet the Viking forces, this was not luck, he had planned his attack; Harold's tactic to get his army across the bridge to fight the main body of the Viking army was not luck; this resulted in Hardrada being killed.
Conclusion to explain how far you agree.

6. By an arrow that hit him in the neck.

Page 54: The Battle of Hastings

1. 14 October 1066

2. Housecarl – the most professional soldier in Harold's army; Thegn – good fighters but not as well trained as the housecarls; Fyrd – peasants that Harold would have recruited on his march south. These were not well trained and would have been armed with tools they worked with on the land.

3. It shows William's men carrying weapons: arrows, chainmail, lances and helmets; William ensured he brought with him everything he would have needed for the invasion, this source shows the thorough preparation by William.

4. Harold's men protected themselves at the start of the battle with a shield wall on top of Senlac Hill; William's men found it difficult to break through the shield wall during the first hours of the battle; a rumour was spread that William had been killed and his men started to retreat off the hill; William lifted his helmet and gave an encouraging speech to re-energise his men; the Saxons had broken ranks and had run down the hill after the retreating Normans; the cavalry were able to kill the Saxons who were unprotected on the hill; Harold was killed and William was able to march to London to claim the throne.

5. Agree – his troops broke rank and ran down the hill; this meant his shield wall was broken; his army had held off the Norman advances in the early hours of the battle.
Disagree – William's men were superior to Harold's (his soldiers were better prepared and trained); Harold should have let his troops rest and recover from the battle with Hardrada and the long marches they had done; William was a great tactician in battle, this paid off and gave him victory.
Conclusion to explain how far you agree.

6. 25 December 1066

Page 55: Anglo-Saxon Resistance and the Norman Response

1. He was French; he had invaded England; he had killed the king, Harold Godwinson; he had destroyed many villages on his way to Hastings.

2. To ensure that there were loyal Normans in charge of different areas of England; to prevent any Saxon earls from trying to rebel against his reign; to ensure that the ordinary Saxon people knew that William was in charge; to reward his followers for their support and loyalty at Hastings.

3. Earl Ralph and Earl Roger led forces to rebel against William's reign; this could have proved difficult to stop if the Saxons had supported the rebellion; Earl Ralph fought in Norwich but fled to Denmark to get help leaving his wife to continue with the rebellion; Ralph's wife was defeated before Danish help arrived; Roger started his

rebellion in the West but this got cut short because the locals would not support him against William. (Any two)

4. The king > the barons > the knights > the peasants (villeins) the Normans held positions of power and the Saxons were at the bottom of the social structure.

5. Agree – people in the north had tried to ally with the Danes; this was difficult for William because it meant that another nation would have invaded the country and he would have had to fight a coalition rebellion force; William dealt with the rebellion in the north so severely because of the great importance of it and the challenge it meant to his reign.
Disagree – the revolt of the earls in 1075 showed that the people William thought he could trust were capable of rebellion; if the Saxons had supported the Norman earls in rebellion William would have found it very difficult to deal with; William also had issues with his own sons to contend with – Robert, William and Rufus fighting and leaving him big decisions to make regarding the future of his kingdom.
Conclusion to explain how far you agree.

6. William ordered villages and crops to be destroyed in the north as punishment for rebellion and Danish alliances. The source mentions famine, which was a direct result of his actions; people were killed by the Normans. The source supports this with 'human corpses'; in the Domesday Book large parts of the north are classed as 'waste'. This could be used as evidence to support that: 'no village inhabited between York and Durham'.

Page 56: Life Under Norman Control

1. It protected William's love of hunting; deer, boar and the vegetation the animals ate became protected by law; poaching was illegal and anyone caught doing it faced severe punishments; William increased the forest – some villages were destroyed to make way for new areas of forest. (Any two)

2. To ensure that villages would be scared to kill a Norman lord; the burden placed on families and villages would hopefully deter anyone planning an attack on the Normans; the law used collective responsibility to ensure loyalty towards William and the Normans.

3. It is busier than a medieval village – more houses, traffic and people; it shows the trade associated with medieval towns – boats arriving with produce, travelling traders going to market, animals being prepared for market; it shows that animals still played an important role – this links with the growth of trade in meat and wool; there are lots of women in the image, which could represent that women had a vital role to play in medieval society; women can be seen trying to sell produce which highlights the roles they had; men can be seen fishing, hunting and tending to the land – shows that people's lives still relied heavily on animals and agriculture to survive; however, we cannot be completely sure that this is exactly how a town would look. More cross-referencing of sources would be needed to make an accurate conclusion.

4. Agree – many areas of government continued from the reign of Edward, William saw no need to change things that worked well; the law courts continued in much the same way; ordinary people would have continued with their lives in much the same way as during the reign of Edward (although with a Norman lord rather than a Saxon one).
Disagree – the feudal system meant that Saxons were at the bottom of the social ladder and this system was used to collect more tax for William; the people had Norman lords with a new language; forest laws impacted on people who would hunt and forage for food; large areas in the north were destroyed following the Harrying of the north – for people in this area life changed dramatically.
Conclusion to explain how far you agree.

5. The Curia Regis

6. Would help the king run the country; would ensure that any instructions from the king would be administered and followed; would ensure that day-to-day decisions were being made according to the king's wishes.

Page 57: Norman Castles and the Domesday Book

1. He brought prefabricated castles with him on his invasion fleet; these were easy and quick to assemble; he built castles in the south of England to act as a base to rest his soldiers and keep his resources; the castles were big and images of power to the Saxons.

2. The castles were easy to defend; the castles could house soldiers to quash a Saxon rebellion; the castles offered great protection against the Saxons; the castles were built in strategic positions to keep the Saxons loyal and subservient to the Norman barons.
3. The first castles built were motte and bailey castles; the motte was a hill where the castle keep was built; the castle keep was usually a tower, it was the last line of defence in an attack on the castle; the bailey had a fence around it and was where animals, soldiers and resources were kept/stayed; the first castles were built of wood. (Any two)
4. Agree – castles helped control the Saxons because the barons could use them as protection and to keep an eye on rebellious locals; the castles were big structures and acted as a constant reminder to the locals that the Normans were in charge. Disagree – other features of William's conquest of England were important in maintaining control; the feudal system worked alongside the castles to change the social structure of England; William used violence and force to control the Saxons, a powerful tool in maintaining control. Conclusion to explain how far you agree.
5. William's treasury was low – fighting costly wars in northern France; he wanted to know the economic and social features of England following the conquest and the rebellions that resulted.
6. William sent his men around England to ask questions; the questions they asked were based on the land, animals, people and money; own knowledge – each village was visited twice by two different sets of questioners. This ensured that the survey was accurate.

Page 58: The Norman Church and the Death of William I
1. People were encouraged to go on pilgrimages; people were encouraged to have a greater sense of religious devotion. (Any one)
2. People believed that the clergy were God's representatives on Earth; people were desperate to get to heaven (it was seen as a reward for the tough life they faced on Earth); people believed that the only way to get to heaven was to follow the teachings of the church; people were scared of going to hell.
3. In 1082 he tried to travel to Rome to buy himself the Papacy; after William's death, Odo allied with Robert to try to depose William Rufus. Odo saw Robert as the weaker brother and thought he would be able to manipulate Robert if he were king.
4. 1077
5. Robert – Normandy; William Rufus – England; Henry – money
6. He was right – Robert had fallen out with his father and brothers and tried to rebel against them; Robert was easily manipulated and viewed by many as weak – this would have caused problems had he been left England and Normandy to rule.
He was not right – tradition stated that the first son inherited everything from his father; by breaking tradition the tension between the brothers was cemented.
Conclusion to explain how far you agree.

Pages 59-67 **Practice Questions**

Page 59: Elizabeth I and Her Government
1. Economic problems – Elizabeth inherited an almost bankrupt country; political problems – many people did not want her as Queen; social problems – impact of bad harvests; foreign policy problems – war with France.
2. Use of portraits; the messages she tried to convey, such as legitimacy and power and wealth.
3. Marriage question; national security; desire to secure an alliance with a strong foreign nation.
4. He was Elizabeth's chief advisor and key ally; he was an important member of the Privy Council.
5. Role and functions of Parliament; you should compare with other parts of Elizabethan government, such as the Privy Council; did Parliament's role change during Elizabeth's reign?
6. Agree – England had lost Calais, its last military outpost in France; declining prestige; England had debt and was on the verge of bankruptcy; high unemployment.
Disagree – England was at war with France; three million people lived in England and Wales; it was a structured society.
Conclusion to explain how far you agree.

Page 60: The Elizabethan Religious Settlement
1. Changes in religion from 1530s; religious divisions – Elizabeth was a Protestant and was supported by the House of Commons and the Privy Council: the clergy and House of Lords remained Catholic.
2. The Act of Uniformity – dealt with acts of worship is the Church of England. The Act of Supremacy – dealt with the nature and leadership of the Church of England.
3. Reaction from Catholics – Catholic bishops resigned; reaction from Protestants; reaction from extremists – extreme Protestants (Puritans) increased preaching of their vision of the church in services.
4. Quality of clergy – resignation of Catholics left a gap; undefined position of doctrine; compromise left confusion.
5. The creation of a moderate Church of England; Elizabeth wanted to find a 'middle way'.
6. Look at the Catholic and Protestant elements of the Settlement; reach a judgement about whether the Catholic and Protestant elements were balanced or was there a bias.

Page 61: Elizabeth I and Spain, 1558–1587
1. Spain wanted to have England as an ally against France; Spain needed access to the Netherlands via the English Channel; Elizabeth could not afford war in the 1560s.
2. The Ridolfi Plot; Elizabeth's intervention in the Netherlands against Spain; actions of English privateers against Spanish treasure ships, which enraged Philip.
3. Strategic importance of the Netherlands; Dutch Revolt; Elizabeth's intervention in the Netherlands and support for Dutch exiles.
4. The impact of Drake's world voyage on Spain – he attacked the Spanish empire in the New world; attacking treasure ships; Elizabeth's support for Drake.
5. Religious differences; actions of English privateers; English intervention in the Netherlands; desire of Spain to replace Elizabeth with a Catholic monarch.
6. Philip II had married Mary, Elizabeth's sister; Philip II proposed marriage to Elizabeth after Mary died, which she rejected.

Page 62: Elizabeth I and Mary, Queen of Scots
1. The role of Mary's marriages; the differences between Mary and most of the Scottish nobles; the most important reason in your opinion.
2. The options open to Elizabeth – her councillors did not want to assist Mary; the reaction of the English Catholics; reach a judgement about the extent of the threat Mary posed to Elizabeth I – there were a number of catholic plots to liberate Mary and overthrow Elizabeth.
3. Describe the reaction of Elizabeth I – Elizabeth was furious – never intended death warrant to be used; French protests; Philip II was furious – continued Armada plan.
4. The differences between what Elizabeth and her councillors wanted; the house arrest that Mary endured.
5. Bothwell's possible involvement in Darnley's murder; the fact he was hated by many powerful Scottish nobles.
6. The importance of the Babington Plot – Walsingham found a letter by Mary in which she approved the plot; the role of Elizabeth's ministers in persuading her to put Mary to trial; signing of death warrant.

Page 63: The Attack of the Spanish Armada, 1588
1. Religious differences; the execution of Mary, Queen of Scots; there was long-term friction between England and Spain.
2. 130 ships; large ships with cannon; trained soldiers; the strong, crescent formation.
3. No ports were secured by the Spanish to land in either the Netherlands or England; there was no co-ordination of the Spanish troops in the Netherlands; they tried to build ships and supplies too quickly after Drake's Cadiz raid in 1587.
4. It broke the crescent formation; it ran into bad weather; they ran out of food/water; they crashed on rocks in Scotland and Ireland and soldiers were killed.
5. Drake's surprise attack on Cadiz harbour destroyed much of the Spanish Armada; the Spanish Admiral, the Marquis de Santa Cruz died and was replaced with the Duke of Medina Sidona, who did not want the job; the Spanish Armada set sail in April 1588 only to be blown off course by a series of bad storms.

6. Impact of the Battle of Graveines – the Armada was out of formation; many Spanish ships were damaged and they were forced to flee north around the British Isles; impact of the Battle across the English Channel – lasted 10 days; neither side gained an advantage; compare the impact of both events and reach a judgement.

Page 64: Threats Posed to Elizabeth I, 1558–1601

1. Strategic errors of the leadership – there was no clear plan; lack of support from Mary, Spain and Papacy; apathy of English Catholics.
2. Political slights towards Earl of Essex; deterioration of the Earl of Essex's relationship with Elizabeth.
3. Consider the methods of opposition the Puritans adopted – they never threatened to overthrow Elizabeth; the Puritan role in Parliament; the aims of Puritans and attitudes towards Elizabeth I.
4. The spy network; his role in the Babington Plot – he presented evidence of the plot to Elizabeth.
5. Babington was arrested; execution of Mary, Queen of Scots; Spain launched its armada.
6. Agree – Northern Rebellion led by leading Catholic nobles; aimed to rescue Mary, overthrow Elizabeth and return England to Catholicism; 6000 soldiers gathered.
   Disagree – Lack of support from Mary, Spain and the Papacy (Ridolfi plot was supported by Philip II, Babington plot was supported by Mary); strategic errors from rebels; Elizabeth's army easily crushed the rebellion.
   Conclusion to explain how far you agree.

Page 65: Elizabethan Society

1. Food shortages; inflation; bad harvests; charges in farming; collapse of European cloth market; population increase.
2. Poor Laws; role of local government; lack of action of the Privy Council.
3. Investments in successful voyages and new trading companies; increasing availability of land following the Dissolution of the monasteries in the 1530s/1540s; rising prices of food helped landowners make money.
4. Family structures and bonds with extended family; emphasis on married life; average of 3 children; high infant mortality.
5. Rise of the grammar school; increasing numbers in university education; increasing education provision for the poor – petty schools.
6. Agree – The impact of the collapse of the European cloth market; many workers lost their jobs – led to poverty.
   Disagree – Series of bad harvests meant less food was produced; food prices rose; changes in farming led to rising unemployment; population of England and Wales rose by over a million during Elizabeth's reign; inflation was also a factor.
   Conclusion to explain how far you agree.

Page 66: Elizabethan Culture

1. Quality of playwrights was high, e.g. Shakespeare; sponsorship of acting groups by important people; Elizabeth enjoyed the theatre; it was a cheap form of entertainment.
2. Some feared that it was a source of social disorder due to gatherings of large crowds; plays were seen by some as rude and distasteful.
3. Music – particularly religious music; art – particularly miniatures; fashion.
4. Compare the pastimes of the rich and the poor; identify similarities, such as both enjoyed the theatre and sports; contrast that some pastimes required money which the poor did not have, such as buying fashionable clothes; literature was also popular and the growth in printing of cheap books meant the poor had more access to it; the rich generally enjoyed pastimes at home while the poor went out, e.g. to alehouses.
5. Growth of cheap books; rising popularity of the theatre; gambling on blood sports.
6. Different parts of the theatre, such as the stage and its shape; different sections for the audience – groundlings and seated, covered areas.

Page 67: Elizabeth I and the Wider World

1. The work of Richard Hakluyt in his influential book; the collapse of the European cloth trade meant merchants had to travel further to sell goods; developments in technology, e.g. compasses, caravels.

2. The development of companies such as the East India Company; the demand for luxury goods; success of English privateers.
3. Increased world prestige; booty collected on the world voyage – gold, silver, luxury goods; deterioration of relations with Spain, due to attacks on Spanish settlements.
4. Strategic mistakes, such as landing areas; divisions in crew and its leadership, as well as bad weather.
5. He was an early slave trader; he became a naval expert and leader of the English navy.
6. Wealth – investors, such as merchants and the royal court, became very wealthy; overseas trade – new trade routes opened up during the reign of Elizabeth I; power – England became a great sea power in the world; the navy – England developed a very strong navy which used cutting edge technology; which one do you think was the most important?

Pages 68-85 Revise Questions

Page 69 Quick Test: Medieval Medicine (Middle Ages) 1

1. Black bile, blood, yellow bile and phlegm.
2. Because the Christian Church grew in this period, the main belief was that illness was caused by God.
3. There were very few of them; they were small; they did not admit patients with contagious illnesses; they focused on 'care not cure'.

Page 71 Quick Test: Medieval Medicine (Middle Ages) 2

1. People believed God caused illness so no research was conducted; the Romans took away their public health system; poor living conditions.
2. Punishment for disobeying God/sinning; bad air; planets such as Mars and Jupiter were too close together; Jews, strangers, witches or 'outsiders'. (Any three)
3. Whipping to be given forgiveness from God; carrying sweet smelling herbs; praying; staying indoors; lighting fires; clearing up street rubbish. (Any three)
4. Buboes, high fever, headache, vomiting and diarrhoea, shaking, seizures, stomach cramps. (Any three)

Page 73 Quick Test: Renaissance Medicine (1400s–1600s) 1

1. *The Fabric of the Human Body*.
2. He found the jaw bone was made of one bone, not two; there were no invisible holes in the septum.
3. *An Anatomical Account of the Motion of the Heart and Blood in Animals*.
4. Blood was carried around the body through veins and the heart acted as a pump to allow the blood to travel through the body.
5. The printing press allowed ideas to spread very quickly. Before the creation of the printing press, books were written by hand (usually by monks) and therefore few books were written and circulated widely.

Page 75 Quick Test: Renaissance Medicine (1400s–1600s) 2

1. Towns and cities were increasing in size; people still left rubbish and sewage in the streets, still drank dirty water and let animals roam around towns; people did not know what caused disease. (Any two)
2. Burning cats and dogs; banning large crowds of people in public places; praying; whipping; boarding up. (Any three)
3. They increased in size; some hospitals started to admit patients with infectious diseases; simple surgeries were carried out; the majority of physicians and doctors in hospitals had been trained at university; the idea of observation of patients increased in importance. (Any two)
4. Still 'care not cure'; those with money would still pay for a doctor to visit their home rather than go to hospital; nurses still used herbal remedies; most women working in hospitals had no medical training. (Any two)
5. Installation of public toilets; installation of public baths; laws passed that stated streets needed to be kept clean; people who did not keep streets clean were fined. (Any two)

Page 77 Quick Test: Industrial Medicine (1700s–1900) 1

1. Increase in number of people in small spaces; cheap, poor quality, damp, back-to-back housing created; poor, unclean drinking water; poor working conditions in factories such as cotton factories led to breathing problems; lack of availability of fresh food in towns and cities. (Any two)
2. Cholera, typhoid, smallpox. (Any two)

3. Sewers should be improved; rubbish should be removed from the streets; drinking water should be clean; medical officers should monitor the cleanliness of towns. (Any three)
4. Councils appointed medical health officers to each town; councils were forced to clear up streets; councils were forced to create sewer systems and provide clean drinking water.

Page 79 Quick Test: Industrial Medicine (1700s–1900) 2
1. Successfully vaccinated a person against smallpox in 1796; the government paid for people to receive vaccinations against smallpox in 1840; in 1853 it became compulsory to be vaccinated against smallpox; in 1979 smallpox was finally wiped out around the world. (Any two)
2. The period after anaesthetics came into use but before antiseptics were discovered where more people died from blood loss and infection during surgery because surgeons could take longer over their surgery as their patients were no longer in pain.
3. Germ Theory.

Page 81 Quick Test: Modern Medicine (1900s–Present) 1
1. Plastic surgery; X-rays; transplant surgery; prosthetic limbs, blood transfusions.
2. Salvarsan 606, Prontosil.
3. The USA funded their development; the NHS allowed people to afford them.

Page 83 Quick Test: Modern Medicine (1900s–Present) 2
1. 1906, introduction of school meals for poor children; 1907, health visitors monitored young children and their mothers; 1908, Old Age Pensions Act introduced; 1911, National Insurance Act. (Any two)
2. The School Meals Act only improved children's health during term time; the National Insurance Act was only given to some workers, meaning some workers and the majority of women were not covered.
3. Disease, squalor.
4. World War Two highlighted the poor health of British citizens; evacuation of children emphasized the varied level of public health in Britain; in 1944, William Beveridge wrote a report that stated there were 'Five Evils' in Britain that the government needed to tackle, including disease and squalor. (Any two)

Page 85 Quick Test: Modern Medicine (1900s–Present) 3
1. Chemotherapy, radiation, endocrine therapy. (Any two)
2. 1967, Christiaan Barnard performed the first heart transplant; in the 1970s and 80s the first MRI scans were completed; also in the 1970s and 80s the first ultrasounds were used. (Any two)
3. AIDS, Ebola.
4. 'No Smoking' campaigns; reduction in alcohol campaigns; Change4Life; flu campaigns; national anti-drugs campaigns. (Any two)
5. Some scientific developments have caused problems, such as thalidomide; some people disagree with scientific involvement for moral and religious reasons; there is a move towards alternative medicines such as herbal remedies, acupuncture and meditation. (Any two)

Pages 86-94 Review Questions

Page 86: Elizabeth I and Her Government
1. It passed laws; it was responsible for taxation.
2. It was divided due to religious differences – catholics and protestants; social differences – a strict social hierarchy.
3. Portraits were the main methods she used to project an image of legitimacy; success and wisdom; power and control; wealth.
4. Elizabeth never explained why she never married. Some of the possible reasons were: the potential for any husband to try and control Elizabeth and rule himself; the potential to upset factions if she married someone from England; the potential to upset countries if she married a foreign prince.
5. A love interest for Elizabeth and this created divisions within the Privy Council; he became an experienced minister in a variety of positions.
6. You need to look through the roles of the key ministers William Cecil, Lord Burghley; Robert Dudley, Earl of Leicester, Sir Francis Walsingham and reach a judgement about who is the most important; look at the influences of the different ministers; look at the roles of the different ministers and how successful they were in carrying them out.

Page 87: The Elizabethan Religious Settlement
1. Most accepted it and were pleased with the changes; some, such as the Puritans, felt the Settlement did not go far enough and was too Catholic.
2. Consistent church practices; everyone to use the Book of Common Prayer; standardising services and ensuring attendance; punishing recusants.
3. Restoration of the Royal Supremacy; it gave Elizabeth the title of Supreme Governor.
4. He was appointed Archbishop of Canterbury; he aimed to make the Church more inclusive; he was a moderate.
5. The Pope did not excommunicate Elizabeth; there were some Catholic practices within the Settlement; the Settlement was not strictly enforced.
6. Mass resignation of Catholic bishops led to the problem of a lack of trained clergy; Puritans began to increase preaching of their vision of the church in services; most clergy took oath of loyalty.

Page 88: Elizabeth I and Spain, 1558–1587
1. He wanted an anti-French alliance with England; friendship with England meant he could still use the English Channel as a link to the Netherlands.
2. Hawkins and Drake successfully attacked Spanish interests in the New World; they became hate figures in Spain; Elizabeth approved of their actions – they brought her riches.
3. Spain was seen as a supporter of some plots against Elizabeth; some Spanish people were actively behind some of the plots, such as Roberto Ridolfi; the Spanish ambassador was expelled from the English Court for his role in the Throckmorton Plot.
4. Elizabeth had rejected Philip's marriage proposal; Elizabeth was not a Catholic, and established a new Protestant church.
5. Antwerp was Europe's largest cloth market; England needed access to Antwerp as its economy depended upon cloth; Spain controlled Antwerp.
6. France in 1562 suffered a civil war; France was no longer a threat to either Spain or England; Spain needed England less now France was no longer a threat.

Page 89: Elizabeth I and Mary, Queen of Scots
1. Darnley's behaviour whilst Mary was pregnant; split Scottish nobles – some wanted to murder him; Darnley was implicated in Rizzio's murder.
2. Mary and Elizabeth were cousins, and as Elizabeth's closest relative Mary was heir to the throne. Mary was a Catholic and declared that she was the rightful Queen of England as Elizabeth I was really a bastard (her parents' marriage was invalid); Mary was a potential figurehead for any Catholic plot and rebellion against Elizabeth.
3. Mary had been deposed as Queen of Scotland; Mary did not have significant support in Scotland; Mary had nowhere else to go after escaping from prison.
4. Bothwell was hated by many Scottish nobles and the marriage led to a Protestant uprising against Mary's rule; Mary was forced to abdicate and her baby son, James, became King; Mary was imprisoned in Loch Leven Castle but a year later in 1568, she escaped captivity and fled to England.
5. Walsingham was a staunch protestant; explain why he saw Mary as a threat to Elizabeth – Mary was legitimate claimant to the English throne, and a devout Catholic; explain his role in the Babington Plot – he uncovered the plot, which ultimately led to Mary's execution.
6. Explain the role of Darnley – drunkard, had lots of enemies and was a Catholic sympathiser; implicated in Rizzio's murder; explain the role of Bothwell – unpopular with Scottish nobility and had a role in the murder of Darnley.

Page 90: The Attack of the Spanish Armada, 1588
1. Bad weather; poor planning; English skill – English military leaders had more naval experience.
2. Spain lost a very effective naval leader; his replacement, Medina Sidonia, did not want the job, hated sailing and had no naval experience.
3. Spain failed to land in England; English ships fended off the attack but did not defeat it; Armada still in crescent formation.
4. The Cadiz raid in 1587 was significant in destroying preparations; Drake was an important leader in the English navy.
5. Agree – The Armada was hindered by a series of bad storms and bad weather which would have been unexpected at the time of

year; the Spanish admiral died (and was replaced with the Duke of Medina Sidonia who didn't want the job).

Disagree – The Spanish didn't have a clear plan of where to land in the Netherlands; the English ships were better suited to fighting; the English had more naval experience.

Conclusion to explain how far you agree.

6. Compare the type of ships both navies had – identifying their strengths and weaknesses; compare the leadership of each navy – look at their experiences and past records; compare the armies of each country – look at their numbers and extent that they were trained for combat; reach a judgement.

Page 91: Threats Posed to Elizabeth I, 1558–1601

1. Led by leading Catholic nobles in the north of England, Earls of Northumberland and Westmoreland; although 6000 rebels were gathered, they were easily crushed by Elizabeth's army.
2. It was well financed – Ridolfi had business connections; significant number of Spanish troops prepared but Spain backed down and the troops did not materialize; plot was uncovered by the privy council.
   Conclusion to say how much of a threat you think the plot was.
3. Source of organised opposition in Parliament; they campaigned against the Elizabethan Religious Settlement; campaigned for more protestant changes but never threatened to overthrow Elizabeth.
4. Dangers of a Spanish-Franco alliance to England.
5. To overthrow Elizabeth I; to then secure Mary, Queen of Scots as Queen of England.
6. Compare the aims of both plots; compare the success and failures of both plots; compare the extent of support for each plot and who was involved; Conclusion to say which plot you think was a greater threat, if either.

Page 92: Elizabethan Society

1. Local government was inconsistent in its approach; some excellent provision in places like Ipswich; supported by government in the 1570s which gave some poor relief.
2. Increased provision for the poor in petty schools; a rising number of universities were being opened; the curriculum widened.
3. Fear from people who believed in evil magic; people looking for something or someone to blame for bad occurrences that they could not explain, such as bad harvests.
4. Increased land ownership; rising food prices; investment opportunities.
5. New farming techniques such as drainage and fertilisation increased yields and crops; led to more sales and greater profits.
6. Changes in farming – new technology meant many jobs were lost; collapse of the European cloth market; lack of government support.

Page 93: Elizabethan Culture

1. Plays; arena for meetings; arena for secret affairs; food and drink offered.
2. They believed they encouraged bad behaviour; the plays were vulgar; the plays provided a distraction from godly behaviour.
3. Humanist and classical styles tapped into the interest in the Renaissance; the growth in printing cheap books gave more access to literature.
4. It was a sign of wealth and prestige; showing off and getting noticed at court.
5. A distraction from daily life; to get out of their homes; to socialise with others; gambling offered the prospect of quick and easy money.
6. Blood sports such as bear baiting and cock fighting; alehouses and drinking beer; theatre; tobacco.

Page 94: Elizabeth I and the Wider World

1. Competition for new markets; English attacks on Spanish treasure ships angered the Spanish; role of Drake, which was a significant cause of war with Spain.
2. Prestige; attacking Spanish interests to capture gold, silver and luxury goods.
3. It was a source of income; England needed to find alternative trade routes; acquisition of luxury goods.
4. Damaged relations with Spain; power and glory; wealth and trade.
5. It was a source of great wealth; it developed the navy; explorers were seen as heroes; successfully defiant against the Spanish.
6. Choose the three most significant explorers – Drake, Raleigh, Hawkins; examine each one's achievements (and failures); reach a judgement.

Page 95: Medieval Medicine (Middle Ages) 1

1. The body is made up of four main elements ('humours'), and in order to remain healthy these should stay balanced. The four humours consisted of: black bile, blood, yellow bile and phlegm.
2. Regressed
3. Developed from Hippocrates' ideas of the four humours. For example, if a person felt cold, they should eat something hot to improve their health.
4. Alchemy – a mixture of philosophy, superstition and Medieval 'science'; family treatments; herbal remedies, e.g. poppy juice; bloodletting by barber surgeons; praying; amputation.
5. Few hospitals; small in size (around 12 beds per hospital); 'care not cure'; cared for the old and poor rather than the sick; those with contagious diseases were turned away; herbal remedies were used.
6. Agree – The Christian church was in charge of hospitals; the Church did not like to contradict Galen so progress was not made; as people were taught that God caused illness, people prayed to be made better rather than search for treatments that would work; Muslims believed it was wrong to oppose Galen because the Koran supported his beliefs.
   Disagree – People didn't question Galen's ideas because it would have seemed wrong to do so; his beliefs were widely accepted throughout the world; the Romans had taken away the public health system; the belief was that people should be cared for rather than cured; there was a lack of scientific knowledge and understanding.
   Conclusion to explain how far you agree.

Page 96: Medieval Medicine (Middle Ages) 2

1. They were not based on science; based on superstition; herbal remedies did not work.
2. Poppy juice; sweet smelling herbs (Any one)
3. Flagellants would whip themselves; through prayer.
4. People didn't understand what caused illness – they believed it was God; living conditions were poor and dirty; the Romans had taken away Britain's public health system; famine was rife; there was little clean, healthy food; people would leave their waste in the streets; animals roamed towns and cities and the diseases from these animals would easily spread to people; sewage was left near water sources; war caused diseases as wounds would become quickly infected due to the dirty living conditions.
5. People believed that there was 'bad air'. Although not entirely correct, the bad smells in the air were caused from the bacteria in the sewage that caused disease; some people believed that the streets should be cleaned up.
6. Agree – People did not try to find a cure because they believed God caused the Black Death; treatments and preventions were based on religious beliefs such as prayer.
   Disagree – The government did not take purposeful action (this could be explained because of religious beliefs); there was a lack of scientific understanding about the causes of the Black Death; poor public health caused the Black Death to spread quickly; animals roamed the streets so the fleas on the rats spread more quickly.
   Conclusion to explain how far you agree.

Page 97: Renaissance Medicine (1400s–1600s) 1

1. New discoveries were made which allowed people to question other beliefs such as those held by Galen; increasingly, individuals such as Andreas Vesalius and William Harvey started to criticise Galen; Vesalius found that Galen had been wrong about the jaw bone. Because Galen was proved to be wrong in one area, people started to question his views in other areas.
2. Fabricius had proved that veins had valves.
3. Vesalius found that there was only one jaw bone, not two; Vesalius found that there were no invisible holes in the septum so blood did not flow into the heart through these.
4. Increase in the importance of technology; the Protestant Church created by Henry VIII took away authority from the Catholic Church; groups such as The Royal Society were created where people met to discuss scientific thinking and ideas rather than religious beliefs.
5. Their discoveries helped increase understanding about anatomy, not how to treat poor health.

6. Agree – The Protestant Church created by Henry VIII took away authority from the Catholic Church; groups such as The Royal Society were created where people met to discuss scientific thinking and ideas rather than religious beliefs.
Disagree – Importance of technology increased; microscopes discovered; the printing press allowed ideas to spread very quickly; time spent observing and therefore thinking increased; John Hunter stressed importance of observation; people's attitudes changed – people now more willing to accept new ideas.
Conclusion to explain how far you agree.

Page 98: Renaissance Medicine (1400s–1600s) 2

1. Smelling sweet herbs
2. Burning cats and dogs; banning large crowds of people in public places; prayer; houses would be boarded up. (Any two)
3. Public toilets installed in some towns; public baths installed in some towns; the government fined people who did not keep streets cleaned.
4. Public health became worse; people still left rubbish and sewage in the streets; people still drank dirty water; animals roamed around towns; infectious diseases such as the Sweating Sickness and the Plague killed thousands.
5. The recommendations and laws were not enforced strongly enough; people still left their sewage in the streets; there were very few new public baths; people did not like the government interfering in their lives; the government did not feel it was their responsibility to improve public health.
6. Agree – Hospitals relied less on the Church; the size of individual hospitals increased; some hospitals started to admit patients with infectious diseases; simple surgeries were carried out; the majority of physicians and doctors in hospitals had been trained at university; the practice of observation became more important through the work of Thomas Sydenham.
Disagree – The focus was still 'care not cure'; poor people would go to hospitals alongside the old, but those with money would pay for a doctor to visit their home; nurses still continued to use herbal remedies; many other women working in the hospitals had no medical training.
Conclusion to explain how far you agree.

Page 99: Industrial Medicine (1700s–1900) 1

1. The size and population of towns increased; back-to-back housing was created; diseases such as cholera, typhoid and smallpox were rife.
2. Pill machines allowed pills to be mass produced.
3. The policies created by the government on the back of Chadwick's report were only advisory policies; towns did not legally have to put them into place; the government and public believed in a 'laissez-faire' approach to government involvement in people's health. (Any two)
4. Pharmacies became more popular; patent medicines became more popular; pills were increasingly used; there was a decrease in the use of herbal remedies. (Any two)
5. Snow believed cholera spread through water rather than air; Snow jotted down the area where deaths from cholera took place during the 1854 epidemic; found all victims were using the same water pump down Broad Street; the handle was removed and no more people died of cholera; people's attitudes did not change quickly and there was no public health act in the 1850s; Further outbreaks of cholera in 1865 occurred.
6. Differentiate between the effects of the 1848 and 1875 acts.
Agree – The 1848 policies were not made law; the majority of people did not change their actions; the government and public believed in a 'laissez-faire' approach to government involvement in people's health and did not want laws created.
Disagree – Even though the recommendations of 1848 were not made law, they did show progress; The 1875 act: forced councils to appoint medical health officers to each town, forced councils to clear up streets, forced councils to create sewer systems and provide clean drinking water, increased people's living conditions, increased people's health, increased life expectancy.
Conclusion to explain how far you agree.

Page 100: Industrial Medicine (1700s–1900) 2

1. In 1796 Edward Jenner inoculated people with cowpox; he found they did not contract smallpox; in 1840 the government paid for people to receive vaccinations against smallpox; in 1853 it became compulsory; in 1979 smallpox was wiped out.

2. They focussed on care and cure; there was an increase in hospital hygiene; cleanliness increased after Semmelweis' discovery.
3. Joseph Lister discovered carbolic acid in 1865; he found that carbolic acid would decrease infection during surgical procedures; a negative impact of this was the 'black period' of surgery.
4. Robert Koch discovered which specific germs caused disease; through staining a microbe that caused TB under a microscope, other microbes such as cholera and plague could be identified; Emil von Behring used Koch and Pasteur's work to discover the way in which antibodies worked; in 1890 Behring developed a cure for diphtheria; other scientists also used Koch and Pasteur's work to stop illnesses such as typhoid and tetanus.
5. New hospitals were set up by charities and councils; cottage hospitals were established in 1869 and focussed on care and cure; an increase in hospital hygiene after the publication of Pasteur's Germ Theory and Ignaz Semmelweis' work; reformers such as Florence Nightingale put pressure on the government to ensure hospitals were clean and well organised.
6. Agree – She put pressure on the government to ensure hospitals were clean and well organised; she wrote Notes on Nursing in 1859, thereby improving nursing; she wrote Notes on Hospitals in 1863, improving hospitals and their conditions.
Disagree – The new hospitals created were set up by charities and councils, meaning they relied less on the church; cottage hospitals were established in 1869 and these focussed on care and cure; there was an increase in hospital hygiene after the publication of Pasteur's Germ Theory; Ignaz Semmelweis understood the importance of cleanliness and persuaded labour wards to implement this; Florence Nightingale didn't support Pasteur's Germ Theory; it has been argued that Nightingale's ideas on hospital cleanliness were only implemented because of a change in the government's attitude.
Conclusion to explain how far you agree.

Page 101: Modern Medicine (1900s–Present) 1

1. Allowed the understanding of genetics; Franklin's discovery of the double helix structure of DNA allowed developments such as stem cell research, understanding of Down's Syndrome and conditions such as diabetes, Parkinson's and Alzheimer's.
2. Although DNA was discovered in the nineteenth century, people did not understand it; Crick and Watson experimented and researched throughout the twentieth century; they discovered that DNA was present in all human cells, which led to further understanding of genetics; other individuals were also important in the understanding of DNA; Crick and Watson developed their experiments and research further after Wilkins devised X-ray crystallography.
3. Plastic surgery developed due to the skin grafting techniques devised by Harold Gilles in his plastic surgery unit; improvements in surgery and blood transfusions made due to high demand; as more blood was needed quickly, blood depots were created; blood needed to be stored during the war so refrigerators were introduced by Richard Weil; transplant surgery and prosthetic limbs improved due to their sudden greater need. (Any two)
4. Magic bullets are drugs that kill bacteria; whilst bacteria had been discovered and was understood before 1909, there were no drugs to treat it; the first two magic bullets were Salvarsan 606 and Prontosil. Salvarsan cured diseases such as syphilis.
5. Before the outbreak of World War One, there was the problem of clotting; as more blood was needed more quickly, it put pressure on individuals to find ways to allow this to happen; in 1915 sodium citrate was added to blood by Richard Lewisohn. This stopped the blood from clotting; Richard Weil introduced the use of refrigerators in 1915; Francis Rous and James Turner discovered that blood could be kept fresh by adding citrate glucose in 1916; the first blood depot was created in 1917 before the Battle of Cambrai.
6. Agree – The US government agreed to fund the growth and space needed for mould to develop; the NHS allowed the British public to access penicillin. Otherwise many people wouldn't have been able to afford the drugs.

Disagree – Without Fleming, penicillin wouldn't have been used, as he was the discoverer; without Florey and Chain's testing on humans, penicillin couldn't have been used; during the 1930s, Britain's government did not give the time and space needed to grow the mould.
Conclusion to explain how far you agree.

Page 102: Modern Medicine (1900s–Present) 2

1. Charles Booth found that the government needed to help the poor get out of poverty; Rowntree's 1901 study *Poverty: A Study of Town Life* found that illness and poverty were not the fault of the poor; Rowntree found that poverty was due to lack of money for food and quality housing.
2. 1906 School Meals Act; 1907 Health Act; 1908 Old Age Pensions Act; 1911 National Insurance Act. (Any one)
3. World War Two highlighted the poor health of British citizens; the evacuation of children emphasised the poor public health in towns and cities; in 1944 William Beveridge wrote a report stating that the British government needed to tackle the Five Evils, including disease and squalor. (Any two)
4. Charles Booth's and Seebohm Rowntree's studies highlighted that the government should take a more active role in improving people's health; half of the men were declared unfit to fight in the Boer War. This concerned the British government.
5. Agree – The 1906 School Meals Act improved the health of the poorest children; the 1907 Health Act meant young children and their mothers were checked on by health visitors; the 1908 Old Age Pensions Act gave financial support to the elderly, which improved their health due to them having a better standard of living; the 1911 National Insurance Act gave some workers some sick pay and medical treatment
   Disagree – Despite the School Meals Act children's health worsened during school holidays; most women and some workers were not covered under the National Insurance Act.
   Conclusion to explain how far you agree.
6. Agree – Free access to doctors; creation of family doctors; free prescriptions; creation of health care centres; ambulances.
   Disagree – Some people did not want to pay extra taxes to fund the NHS; doctors felt too heavily controlled by the government; some still believed in the laissez-faire approach; charities and councils felt they were no longer needed for healthcare; the NHS has become increasingly expensive; some believe 'going private' is creating a 'two-tier' system of care, with the more wealthy receiving better treatment.
   Conclusion to explain how far you agree.

Page 103: Modern Medicine (1900s–Present) 3

1. Lasers, radiation therapy, keyhole surgery; heart transplant; MRI; ultrasound (Any one)
2. MRI scan can examine most areas of the body, including the brain, spinal cord and blood vessels; through MRI scans, conditions such as sports injuries and tumours can be diagnosed.
3. In the 1960s thalidomide caused babies to be born with disfigurements such as missing limbs; opposition due to moral and religious reasons; some people still prefer to use alternative medicines such as herbal remedies, acupuncture and meditation. (Any two)
4. Treatment: Surgery, radiotherapy, chemotherapy, radiation and endocrine therapy; the British Lung Foundation established to investigate causes of cancer and fund treatments.
   Prevention: No Smoking campaigns by the government; alcohol awareness campaigns.
5. Successful – Increase in treatments for cancer such as radiation therapy; improvements in treatments and diagnosis such as MRI scanning, ultrasounds, heart transplants, laser surgery and keyhole surgery.
   Unsuccessful – thalidomide; not all people support scientific developments. Many are unsupportive for moral and religious reasons; some still prefer alternative medicines such as herbal remedies, acupuncture and meditation; some diseases (AIDS, Ebola) can still not be cured.
6. Agree – Implementation of the Liberal reforms; creation of the NHS;
   Disagree – Increase in understanding of science and technology; changing attitudes; the role of Booth and Rowntree.
   Conclusion to explain how far you agree.

Page 105 Quick Test: 1000–1500: Crime
1. The king
2. 10%
3. Castles

Page 107 Quick Test: 1000–1500: Punishment
1. An outlaw
2. 12 years old
3. 1215

Page 109 Quick Test: 1500–1700: Crime
1. Elizabeth I
2. 1494
3. A badge

Page 111 Quick Test: 1500–1700: Punishment
1. Local judges
2. 1725
3. 36

Page 113 Quick Test: 1700–1900: Crime
1. Cheap illustrated newspapers
2. Garroters
3. 1888

Page 115 Quick Test: 1700–1900: Punishment
1. Henry and John Fielding
2. 3200
3. *The State of the Prisons in England and Wales*

Page 117 Quick Test: 1900–Present: Crime
1. Technology
2. 1.3 million
3. 1965

Page 119 Quick Test: 1900–Present: Punishment
1. 1920
2. Police Community Support Officer
3. 1948

Page 121 Quick Test: Case Studies
1. Matthew Hopkins
2. 1736
3. 15,000
4. 1916

Page 122: Medieval Medicine (Middle Ages) 1

1. Their focus was on care not cure; cared for the old and poor rather than the sick; those with contagious diseases were turned away; herbal remedies were used.
2. Muslims believed in Galen and Hippocrates' work; Muslims believed it was wrong to oppose Galen because the Koran supported his ideas.
3. The Theory of Opposites
4. Hippocrates devised the idea of the four humours; the body was made up of four main elements; the four humours should stay balanced; consisted of: black bile, red bile, yellow bile and phlegm.
5. Important: Nuns created herbal remedies for their patients; women passed down herbal remedies within their family.
   Not important: Women were not permitted to attend university; it could be argued that women were not important as their herbal remedies largely did not work.
6. Agree – People continued to believe in the four humours and the Theory of Opposites; people did not believe Galen was wrong because the Church and Islam supported his views.
   Disagree – The Romans left Britain without a sewer system; people did not understand the cause of disease; people's public health was poor; the government did not try to improve people's health; people did not try to find ways to improve their health as they believed poor health was caused by God.
   Conclusion to explain how far you agree.

Page 123: Medieval Medicine (Middle Ages) 2

1. Britain's public health system left with the Romans; they left Britain with no money to continue their public health system. (Any one)
2. People's religious beliefs; lack of scientific understanding; lack of government involvement. (Any one)

3. Religious people who whipped themselves to gain forgiveness from God.
4. Arab religion was important as the Koran supported Galen's Theory of Opposites; hospitals were run by churches; remedies in churches were given out by monks and nuns; the Church supported Galen's ideas and did not support further scientific study; most people believed that illness was caused by God.
5. Religious: Praying, flagellants would whip themselves.
   Superstition: Staying indoors and lighting fires, avoiding strangers, using lucky charms.
   Practical: Clearing up street rubbish.
   Medical/herbal: Cutting open buboes, holding bread against buboes, carrying sweet smelling herbs.
6. Agree – Lack of understanding meant people did not invest time and money into science; people agreed with Galen and Hippocrates' views which were limited in scientific knowledge; there was a lack of scientific knowledge because of the importance of religious beliefs; people did not understand the cause of disease.
   Disagree – The Romans left Britain without a sewer system; the government did not try to improve people's health; people did not try to find ways to improve their health as they believed poor health was caused by God; people continued to believe in the idea of the four humours; people continued to believe in the Theory of Opposites; people did not believe that Galen was wrong because the Church and Islam supported his views.
   Conclusion to explain how for you agree.

Page 124: Renaissance Medicine (1400s–1600s) 1
1. People were used to Galen's ideas; it is difficult to accept new ideas; religious beliefs had always supported Galen. (Any one)
2. Their discoveries were based on anatomy not treatments, or how to improve health.
3. Microscopes allowed people to discover capillaries that transport blood to veins from the arteries; the printing press allowed ideas to spread very quickly; it is suggested that Harvey concluded that the heart acts like a pump after seeing a pump used to extinguish a fire.
4. Reduction in importance of religion – people were starting to become more interested in science and new ideas; increase in importance of science and technology – the printing press, pumps and microscopes allowed understanding to develop more quickly; changing attitudes – people were slowly starting to accept Galen was wrong.
5. Important – People were still wary of accepting new ideas because of their religion; people were still religious; even though the Catholic Church's dominance had decreased, the Church of England continued to be powerful.
   Not important – People were wanting to understand new ideas; the Royal Society (where men explored new ideas and scientific thinking) became popular; the Catholic Church had lost its power due to Henry VIII's dissolution of the monasteries.
6. Agree – First person to openly disprove Galen; his book *Fabric of the Human Body* was widely read; he increased people's confidence in criticising Galen's beliefs.
   Disagree – The printing press allowed people to widely read Vesalius' work. Without the printing press, Vesalius' discoveries would have had less impact, less quickly; Harvey's work allowed people to understand how blood was carried through the body; Paré found new ways to tie arteries when limbs were amputated which reduced blood loss during operations; microscopes allowed people to detect capillaries; the printing press allowed ideas to spread very quickly, meaning medical understanding could develop quickly.
   Conclusion to explain how far you agree.

Page 125: Renaissance Medicine (1400s–1600s) 2
1. They were based on superstition; they were based on religion; they were not based on scientific thinking. (Any one)
2. Burning cats and dogs; banning large crowds of people in public places; praying; houses boarded up. (Any one)
3. Public toilets were installed in some towns; public baths were installed in some towns; the government passed a law to keep streets clean; fined people who did not keep streets cleaned.
4. The focus was still 'care not cure'; poor people would go to hospitals alongside the old, but those with money would pay

for a doctor to visit their home; nurses still continued to use herbal remedies; many other women working in the hospitals had no medical training.
5. The size of hospitals increased; some hospitals started to admit patients with infectious diseases; simple surgeries were carried out; the majority of physicians and doctors in hospitals had been trained at university; the practice of observation became more important through the work of Thomas Sydenham.
6. Agree – People started to believe that dirty streets caused poor public health; people believed individuals should be isolated if they had a contagious disease; some towns had public toilets installed; some towns had public baths installed; laws were passed by individual towns that stated streets needed to be kept clean; people who did not keep streets cleaned were fined.
   Disagree – People still left rubbish and sewage in the street; people still drank dirty water and let animals roam around towns; people did not understand infectious diseases such as the Sweating Sickness and the Plague; preventions included burning cats and dogs and banning large crowds of people in places such as theatres.
   Conclusion to explain how far you agree.

Page 126: Industrial Medicine (1700s–1900) 1
1. The size and population of towns increased; back-to-back housing was created; diseases such as cholera, typhoid and smallpox were rife; poor factory conditions; unclean water.
2. Advisory policies, i.e. towns did not legally have to do this; the government and public believed in a 'laissez-faire' style approach to government involvement in people's health; due to traditional attitudes, people still did not enforce change.
3. Known as 'The Great Clear Up'; it forced councils to appoint medical health officers to each town; it forced councils to clear up streets; it forced councils to create sewer systems and provide clean drinking water; it improved people's living conditions; it increased people's health/life expectancy.
4. Hospital treatment improved; pharmacies became more popular; companies such as Beechams invested money into researching patent medicines; pills were increasingly used, especially after the creation of pill machines in 1840 by William Brockedon; there was a decrease in the use of herbal remedies.
5. Important – Snow found that all the victims were using the same water pump down Broad Street; the handle to the water pump was removed and no more people died of cholera.
   Not important – People's attitudes did not change quickly enough; there was no public health act in the 1850s, which lead to further outbreaks of cholera in 1865.
6. Agree – Back-to-back housing was needed for the increase in people in towns; diseases such as cholera, typhoid and smallpox spread quickly because of the high population density; people lived in more cramped conditions than ever before.
   Disagree – There was no fresh drinking water; housing was cheap, poor quality and damp; poor working conditions in factories such as cotton factories led to breathing problems; lack of availability of fresh food in towns and cities; lack of enforcement of the 1848 Public Health Act; the government and public believed in a 'laissez-faire' style approach to government involvement in people's health; due to traditional attitudes, people still did not enforce change.
   Conclusion to explain how far you agree.

Page 127: Industrial Medicine (1700s–1900) 2
1. Florence Nightingale didn't support Pasteur's Germ Theory; it has been argued that Nightingale's ideas on hospital cleanliness were only implemented because of a change in the government's attitude; can be argued she was not a 'hands on' nurse. (Any one)
2. Edward Jenner found a vaccination for smallpox; in 1840 the government paid for people to receive these vaccinations; in 1853 it became compulsory.
3. In 1861 Pasteur developed Germ Theory; Pasteur discovered microbes after experiments on sour milk; he published his theory in 1861 and after more experiments, scientists agreed with his theory; for the first time ever, people understood what caused disease; after Koch's identification of microbes, Pasteur could improve people's health by creating vaccinations such as anthrax; Emil von Behring used Koch and Pasteur's work to discover how antibodies worked; in 1890 Behring developed a

cure for diphtheria; other scientists also used Koch and Pasteur's work to stop other illnesses such as typhoid and tetanus.

4. Chloroform was discovered accidentally in 1847 by James Simpson; it started to be used by women in labour all over Europe; as anaesthetics were increasingly used during operations, panic among patients decreased; antiseptics such as carbolic acid were also increasingly used in decreasing infection after their discovery by Joseph Lister; there was a further move from antiseptic to aseptic surgery. Koch found that the use of hot steam and sterilisation of instruments would rid germs; however, after anaesthetics were used but before antiseptics were discovered, more people died during surgery because surgeons could take longer over their surgery as their patients were no longer in pain; the increase in deaths was due to an increase in blood loss and infection. This was the black period of surgery.

5. Important – Noted poor hygiene when working as a nurse during the Crimean War; put pressure on the government to increase hospital hygiene; wrote *Notes on Nursing* in 1859, and *Notes on Hospitals* in 1863, improving hospitals' conditions and nursing.
Not important – Can be argued that she was not a 'hands on' nurse; didn't support Pasteur's Germ Theory; her ideas on hospital cleanliness were only implemented because of a change in the government's attitude.

6. Agree – Robert Koch discovered which specific germs caused disease; other microbes such as cholera and plague could be identified; Emil von Behring used Koch and Pasteur's work to discover the way in which antibodies worked; other scientists also used Koch's work to stop other illnesses such as typhoid and tetanus.
Disagree – Changing attitudes; Edward Jenner's work; Pasteur's development of Germ Theory; cottage hospitals established; Ignaz Semmelweis put pressure on hospitals to improve cleanliness; Florence Nightingale wrote *Notes on Nursing* in 1859, and *Notes on Hospitals* in 1863, improving hospitals' conditions and nursing; anaesthetics were increasingly used during operations after Simpson's discovery of chloroform in 1847. This decreased panic among patients and increased the likelihood of people willing to undergo surgery; antiseptics were increasingly used during surgery after Joseph Lister's discovery of carbolic acid in 1865; aseptic surgery decreased the likelihood of infection.
Conclusion to explain how far you agree.

Page 128: Modern Medicine (1900s–Present) 1
1. Lack of funds
2. They developed research on penicillin, testing it on humans.
3. Magic bullets are drugs that kill bacteria; while bacteria had been discovered and was understood before 1909, there were no drugs to treat it; the first two magic bullets were Salvarsan 606 and Prontosil. Salvarsan cured diseases such as syphilis.
4. In 1953 Francis Crick and James Watson discovered that DNA was present in all human cells; Maurice Wilkins devised X-ray crystallography to allow Crick and Watson to develop their experiments and research further; Rosalind Franklin was the first person to discover the double helix structure of DNA; the new understanding of DNA and genetics allowed for greater understanding of stem cell research, Down's Syndrome, and illnesses such as diabetes, Parkinson's and Alzheimer's.
5. Important – The USA offered to fund the production of antibiotics to help wounded soldiers in World War Two; Britain did not have the time and space needed to grow the mould required for penicillin due to being involved in World War Two; without the finances of the USA, the production of antibiotics wouldn't have been possible.
Not important: The USA had previously refused to fund the development of antibiotics.
6. Agree – Without World War One, progress in blood transfusions and surgery wouldn't have happened as quickly; storage of blood was made easier through Weil, Rous and Turner's discoveries; plastic surgery developed due to the skin grafting techniques devised by Harold Gilles in his plastic surgery unit; Marie Curie created mobile X-ray machines during World War One; X-ray machines became smaller and mobile in order for them to be used on soldiers on the front line; transplant surgery and prosthetic limbs improved due to their sudden greater need; in 1915 sodium citrate was added to blood by Richard Lewisohn. This stopped the blood from clotting.

Disagree – More funding now supported scientific discoveries; science and technology dominated medical progression; the understanding of DNA meant people could understand genetic diseases; magic bullets had a huge impact in targeting disease; the development of penicillin allowed antibiotics to be created.
Conclusion to explain how far you agree.

Page 129: Modern Medicine (1900s–Present) 2
1. Free access to doctors; creation of family doctors; free prescriptions; creation of healthcare centres; free to call ambulances. (Any one)
2. World War Two highlighted the poor health of British citizens; the evacuation of children emphasised the poor public health in towns and cities; in 1944 William Beveridge wrote a report stating that the British government needed to tackle the five evils, including disease and squalor.
3. They highlighted that the government should take some responsibility for the public's health; the poorest children's health improved through the 1906 School Meals Act; the 1907 Health Act meant young children and their mothers were checked on by health visitors; the 1908 Old Age Pensions Act gave financial support to the elderly, which improved their health as they now had a better standard of living; the 1911 National Insurance Act gave some sick pay and medical treatment to those in work.
4. Some people did not want to pay extra taxes to fund the NHS; doctors felt too heavily controlled by the government; some people still believed in the laissez-faire approach; charities and councils felt they were no longer needed for healthcare; the NHS has become increasingly expensive; some people believe that the option of 'going private' is creating a 'two-tier' system of care, with the more wealthy receiving better treatment.
5. Important – Half of British men were declared unfit to fight; this made the government concerned about Britain's security.
Not important – The studies of Charles Booth and Seebohm Rowntree highlighted the real reasons for poverty: lack of money for food and quality housing; people's attitudes about a laissez-faire approach to government were changing.
6. Agree – The report put pressure on the government to help its citizens further; reaffirmed the discoveries made about people's ill health from World War Two.
Disagree – World War Two highlighted the poor health of British citizens; the evacuation of children emphasised the poor public health in towns and cities; in 1944, William Beveridge wrote a report stating that the British government needed to tackle the Five Evils, including disease and squalor.
Conclusion to explain how far you agree.

Page 130: Modern Medicine (1900s–Present) 3
1. Ebola, AIDS (Any one)
2. Radiotherapy – a treatment for cancer that uses high-energy radiation; chemotherapy – a type of cancer treatment that uses anti-cancer drugs; radiation – the use of electromagnetic waves; endocrine – where hormones are put into the circulatory system so they can be carried to organs. (Any one)
3. MRI scanning, ultrasound
4. AIDS was first reported in 1981; it was feared there was no treatment and was nearly always fatal; once HIV was discovered, effective antiretroviral drugs were developed, this now means people with HIV can lead healthy lives; by 2000, over 30 million people had been infected with AIDS, the majority being in Africa; Ebola was first reported in Africa; it is resistant to antibiotics; so far, Ebola has killed over 10,000 worldwide.
5. The No Smoking campaigns aim to reduce cancers such as lung cancer; the campaigns to reduce alcohol consumption aim to reduce liver diseases; Change4Life promotes the 'five a day' consumption of fruit and vegetables and the importance of exercise; flu campaigns explain what to do if a person contracts flu; national drugs campaigns explain the negative impact of illegal drugs.
6. Agree – Increase in treatments for cancer such as radiation therapy; people are living longer; improvements in treatments and diagnosis such as MRI scanning, ultrasounds, heart transplants, laser and keyhole surgery.
Disagree – In the 1960s, thalidomide caused babies to be born with disfigurements such as missing limbs; not all people support scientific developments. Many are unsupportive for

moral and religious reasons; some people still prefer alternative medicines such as herbal remedies, acupuncture and meditation; some diseases such as AIDS and Ebola can still not be cured. Conclusion to explain how far you agree.

Pages 131-139 Practice Questions

Page 131: 1000–1500: Crime

1. He used brutal methods such as burning villages, destroying crops and animals; survivors also died of starvation; built castles; used the death penalty for serious crimes.
2. To protect people from violence; to protect a landowner's property from damage or theft.
3. The victim or relative of the victim could claim compensation; the level of compensation depended on the seriousness of the crime.
4. They roamed the country, stealing from anyone, particularly the poor; they would steal food, clothing or pots and pans; they used violence including arson.
5. Use of the wergild to pay compensation; death penalty for treason; repeat offenders could be mutilated; blood feuds allowed victims to hunt down the criminals and punish them.
6. They were banned from cutting down trees for fuel or building; they were forbidden from owning a dog, hunting or using bows and arrows; severe punishments, such as being blinded, were used.

Page 132: 1000–1500: Punishment

1. Fines.
2. The death penalty for treason and arson; punishment for reoffenders included mutilation, or having a hand or nose cut off.
3. Manor courts; county courts; royal courts; church courts.
4. Took advantage of the belief in God; used as a way of allowing God to decide upon guilt; belief that God would help innocent people and punish the guilty.
5. A reliance on friends and family because there was no police force; tithings and the hue and cry were used; parish constables were appointed to keep law and order; they were usually leading villagers who commanded respect.
6. Increased influence after the Norman invasion, particularly in everyday lives; belief that punishment should reform the criminal; church courts were set up, but they could not impose the death penalty, but could instead claim 'benefit of the clergy' and recite a Bible passage; the 'right of sanctuary' meant that you could not be arrested in a church.

Page 133: 1500–1700: Crime

1. Changes in people's beliefs; changes of religion of the reigning monarch, between Catholic and Protestant.
2. Public hanging, drawing and quartering was used because it was such a horrific death; it aimed to deter others from committing the crime.
3. Trade between towns grew; improved roads meant that highwaymen could travel easily on horseback.
4. Increase in unemployment – begging; increase in population led to more people in towns – footpads; increase in trade between towns – highwaymen; reduction in common land – poaching; changes in beliefs – heresy; trade restrictions/tax rises – smuggling (Any three)
5. They were forced to work; they could be whipped; they could be branded.
6. End of feudalism led to a reduction in common land; land was fenced off; landowners restricted who could hunt on their land; it was not regarded as a serious crime by the public.

Page 134: 1500–1700: Punishment

1. Only they could impose the death penalty; they heard the most serious cases.
2. King James was Protestant and had treated Catholics very cruelly; they wanted to have a Catholic monarch.
3. The number of crimes punishable by death increased to more than 200; minor crimes such as stealing a rabbit or damaging a tree could result in the death penalty.
4. Watchmen were paid to patrol London; parish officials arrested beggars and petty criminals; thief takers were paid by the victim to catch the criminals and bring them to justice.
5. Smugglers were seen as heroes; unpopular taxes raised the price of luxury goods; smugglers could make huge profits; smuggling

gangs were well organised – smugglers from Sussex could transport their goods straight to London, using the improved roads; wanted posters by the government actually made smugglers more popular.
6. Agree – No national police force; still used parish constables to arrest beggars; the hue and cry was still used.
   Disagree – Thief takers began to track down criminals and collect rewards; watchmen, known as charlies, were paid to patrol London; rewards could be offered for the arrest of criminals, particularly highwaymen.
   Conclusion to explain how far you agree.

Page 135: 1700–1900: Crime

1. Petty theft.
2. Wherever poor people settled in towns and cities.
3. Landowners; factory owners.
4. Crime could now be reported across Britain due to cheap illustrated newspapers; this made people more concerned and scared.
5. Street theft; burglary; drunk and disorderly behaviour; smuggling of illegal goods.
6. Large overcrowded towns and cities made it easy to avoid capture; professional gangs of thieves would hide out in dens and rookeries; extreme poverty increased the level of theft – particularly food.

Page 136: 1700–1900: Punishment

1. As Home Secretary he reduced the number of death penalty offences.
2. They were criticised for being drunk; the public believed that the police restricted their freedom.
3. They were full time and well paid, therefore they wanted to do a good job; 3200 men were recruited to patrol London, particularly high crime areas; a detective department was also set up and police now prevented and detected crime.
4. The use of the death penalty became less acceptable; removing criminals from society and detaining them in prisons instead was seen as a deterrent; a changing emphasis from punishment towards reforming prisoners so that they would not re-offend.
5. She set up education classes to reform female prisoners in Newgate Prison; she worked to ensure women had better food and clothes; she believed women should be treated with respect and kindness, rather than being exploited by warders.
6. Prison conditions improved and they were no longer schools of crime with prisoners crammed together; the aim was to reform prisoners so they would not commit future crime; a fairer system of punishment was introduced: fines and prison rather than transportation and the death penalty; improved working conditions reduced protests and riots; the presence of the police deterred crime and they began to solve crime as well as prevent it.

Page 137: 1900–Present: Crime

1. Britain has become a multi-cultural society; it has become more prosperous; an increased reliance on technology.
2. Less respect for authority; less respect for others; more actions now classed as crimes; victims are more likely to report crime; methods of recording have improved.
3. Due to changing attitudes and opinions; when the government is concerned about issues; public opinion adds pressure.
4. Modern weapons; modern transport; improved communications such as computers and mobile phones.
5. Creating a disturbance; graffiti; drunk and disorderly behaviour.
6. Sex discrimination; computer hacking; race crime; traffic crime; people trafficking; cyber-crime; hooliganism; modern terrorism.

Page 138: 1900–Present: Punishment

1. CCTV and radios; improvements in science such as fingerprinting and DNA; improvements in transport such as cars, motorbikes and helicopters.
2. Community sentences; treatment and rehabilitation programmes; ASBOs; electronic tagging. (Any three)
3. Borstals used work and education to try and reduce youth offending rates, but these still remained high; Youth Detention Centres gave a fixed term sentence, and a tough regime known

as a 'short, sharp shock'; (the government used the media to highlight the tougher regime).

4. To punish someone by removing their freedom; to keep society safe by removing criminals; to attempt to reform prisoners using education and teaching new skills; to separate different types of criminals according to the severity of the crime, using open or high security prisons.

5. Timothy Evans was hanged in 1950 for murder, yet evidence later proved he was innocent; Derek Bentley was hanged for murdering a policeman, yet he had not fired the gun – he was pardoned in 1998; Ruth Ellis was hanged for murdering her boyfriend – yet she had been subjected to violent abuse for many years.

6. Successful – Attempt to reduce reoffending rates through education; prisoners receive work and skills to help them rehabilitate and have a place in society when the sentence is served. Unsuccessful – Mixed success with regard to reoffending as rates remain high; prison numbers have increased; general public do not always support the idea of 'easy' prisons such as open prisons for minor crimes.

Page 139: Case Studies

1. They were poorly educated, single or widows with no one to support them; often these women were vulnerable and isolated from their own community.

2. Unusual marks, spots, freckles or pimples on the body; if the accused did not bleed when pricked with a needle or knife; if they survived the floating test.

3. Agree – He got paid for each witch that was executed; he used torture to gain confessions.
   Disagree – He was a religious man and believed he was doing God's work hunting for witches; he was a lawyer and understood that he needed confessions to prove guilt.
   Conclusion to explain how far you agree.

4. They objected on the grounds of religion; they objected due to their own moral beliefs.

5. Conscription had been introduced in 1916; anyone refusing was seen as a coward, traitor or refusing to do their duty for the King and country.

6. They were treated more leniently; prison was only used as a last resort.

Pages 140-149 Review Questions

Page 140: 1000–1500: Crime

1. A lack of reliable evidence or statistics.
2. Those crimes that threatened the power and wealth of the lawmakers.
3. They contained expensive ornaments of silver and gold; they contained money that had been collected to distribute to the poor.
4. They were protected by local people; they were protected by wealthy friends.
5. To prevent rebellions or punish rebellions; to maintain law and order; William wanted to maintain his power as King and ensure his laws were obeyed.
6. Poverty and famine were common; a growing population/lack of work/low wages; bad harvests led to high food prices.

Page 141: 1000–1500: Punishment

1. Punishments such as stocks and pillories took place in public to shame criminals; serious punishment such as execution took place to frighten and deter others.
2. Tithing; hue and cry.
3. The hand was placed in hot water to retrieve an object; the hand was bandaged for three days; if the wound was healing cleanly then the person was innocent, if not the person was guilty.
4. A royal court tried a variety of cases, and the most common sentence was capital punishment; this aimed to keep peace, law and order in the kingdom; a church court dealt with crimes that were deemed immoral, but it could not impose the death penalty.
5. They were leading villagers who tried to keep the peace; they were not paid; they held the job for only a year.
6. Harsh – Executions often took place; capital punishment was a common sentence; trial by ordeal would be very painful.

Lenient – 'Benefit of clergy' and the 'right of sanctuary' meant the church could not pass the death sentence; fines were given for minor crimes; the system of wergild meant compensation was paid to victims instead.
Conclusion to explain how far you agree.

Page 142: 1500–1700: Crime

1. They were usually beheaded rather than being hung, drawn and quartered.
2. A strong government was more likely to punish criminals; this meant a lower crime rate.
3. Deserving – those who were sick or injured. Sturdy – those who were considered to be lazy.
4. Prices of goods and unemployment were high; taxes had been increased due to wars being fought.
5. An increasing population in towns and cities; a decline in feudalism and an increase in movement of people to urban areas.
6. Increasing unemployment; no system to help those in need.

Page 143: 1500–1700: Punishment

1. Flogging; hanging; execution.
2. A way of dealing with petty criminals and political criminals during the late 17th century; they were sent to English colonies to work as labourers.
3. There had been many arguments about the religion of the monarch, and the country had been changing between Catholic and Protestant since Henry VIII. Example – Gunpowder Plot.
4. He was arrested; he was tortured on the rack for three days; he was found guilty of treason; he was hung, drawn and quartered.
5. Hero – He caught over 60 thieves and brought them to justice; he was able to return stolen goods to their owners.
   Villain – He was also a criminal who ran successful gangs of thieves; he used his power to capture and kill rival gang leaders; he was hung in 1725.
   Conclusion to explain how far you agree.
6. Agree – Fewer people were hanged; juries found people not guilty because they did not want to pass the death sentence; transportation and banishment were used as alternative punishments.
   Disagree – The Bloody Code frightened people and deterred criminals; an increasing number of crimes were punishable by the death penalty; severe penalties for criminals.
   Conclusion to explain how far you agree.

Page 144: 1700–1900: Crime

1. The Chartists; the Luddites.
2. To prevent meetings of more than 12 people; to prevent protests.
3. Crime could now be widely reported and this made people more aware; cheap illustrated newspapers caused panic and fear, by reporting sensational stories or crimes such as garroters and Jack the Ripper.
4. Prostitution; public disorder such as rioting and protest.
5. Swearing a secret oath on the Bible; forming a trade union.
6. Due to the brutality and violence associated with the crime; the case was widely reported in newspapers; panic and fear spread through Whitechapel.

Page 145: 1700–1900: Punishment

1. America; The Caribbean; Australia.
2. He built a new prison in Gloucester; individual cells were used to separate prisoners; he provided access to medical care, exercise and religion.
3. Paying gaolers; providing education; inspections were made by doctors and chaplains; women gaolers would look after women prisoners.
4. Fear of rising crime needed to be controlled by using more effective punishments; the work of reformers such as Howard and Fry was important in improving prison conditions; the Bloody Code was too severe and transportation was seen to be too harsh.
5. The Metropolitan Police Force was set up in 1829 and 3200 men were recruited; the police were well trained and had a uniform; a detective department was set up in 1842 to prevent and solve crime; in 1856 it became compulsory for all counties to have a police force.

6. Similar – Both aim to catch criminals; both are paid to patrol London.
   Different – Police aimed to prevent crime but the Bow Street Runners simply wanted to catch criminals; the police worked day and night, they had a detective department and by 1856 had become compulsory in every county.

Page 146: 1900–Present: Crime

1. Car crime and driving offences; assault; mugging; burglary. (Any three)
2. Cyber crime has developed using computers and the internet.
3. Restrictions on immigration; huge amounts of money to be made; strengthened links to organised criminal gangs. (Any two)
4. Stealing money; defrauding people for their identity; 'phishing' (Any two)
5. Made it illegal to discriminate in businesses and workplaces; illegal to stir up racial hatred; racism is now treated as a serious crime; important cases such as Stephen Lawrence have helped to highlight this crime.
6. Theft – this had always been common but now due to technology it has developed into computer crime such as hacking and phishing. Smuggling – has now become drugs, people, alcohol and tobacco with huge profits being made.

Page 147: 1900–Present: Punishment

1. National Crime Agency. Detect and prevent serious organised crime, including drug smuggling and people trafficking.
2. A reduction in the number of police 'on the beat'.
3. DNA evidence; fingerprinting; CCTV; transport (Any two)
4. Community sentences require people to work on community projects for a required number of hours; electronic tagging – a form of probation that lets the police know where an offender is at any time; restorative justice – the offender and victim meet to discuss why the crime was committed and for the offender to express remorse; ASBOs – require people to conform to rules; treatment programmes for criminals with drug / alcohol problems (Any three)
5. CID – investigates serious crimes. Special Branch – works to prevent all types of terrorism. Traffic Department – responsible for dealing with issues related to road use; PCeU – deals with cyber crime; NCA – detects and prevents serious organised crime (Any three)
6. Agree – CCTV, radios and science have made it easier to detect and record crime; motorised transport, cars, bikes and helicopters allow the police to be more mobile and can react to crime and crime scenes quicker.
   Disagree – Specialised police units have improved policing because the work is so varied that officers can now focus on specific areas of crime and policing; closer links with the community such as Neighbourhood Watch, PCSOs and social media have had a significant impact on policing.
   Conclusion to explain how far you agree.

Page 148–49: Case Studies

1. They were scared of being tortured, and it was easier to just confess; they were uneducated or couldn't defend themselves.
2. Improvements in science and education helped to provide common sense explanations for events; increasing political and religious stability meant people were less superstitious; these rational explanations caused witchcraft accusations to decline.
3. Changing attitudes of people worried about being cursed by the poor; the authority of the King: James I strongly believed in witches; prejudice towards others, particularly towards the old and vulnerable in society; religion and the belief that the devil was doing evil acts; wars and conflicts had made people scared and suspicious of each other.
4. Work in hospitals; drive injured soldiers around; work on farms or in factories.
5. Prison where many received poor treatment; removal of voting rights; (non-combat roles were given including working on farms, factories or in hospitals). Many were abused in the street, beaten up or sacked from their jobs.
6. Agree – Prison was a severe punishment for simply refusing to fight because of religious or moral beliefs; 71 men died in prison due to poor treatment, many others were abused, shamed or shunned.

Disagree – Conscription had been introduced in 1916, and they were breaking the law; the country needed as many soldiers as possible, and thousands of people had made a sacrifice for their King and country.
Conclusion to explain how far you agree.

Pages 150-151 Norman England

1. 1045
2. Edward had promised him the throne in 1051; Harold Godwinson had made an oath to support his claim in 1064.
3. A man who was granted land by the king as a reward for his loyalty. Thegns were responsible for protecting the villagers under their control and providing military assistance to the king when needed.
4. Hardrada's army outnumbered the Saxons; the Saxon army became trapped after being pushed backwards by the Vikings; the Saxons had to fight a three-sided battle that weakened their forces even further; eventually the Saxons were slaughtered after being pushed into a natural pit.
5. Barons were given land and castles to help them keep an eye on the Saxons; castles were used as a base for collecting taxes and completing day-to-day running of local affairs; castles acted as a constant reminder to the Saxons that the Normans were in charge.
6. Agree – the questions focused on land and money, giving William information about how much tax areas of England could and should be paying; William needed this information (and the money) to add to his treasury to pay for wars and battles.
   Disagree – William wanted to assess the effect the conquest had on England – economic and social; William was a foreign king and needed to gather information about his new kingdom once his power was secure.
   Conclusion to explain how far you agree.
7. Archers; cavalry; foot soldiers; crossbowmen (Any two)
8. Agree – Saxons were fighting to protect their country, this gave them a mental determination for the battle; perhaps they also wanted to avenge the defeat at Fulford, which made them fight harder.
   Disagree – the Viking army was a tough opposing force; the warrior on the bridge had held the Saxon forces off; the Vikings had been surprised by the Saxon army which meant that they were not fully prepared for the battle, this was an advantage to the Saxon forces and helped them in the victory.
   Conclusion to explain how far you agree.
9. 28 September 1066
10. Normandy
11. Edward had fathered no children; Edward had promised the throne to two men – William and Harold Godwinson; Hardrada also claimed he had a right to be the king of England; there was no clear successor, which meant that there would be a battle for the throne.
12. 1075
13. Prisoners of war; criminals who couldn't pay their fines; descendants of original British people (from pre-Saxon invasion era).
14. The feudal system ensured that everyone knew their place and was kept under William's control; Saxons had jobs (of high importance) taken from them and were replaced with Normans; boundaries of earldoms were changed and barons controlled new areas; the Anglo-Saxon links with Denmark and Norway were broken and greater links with Normandy and Europe were established; the Saxon language had French incorporated into it.
15. Agree – government, finance and justice continued in much the same manner as Anglo-Saxon times; William did not want to change things if they worked well; he also wanted to ensure that things continued to show that he was the rightful heir to Edward and would continue with Edward's work.
   Disagree – lots of towns and villages were destroyed to make way for castles; most important jobs were taken from Saxons and given to Normans; new laws were introduced (Murdrum Law and Forest Law).
   Conclusion to explain how far you agree.

16. Agree – he was a blood relative; he had direct links with Anglo-Saxon kings – descendant of Alfred the Great.
Disagree – he was only a child; he did not have the support of the Witan; he was no match for the other contenders claiming the throne.
Conclusion to explain how far you agree.
17. Edward had spent time in Normandy as a young man and had developed a strong relationship with William; William had sent soldiers to help him when he had returned to England to become king.
18. Bishop Odo
19. The Normans pretended to retreat down the hill. The Saxon soldiers broke rank out from their shield wall on the top of Senlac Hill and chased them into the open field. The Norman cavalry could then easily kill the Saxons who were defenceless on the hill away from the shield wall. Eventually the shield wall was weakened enough for the archers to be able to hit their Saxon targets.
20. Agree – when the Norman earls revolted in 1075 the Saxons could have joined forces to depose William; although there were many rebellions in William's early reign, none were successful – perhaps better planning and organisation should have been used to ensure a successful outcome.
Disagree – in the early years of William's reign he faced many rebellions from the Saxons; it was difficult for the Saxons to mount a successful rebellion because the Normans used the feudal system and castles to keep them weak and subservient; after the Harrying of the North people did not dare risk the wrath of William.
Conclusion to explain how far you agree.

Pages 152-153 Elizabethan England
1. Philip II of Spain was married to Mary, Elizabeth's sister; trade links – Antwerp, the most important cloth market in Europe was controlled by Spain; Philip II of Spain wanted to marry Elizabeth I to keep his alliance with England.
2. Agree – Poverty was not a high priority for Elizabeth (focused on religion and foreign policy); poverty problem passed to local government.
Disagree – Privy Council and Elizabeth discussed the problem; passed Elizabethan Poor Law.
Conclusion to explain how far you agree.
3. Agree – the importance of the new trade routes established under Elizabeth – Eastland Company to import goods from the Baltic, East India Company opened a trade route to India, luxury goods imported from Mediterranean region; collapse of European trade markets.
Disagree – developments in technology encouraged exploration – compass; faster lighter ships (caravels); sponsorship from monarchs and merchants encouraged voyages; role of Richard Hakluyt's book.
Conclusion to explain how far you agree.
4. Act of Uniformity – key changes in acts of worship; Act of Supremacy – nature of the church leadership and Supreme Governor of the Church of England.
5. Mary, Queen of Scots was spared; Mendoza, the Spanish ambassador, was expelled from the English Court; a decline in Anglo-Spanish relations – another step closer to war.
6. Mary was heir to the English throne and a Catholic; Mary was a figurehead for Catholic plotters; Mary had support in Europe to overthrow Elizabeth.
7. War with France was not going well and was very expensive; series of bad harvests in the mid-1550s; rising inflation since the 1540s.
8. Agree – differences in religion had become an increasing cause of tension. Elizabeth was Protestant and Philip was Catholic.
Disagree – long-term friction existed between Philip and Elizabeth after Elizabeth rejected his marriage proposal; execution of Mary; English assistance for Dutch rebels against Spanish; English privateers' attack on Spanish ships.
Conclusion to explain how far you agree.
9. Who opposed theatres – Puritans and local government officials; reasons for opposition – law and order and content of plays; who liked theatres – many people from different areas of society including Elizabeth I; why theatres were popular – cheap entertainment; compare opposition with those who supported the theatres.

10. Use of portraits; extensive use of imagery.
11. She did not want to commit to a marriage alliance with another country for fear of upsetting rivals; fear of any potential husband wanting to control her and act as a King; she saw the reaction of the people to Mary's marriage – which was very unpopular; any marriage to a noble could cause significant divisions within the Court.
12. Catholic opposition – felt Catholicism was being suppressed as the settlement had a Protestant bias; Puritan opposition – thought agreement was not Protestant enough.
13. Rise of the merchant and gentry classes; still significant poverty evident in society. Therefore, some people become much better off, but others became worse off – many lost their jobs.
14. Overseas trade; wealth and power; development of colonies; sea power and the navy.
Compare these factors and reach a judgement.
15. Look at achievements – such as world voyage and riches brought to England; look at failures – antagonises Spain into war with Cadiz raid of 1587.
Reach a judgement.
16. Elizabeth did not marry; Elizabeth did not name a successor until she was on her deathbed; pressure from Elizabethan ministers.
17. There were many cultural developments – theatre, literature and architecture; rising living standards for many and social mobility; counterpoint – war and poverty.
18. Problem of marriage and succession; attitudes within Parliament; plots and rebellions.
19. English tactics and navy – fireships and type of smaller, faster fighting ships; bad luck – weather; mistakes – inexperienced leadership and unclear plan of attack.
20. Look at each plot (the Northern Rebellion; the Ridolfi plot; the Throckmorton plot; the Babington plot; the Earl of Essex rebellion) and decide which one was the greatest threat; look at how close each one was to achieving its objectives; look at the role of Sir Francis Walsingham and how far he blocked the plots.

Pages 154-155 Health and Medicine
1. Treatments not based on science; most popular forms of treatments included: Alchemy – a mixture of philosophy, superstition and Medieval 'science', herbal remedies, bloodletting, praying.
2. Sweating, fever, headache, sickness, shortness of breath. (Any one)
3. The Second Public Health Act of 1875
4. Agree – Microscopes were discovered; the printing press allowed ideas to spread very quickly; time spent observing and therefore thinking increased; John Hunter stressed the importance of observation; groups such as The Royal Society were created where men met to discuss scientific thinking and ideas rather than religious beliefs; people's attitudes changed – people were now more willing to accept new ideas.
Disagree – The reduction in the importance of the Church had an impact; the role of the individual such as Vesalius, Harvey and Fabricius; a change in attitudes allowed people to question more.
Conclusion to explain how far you agree.
5. Pills, drugs issued by pharmacies, herbal remedies (Any one)
6. Crick and Watson, Wilkins, and Franklin
7. Agree – Allowed people to understand how the blood flowed through the body; enabled Fabricius to make discoveries about valves; realised that the heart was a pump.
Disagree – The printing press allowed people to widely read Harvey's work. Without the printing press, Harvey's discoveries would have had less impact, less quickly; Vesalius was the first person to openly criticise Galen's beliefs; Paré found new ways to tie arteries when limbs were amputated which reduced blood loss during operations; the discovery of microscopes allowed people to detect capillaries.
Conclusion to explain how far you agree.
8. Burning cats and dogs; banning large crowds of people in public places; prayer; houses would be boarded up. (Any one)
9. People still left rubbish and sewage in the streets; people still drank dirty water; animals roamed around towns; infectious diseases such as the Sweating Sickness and the Plague killed in their thousands.
10. Successes – The size of hospitals increased; some hospitals started to admit patients with infectious diseases; simple

surgeries were carried out; the majority of physicians and doctors in hospitals had been trained at university; the practice of observation became more important through the work of Thomas Sydenham.

Limitations – The majority of hospitals still cared rather than cured. Patients were given food, water and warmth; poor people would go to hospitals alongside the old, but those with money would pay for a doctor to visit their home; nurses still continued to use herbal remedies and many other women working in the hospitals had no medical training.

11. Their aqueducts and sewage system were abandoned when they left; they did not leave Britain any money to continue the public health system.

12. In 1842, Edwin Chadwick published a report on the 'Sanitary Conditions of the Labouring Population'; his report highlighted the poor conditions in which working-class people lived; his suggestions were put into action in the Public Health Act of 1848. The Act suggested: sewers should be improved, rubbish should be removed from the streets, drinking water should be clean, medical officers should monitor the cleanliness of towns; contribution was limited as the policies created by the government were only advisory policies.

13. The size and population of towns increased; back-to-back housing was created; diseases such as cholera, typhoid and smallpox were rife. (Any one)

14. Cottage hospitals

15. Galen devised the idea of the Theory of Opposites; the Theory of Opposites stated that if a person was cold for example, they should be given something hot to improve their health.

16. She put pressure on government to ensure hospitals were clean and well organised; wrote *Notes on Nursing* in 1859, thereby improving nursing; she wrote *Notes on Hospitals* in 1863, improving hospitals and their conditions; it could be argued she was less effective as she was not seen to be a 'hands-on' nurse.

17. People were used to Galen's ideas; it is difficult to accept new ideas; religious beliefs had always supported Galen. (Any one)

18. World War Two highlighted the poor health of British citizens; the evacuation of children emphasised the poor public health in towns and cities.

19. Important – The studies highlighted the real reasons for poverty – lack of money for food and quality housing.
Not important – The Boer War highlighted the fact that many of the men were declared unfit to fight; this concerned the government regarding Britain's security; people's attitudes about a laissez-faire approach to government were changing.

20. Agree – There was a lack of scientific knowledge and understanding; as people were taught that God caused illness, people prayed to be made better rather than search for treatments that would work.

Disagree – The Christian church was in charge of healthcare in Britain; the Church did not like to contradict Galen so progress was not made; Romans had taken away the public health system; the belief that people should be cared for rather than cured. Conclusion to explain how far you agree.

Pages 156-157 Crime and Punishment

1. John Howard; Elizabeth Fry.
2. Increasing unemployment; no system to help those in need; they were seen as a threat to society.
3. Computer hacking; traffic crime; sex discrimination; race crime. (Any two)
4. The rack.
5. To protect a landowner's property from damage or theft or to protect people from violence.
6. Only lasted 18 months; crime in London was increasing rapidly during this period; there were not enough patrols.
7. The Forest Law.
8. High prices and high unemployment; increased taxes during wars.
9. Through education; by giving prisoners work that teaches them new skills.
10. They were beheaded
11. They were known as charlies.
12. The ruler of the kingdom, after consulting with nobles and bishops.
13. Increased political stability; increase of education and scientific ideas.
14. Insurance claims require a police reference number; methods of recording crime have improved.
15. Compensation was paid to the victim or relative, with the amount determined by the seriousness of the crime.
16. Smugglers themselves; traders; buyers; those who hid the smuggled items. (Any two)
17. Revenge attacks often led to more violence.
18. Deserving – those who were sick or injured. Sturdy beggars – those who were considered lazy and would be punished.
19. Agree – 'Separate' and 'Silent' systems isolated prisoners and this encouraged self-reflection and remorse; aim was to reform rather than punish.
Disagree – Prison systems were expensive to run and maintain; hard labour and harsh punishments continued to be used. Conclusion to explain how far you agree.
20. Agree – Crimes punishable by death rose from 50 to more than 200; aimed to frighten people to prevent them committing crime.
Disagree – Fewer people were hung because juries avoided giving the death penalty; transportation was increased to remove prisoners to English colonies.
Conclusion to explain how far you agree.

Glossary

Norman England

Alfred the Great   King of Wessex, 849–899
Anglo-Saxons   invaders that came to Britain in the 440s from Germany, Denmark and the Netherlands

banished   to be banned or thrown out of the country
baron   barons were given areas of land as part of the feudal system and helped the king run England after the Battle of Hastings
burh   a fortified town

cavalry   soldiers on horseback
ceorls   free men in Anglo-Saxon times
Chancellor   the man who helped the king run the country and made sure his wishes were fulfilled
claimant   a person who claims something (in this instance that they should be king of England)
clergy   priests
Cluniac Reforms   a series of changes focused on restoring traditional monastic life
Curia Regis   a meeting of the king's barons, bishops and abbots where they helped him run the country; a Norman version of the Witan

deposed   overthrown/removed

earldom   an area of land looked after by an earl
excommunicate   to be banned from the church; in medieval times it was thought you would not be able to get to heaven if you had been excommunicated

feudal   the Latin word for land – describes a system of landowners holding the power and control
fyrd   amateur (peasant) soldiers who had to fight for their lord for 40 days when needed, often armed only with tools brought from their farms

geld   an Anglo-Saxon tax where money was paid to the king based on how many hides of land were owned by an individual; some historians say it's the first national tax system in Western Europe, one which William chose to keep

Harrying   persistently carrying out attacks on an area
heir   the next in line to the throne
hide   an area of land, usually 50–100 acres
housecarl   Harold's most professional and well-trained soldier

infantry   foot soldiers

monastery   the building where monks lived and worked
motte and bailey   the first type of Norman castle where the keep (tower) of the castle was built on a hill (the motte) and the bailey was where the resources would have been stored (in a fenced area below the motte)

Papal   relating to the Pope
pillaged   when a place is robbed using force
prefabricated   ready-made sections of a castle that could be easily transported and built anywhere

rebellion   an organised attempt to overthrow the king

sedition   treason
sheriff   the person responsible for collecting taxes from the people in the shire and looking after its day-to-day issues
strategic   a plan of tactics or strategy to give an advantage
succession   the following on of one king/queen after another

thegn   knights who must fight for their king when required as a condition of being given land
thralls   slaves in Anglo-Saxon times
tithe   a tax paid to the church (10% of income) in either money or goods
treasury   stores of money

villein   a peasant

wergild   the price put on someone's life (a thegn's life would be worth more than a ceorl's)
Witan   an Anglo-Saxon assembly comprised of thegns and sometimes bishops and abbots; all were advisors to the king, who could choose to ignore their advice if he wished

Elizabethan England

abdicate to resign from a position of power, such as a Queen or a Pope

admiral a leader of a navy

alliance a union from which both parties will usually benefit, generally formalised in an agreement, such as a treaty

Armada the Spanish navy

bastard a child born to parents who are not married

civil war a war between groups within the same country

colony land or a settlement owned by a country outside its borders and usually taken by force

empire an area made up of provinces which is controlled by one group of people

excommunicate to be dismissed from the church

fireships unmanned ships, covered in tar and pitch, set alight and pushed towards the enemy

galleon a large battleship with several decks

gentry local landowners, who were the Elizabethan equivalent to the lords of the manor in medieval England

heir the person next in line to the throne

inflation rising prices

merchants people who made their money from trade

minister an important position in government with a special responsibility, such as the running of the legal system

moderate someone who does not hold extreme views or opinions

patent an agreement that protects an idea or an interest from being copied by outsiders

predecessor the previous holder of a position (e.g. the person who was the monarch before the king or queen being discussed)

privy secret

Puritan an extreme Protestant

rebellion an act of resistance, often armed, towards a leader

recusant someone who refused to go to church

Renaissance a period, beginning in the early sixteenth century in England, in which classical learning was very fashionable

sponsor to provide money for a project, like a voyage

treason the crime of plotting against the monarch, punishable by execution

vagabond a wandering beggar who often turned to crime

vestments a clergyman's clothes of office

Health and Medicine

acupuncture an ancient Chinese treatment where thin needles are inserted to areas of the body to improve health

AIDS acquired immune deficiency syndrome – when the body cannot fight life-threatening infections and so is the last stage of HIV infection

anaesthetics drugs that stop patients feeling pain in surgery

anatomy the focus on the structure of the body

antibiotics medications that destroy or reduce the speed of growth of bacteria

antiseptics substances used or applied to skin or surfaces to reduce the chance of infection

apothecaries medieval medicine makers

aqueducts bridges that carry fresh water

aseptic where an area is sterile through the use of hot water or steam, leaving no chance of infection

back-to-back housing poor quality, cramped housing that was built back-to-back without outside space

black period of surgery the time between the introduction of anaesthetics and the introduction of antiseptics; surgeons took longer over surgeries as their patients were not in pain, but this increased infection and resulted in a high death rate

bloodletting withdrawing blood to improve health; an example of putting the theory of 'the four humours' into practice

Boer War a war that took place between 1899 and 1902 between the UK and Ireland and the South African Republic and the Orange Free State

Brockedon, William an English manufacturer who patented the tablet press in 1843

buboes swellings filled with blood, usually found in the groin or armpit

bubonic the more common type of plague, with one of the main symptoms being the growth of buboes

cauterise the burning of the skin or a wound by a heated instrument to stop infection and bleeding

Change4Life a public health programme that began in 2009

chemotherapy a type of cancer treatment that uses anti-cancer drugs

cholera a disease spread via dirty water, often through drinking it

chloroform a drug that was used as an anaesthetic during surgery

cottage hospitals small country hospitals

cowpox an infectious disease that can be spread from animals to humans

Crimean War a conflict between 1853 and 1856 concerning Russia and France, the UK and the Ottoman Empire

dissolution of the monasteries took place between 1536 and 1541 when Henry VIII broke away from the Catholic Church, taking lots of its income, properties and power

Ebola a deadly viral disease that became an epidemic in 2014

endocrine where hormones from glands are put into the circulatory system so they can be carried to organs

evacuation the movement of people from an area of danger to an area of safety – during World War Two, children and pregnant mothers were moved from the city to the countryside to escape the bombing of cities

Fabricius teacher of William Harvey

flagellants extremely religious individuals who would whip themselves for forgiveness by God

Galen (130AD–200AD) a Greek philosopher, surgeon and physician

genetics the study of the genes of living organisms

Germ Theory developed by Louis Pasteur and then Koch; the theory states that some diseases are caused by miniscule microorganisms

Gilles, Harold considered to be the 'father of plastic surgery'; he created the first skin grafts

Harvey, William English physician who discovered that the heart pumped blood around the body

Hippocrates (460BC–370BC) a Greek physician

HIV human immunodeficiency virus – causes infection and acquired immunodeficiency syndrome

Hunter, John Scottish surgeon who believed in the importance of observation and scientific thinking

inoculated treatment with a vaccine to render the body immune to a disease; in Jenner's time what was called inoculation was the unsafe practice of injecting patients with a small amount of smallpox; Jenner called his practice 'vaccination' – 'vacca' was the Latin for 'cow'

Knights Hospitillars Roman Catholic military orders during the medieval period

laissez-faire translates as 'leave well alone'; the idea that the government should not interfere in people's daily lives

life expectancy a measure of how long a person will live based on factors including when they were born, and their gender

magic bullet a drug that targets and kills disease without affecting other parts of the body

medical health officer a member of government who oversaw the health of people in an area

miasma the belief that bad or dirty air caused disease

microbes tiny organisms that can only be observed with a microscope

MRI scan magnetic resonance imaging scan that uses strong magnetic fields and radio waves to produce a scan of the body

NHS the National Health Service, set up by the UK Government in 1948

patent exclusive rights given to a person who has invented a product

Penicillin an antibiotic that fights bacteria in the body

Plague highly contagious disease that spread in the 17th century; it is estimated that 15% of the English population died of it in 1665

pneumonic the less common, but more deadly type of plague with one of the main symptoms being lung infection

Prontosil an antibacterial drug

prosthetic limbs false limbs

public health the health of the population, affected by factors such as sanitation, cleanliness and government involvement

Public Health Act (1848) one of the first acts created by the government to try to improve public health in Britain; this act saw the creation of the Central Board of Health

quack methods methods used by medieval 'doctors' who had no training or scientific knowledge – treatments would include smelling sweet herbs and other herbal remedies

radiation the use of electromagnetic waves

radiotherapy a treatment that can be used for cancer that uses high-energy radiation

reforms changes that take place

regression where understanding gets worse

Renaissance the period when a revival of art, literature and learning took place between the 14th and the 17th centuries

The Royal Society a group created by physicians in London who were interested in science and knowledge

Salvarsan 606 the first magic bullet discovered; it could cure syphilis

Second Public Health Act (1875) an improvement of the first act of 1848; this Act aimed to end dirty living conditions

septum the dividing wall between the left and right sides of the heart

skin grafting where a piece of skin is transplanted to another place on the patient's body or to a different patient

smallpox previously one of the most infectious, deadly diseases that has now been wiped out around the world

squalor dirty and unpleasant, often through poverty and neglect

sterilisation the killing of all bacteria in an area

sulphonamide the ingredient in magic bullets that kills disease

thalidomide a drug given to pregnant women during the 1960s to ease morning sickness that caused deformities in the babies while in the womb

Theory of Opposites Galen's belief that in order to stay in good health, the humours must be balanced; if there is more of one humour than another, the 'opposite' of a patient's symptom should be administered

Theory of the Four Humours Hippocrates' belief that the body is made up of four main liquids (known as humours)

ultrasound a type of scan, also known as a sonogram

vaccinations material that is given to a patient that will stimulate a person's immune system to develop immunity against a disease

Vesalius, Andreas Belgian anatomist and physician who wrote *The Fabric of the Human Body*; he was the first person to publicly contradict Galen

welfare state where the government plays an important role in protecting its citizens

Crime and Punishment

abolish to end a particular law

anti-social behaviour poor behaviour which causes, or is likely to cause, harassment, alarm or distress to others

arson deliberately starting a fire with the intent to cause damage

Bloody Code the harsh laws gradually introduced between 1500 and 1750

blood feud the legal right of a murder victim's family to hunt down and kill the murderer in revenge

capital offence an offence punishable by death

community sentences an alternative to prison where offenders perform duties for the public

conscription a government law that forced men to join the army

confession admitting to committing evil deeds

constable men from every village or town, appointed to uphold law and order

deterrent a measure that frightens or prevents people from committing a crime

discriminate to treat someone differently on grounds of race, religion, gender or sexuality

exemption given permission not to fight in the war

garroters criminals who would strangle the victim before robbing them

heresy the crime of holding different beliefs from the Church or monarch

hue and cry raising the alarm by loud shouts when a crime has been committed

moral acting in a manner that is considered right or fair

outlaw an outcast from society, without protection from the law

pillory a wooden frame with holes for the head and hands used for public humiliation

people trafficking illegally selling people for prostitution or forced labour

petty crime minor crimes such as stealing inexpensive items

poaching illegally hunting animals on someone else's property

prejudice to judge a person without knowing them

prison reformers people trying to make changes to improve prison conditions

probation a system that allows offenders their freedom on condition of good behaviour

rational common sense explanations for events

reform improve and change criminals so that they no longer commit crime

sanctuary a safe place within a church

smuggling illegally importing or exporting goods without paying tax

stocks a punishment device made of a wooden frame with holes for the feet

tithing a group made up of ten men, who were responsible for each others' behaviour

transportation sending convicted criminals overseas

treason disobedience or disloyalty to the monarch or government

trial by ordeal a test that an accused person would undergo if a court could not decide on a verdict

urbanisation the growth and development of towns and cities

vagrancy wandering from place to place without a settled job

wergild a form of compensation paid to the victims in Saxon times

Notes

Notes

Index

Collins

GCSE Revision

History

British

GCSE

Workbook

Kelly Mellor, John Mitchell,
Rachelle Pennock and Steve McDonald

Contents

Norman England

Elizabethan England

Contents

Health and Medicine

Crime and Punishment

Exam-style Questions: Norman England

Anglo-Saxon Society on the Eve of Conquest

Edexcel

1 Describe **two** features of the legal system in Anglo-Saxon England. [4]

2 Explain why law and order wasn't always completely fair in Anglo-Saxon times.

You may use the following in your answer:
- Trial by ordeal
- Entire families being punished for one individual

You **must** also use information of your own. [12]

OCR B

1 In Interpretation A, the writer discusses the structure of Anglo-Saxon England.

Identify and explain **one** way in which kings could be chosen to succeed as heir in Anglo-Saxon England. [20]

> **Interpretation A – From a modern website.**
>
> The Anglo-Saxon community in England was basically a rural one, where primarily all classes of society lived on the land. At the top of the social system was the royal house. This consisted of the king and princes, who claimed a common ancestry with the king; they had special privileges and responsibilities, which included military service and command in the field. By the middle of the ninth century the royal family of Wessex was universally recognised as the English royal family and held a hereditary right to rule. Succession to the throne was not guaranteed as the *witan*, or council of leaders, had the right to choose the best successor from the members of the royal house.

2 If you were asked to do further research on one aspect of Interpretation A in Q1, what would you choose to investigate? Explain how this would help us to analyse and understand the succession of Anglo-Saxon kings. [5]

The Succession Crisis of 1066

AQA

1 Write an account of why the issue of succession was unclear in 1066. [8]

2 'Edgar had the strongest claim to the throne in 1066.' How far does a study of the Anglo-Saxon family tree support this statement? Explain your answer. You should refer to the family links of Edgar to Edward and your contextual knowledge. [16]

Edexcel

1 Describe **two** features of how Edward dealt with the issue of succession in England before his death. [4]

2 'Edward plunged England into crisis after his death because he promised the throne to William in 1051.' How far do you agree? Explain your answer.

You may use the following in your answer:
- William of Normandy
- Harold Godwinson

You **must** also use information of your own. [16]

OCR B

1 In Interpretation A, the writer discusses the succession crisis.

How far do you agree with this interpretation of the succession crisis of 1066? [20]

> **Interpretation A – By historian Stephen Baxter.**
>
> [Edward's] handling of the succession issue was dangerously indecisive, and contributed to one of the greatest catastrophes to which the English have ever succumbed.

2 If you were asked to do further research on one aspect of the source in Q1, what would you choose to investigate? Explain how this would help us to analyse and understand how Edward handled the issue of his successor. [5]

The Rival Claimants to the Throne in 1066

AQA

1 English monks wrote:

> '… on his deathbed that wise king promised the kingdom to Harold.

Explain why this was important when Harold claimed the throne in 1066. [8]

2 How convincing is Interpretation A about the events following Edward's death? Explain your answer using Interpretation A and your contextual knowledge. (The men in the right of the tapestry are Bishop Odo and William receiving news that Harold has been crowned king.) [8]

Interpretation A

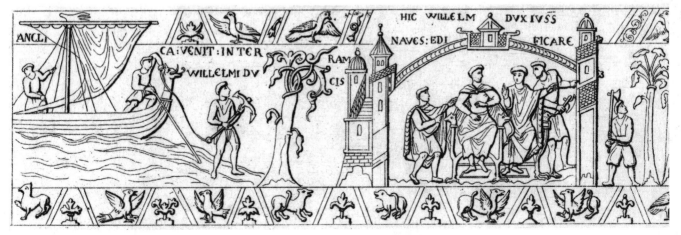

Edexcel

1 Explain why Harold claimed the throne after Edward's death in 1066.

You may use the following in your answer:
- He was promised the throne by Edward
- The Witan supported his claim

You **must** also use information of your own. [12]

2 'Harold Godwinson had the strongest claim to the English throne after King Edward's death.' How far do you agree? Explain your answer.

You may use the following in your answer:
- He was English
- He was the Earl of Wessex

You **must** also use information of your own. [16]

OCR B

1 In Interpretation A, the writer discusses the events around Edward's death.

Identify and explain **one** reason why Harold was named successor after the death of Edward. [3]

> **Interpretation A – From the Britannica website.**
>
> **Despite his promise of the throne to William, Edward from his deathbed designated Harold his heir. On Jan. 6, 1066, the day after Edward's death, Harold was elected by the English nobility and crowned and anointed king at Winchester Abbey by the archbishop of York.**

2 'Harold Godwinson had the strongest claim to the English throne after King Edward's death.' How far do you agree with this interpretation? [20]

The Battles of Fulford and Stamford Bridge

AQA

1 'The Battle of Stamford Bridge was not a significant battle in the events of 1066.' How far do you agree with the statement? Explain your answer. [16]

2 How convincing is Interpretation A about the Battle of Stamford Bridge? Explain your answer using Interpretation A and your contextual knowledge. [8]

Interpretation A

Edexcel

1 Describe **two** features of the Battle of Fulford. [4]

2 Explain why Harold Godwinson was victorious at the Battle of Stamford Bridge.

You may use the following in your answer:
- The Viking army had not expected the Saxons to arrive so quickly
- Hardrada was killed

You **must** also use information of your own. [12]

OCR B

1 In Interpretation A, the writer talks about the Battle of Fulford.

Identify and explain **one** reason why the Anglo-Saxons were defeated at the Battle of Fulford. [3]

> **Interpretation A – From Wikipedia.**
>
> Harald brought more of his troops from the right flank to attack the centre, and sent more men to the river. The invaders were outnumbered, but they kept pushing and shoving the defenders back. The Anglo-Saxons were forced to give ground. Edwin's soldiers who were defending the bank now were cut off from the rest of the army by the marsh, so they headed back to the city to make a final stand. Within another hour, the men on the beck were forced off by the Norwegians. Other invading Norwegians, who were still arriving, found a way to get around the thick fighting and opened a third front against the Anglo-Saxons. Outnumbered and outmanoeuvred, the defenders were defeated.

2 Examine Interpretations A and B. How far do they differ and what might explain any differences? [12]

> **Interpretation A**
>
> Harald Hardrada lost the Battle of Stamford Bridge because he did not expect Godwinson's forces to arrive north so quickly.

> **Interpretation B**
>
> Harald Hardrada was defeated at Stamford Bridge because the Saxons were fighting to protect their country from Viking invaders and so had a mental advantage during the battle.

AQA

1 Write an account of why William won at the Battle of Hastings. [8]

2 'Harold's defeat at the Battle of Hastings was inevitable.' How far does a study of the battle ground at Hastings support this view? You should refer to the battlefield and your contextual knowledge in your answer. [16]

Edexcel

1 Explain why William won at the Battle of Hastings.

You may use the following in your answer:
- William's army had been blessed by the Pope
- William used clever tactics

You **must** also use information of your own. [12]

2 'Harold's defeat at Hastings was inevitable.' How far do you agree? Explain your answer.

You may use the following in your answer:
- The Saxon army was tired and battle weary
- William's army outnumbered the Saxons

You **must** also use information of your own. [16]

OCR B

1 Examine Interpretations A and B. How far do they differ and what might explain any differences? [12]

> **Interpretation A – written by a Norman**
>
> It was only William's courage that saved us. Three times he had horses killed beneath him; each time he leapt to the ground and killed the footman who had killed his horse. Fighting on foot he split shields, helmets and coats of mail with his great sword. Seeing his men fleeing he took off his helmet and cried, 'Look at me well! I am still alive and by God's grace I shall yet prove victor'. This inspired his tired men who gathered for a final charge in which Harold was killed.

> **Interpretation B – *Chronicle of Battle Abbey* (c. 1155)**
>
> In the year 1066, the most noble William, duke of the Normans, sailed with a mighty army against England... William called together his barons and knights and roused them to fight faithfully in battle. His speech made the men more courageous; they entered the fight determinedly, and at last, as God had planned, on 14th October they won the victory.

2 If you were asked to do further research on one aspect of Interpretation B, what would you choose to investigate? Explain how this would help us to analyse and understand the victory of William at Hastings. [5]

AQA

1 Explain why castles were important in helping the Normans gain and keep control of England. [8]

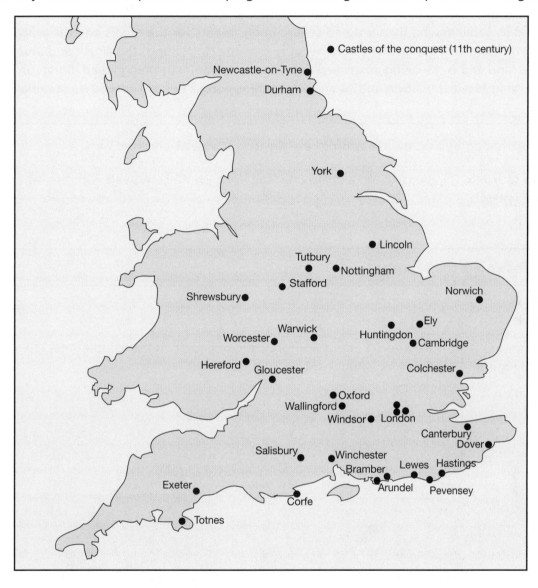

2 Explain why William dealt so severely with the rebellion in the north of England. [8]

Edexcel

1 Give **two** features of Hereward's rebellion. [4]

2 Explain why William dealt so severely with the rebellion in the north of England.

You may use the following in your answer:
* The north had allied with the Danes
* William wanted to set an example to the rest of the country

You **must** also use information of your own. [12]

OCR B

 1 A modern Historian wrote:

> William faced a dangerous rebellion in the north of England in 1069. Edgar the Atheling led the rebels and people supported him because of his blood link with King Edward. Edgar allied with the Danes and Scots to try and overthrow William. The rebellion was ultimately defeated by William who then ordered severe punishments for the rebels and the places they were from. This punishment became known as the Harrying of the North and involved villages, land and crops being destroyed and people and animals being killed. Survivors of the Harrying faced starvation and some even were reported to have turned to cannibalism to survive.

How far do you agree that the Harrying of the North was excessively cruel? [20]

2 Using the source in Q1, identify and explain one way in which William dealt with the rebellion in the north of England. [3]

> ## Life Under Norman Control

AQA

 1 How convincing is Interpretation A about life for ordinary people in the Middle Ages? Explain your answer using Interpretation A and your contextual Knowledge. [8]

Interpretation A

2 Explain how much England changed as a result of the Norman victory at Hastings. [8]

Edexcel

1 Give **two** features of the feudal system. [4]

2 'After the Battle of Hastings, England was changed beyond recognition'. How far do you agree? Explain your answer.

You should refer to the following in your answer:
- The government
- Towns and villages

You **must** also use your own information. [16]

OCR B

1 Interpretations A and B are both written by Historians. How far do these interpretations differ about what the Normans did to the places they ruled? [12]

> **Interpretation A – written by Historians, Shephard and Rees**
>
> William made no changes to the Saxon system of government, except for making sure that it was run by Normans. It wasn't simply that the old system worked, although that had a lot to do with it. William, although he had won England by conquest, was anxious to show that he was, in fact, the true heir to Edward the Confessor and so he couldn't be seen to change too much – he had to make sure there was more continuity than change in the ways in which the Normans governed England.

> **Interpretation B – a modern Historian writing in 2015**
>
> The Normans had many skills which they brought to England after the conquest. They built great architecture, were efficient at governing and were superb fighters.

2 If you were asked to do further research on one aspect of Interpretation A, what would you choose to investigate? Explain how this would help us to analyse and understand what the Normans did to the places that they ruled. [5]

AQA

1 How convincing is Interpretation A about the collection of material for inclusion in the Domesday Book? Explain your answer using Interpretation A and your contextual knowledge. [8]

Interpretation A

2 How convincing is Interpretation B, a motte and bailey castle, to explain how they were designed and used? Explain your answer using Interpretation B and your contextual knowledge. [8]

Interpretation B

Edexcel

1 'Castles were the most significant change that the Normans made to England after the conquest.' How far do you agree? Explain your answer.

You should refer to the following in your answer:
* Motte and bailey castles
* The feudal system

You **must** also use your own information. [16]

2 Give **two** features of how the Domesday Survey was structured. [4]

OCR B

1 Examine Interpretations A and B. How far do they differ and what might explain any differences? [12]

> **Interpretation A – an extract from the Domesday Book**
>
> In the city of York, before 1066 were 6 shires besides the Archbishop's. One of these has been laid waste for the castles. In 5 shires there were 1418 inhabited dwellings. Out of the aforementioned dwellings there are now inhabited, and paying customary dues, 400 less 9, both large and small; 400 dwellings not inhabited of which the better ones pay 1 penny and the others less; and 540 dwellings so empty that they pay nothing at all; and the Frenchmen hold 145 dwellings.

> **Interpretation B – a History teacher writing in 2015**
>
> The main focus for William after his victory at Hastings was to strategically place loyal barons around England to ensure the Saxons accepted him as their new king. By 1086 William needed to assess the economic and social impact the invasion and conquest had had on England. The Domesday survey would discover who owned the land, both in the time of King Edward and after the invasion, what taxes the king could claim in order to support his never-ending military campaigns, and ensure that he knew what resources his barons had to support him as and when he needed it.

2 'Castles were the most significant change that the Normans made to England after the conquest.' How far do you agree with this view? [20]

The Norman Church and the Death of William I

AQA

1 Explain what was important about the church in the Middle Ages. [8]

2 Write an account of why there was a succession crisis after the death of William I. [8]

Edexcel

1 'The church had more power than kings in the Middle Ages'. How far do you agree? Explain your answer.

You should refer to the following in your answer:
- The Investiture Controversy
- Monasteries

You **must** also use your own information. [16]

2 Explain why there was a succession crisis after the death of William I.

You should refer to the following in your answer:
- William Rufus being named heir to the English throne
- Archbishop Lanfranc

You **must** also use your own information. [12]

Exam-style Questions: Elizabethan England

Elizabeth I and Her Government

AQA

1 Write an account of how Elizabeth dealt with the succession question. [8]

2 Explain how Elizabeth used propaganda to promote her role as Queen of England. [8]

Edexcel

1 Explain why the succession remained a problem during the reign of Elizabeth I.

You may use the following in your answer:
- Elizabeth's reluctance to name a successor
- Elizabeth's reasons she never married

You **must** also use information of your own. [12]

2 'The threat of invasion was Elizabeth's main problem when she became Queen in 1558.' How far do you agree? Explain your answer.

You may use the following in your answer:
- France
- Elizabeth's legitimacy

You **must** also use information of your own. [16]

Eduqas

1 Study the source below and then answer the question which follows.

> **Prices had been rising since the beginning of the sixteenth century. They rose very fast in the 1550s. Farmers faced higher rents and many people found that their wages were losing value.**

[Andy Harmsworth, *Elizabethan England*]

To what extent does this source accurately reflect the seriousness of England's economic position in 1558?

In your answer you should refer to the strengths and limitations of the source and use your own knowledge and understanding of the historical context. [8]

2 Explain the connections between **TWO** of the following that are to do with Elizabethan government:
- Privy Council
- Parliament
- House of Commons
- Lord Burghley [10]

OCR B

1 'William Cecil was Elizabeth's most important minister.' How far do you agree with this view? [20]

2 In Interpretation A the artist presents Elizabeth I as the rightful Queen of England. Identify and explain how the artist does this. [3]

Interpretation A – Elizabeth I Coronation Portrait, 1559

The Elizabethan Religious Settlement

AQA

1 Explain the reaction towards the Elizabethan Religious Settlement. [8]

2 Write an account of the Elizabethan Religious Settlement. [8]

Edexcel

1 Describe **two** features of the Elizabethan Religious Settlement. [4]

2 'The Elizabethan Religious Settlement's vague position on doctrine was its most important weakness.' How far do you agree? Explain your answer.

You may use the following in your answer:
*   The mass resignation of the clergy
*   The vague doctrine outlined in the Act of Supremacy

You **must** also use information of your own. [16]

Eduqas

1 Study the source below and then answer the question which follows.

> Although Elizabeth had her own religious views, she thought that her most important task was to unite the country. She wanted people to obey her and not cause trouble.

[Andy Harmsworth, *Elizabethan England*]

To what extent does this source accurately reflect Elizabeth's motives in establishing a religious settlement? [8]

In your answer you should refer to the strengths and limitations of the source and use your own knowledge and understanding of the historical context.

2 Explain the connections between **TWO** of the following that are to do with the Elizabethan Religious Settlement:

* Act of Uniformity
* Act of Supremacy
* Recusants
* Clergy [10]

OCR B

1 'The Elizabethan Religious Settlement caused more problems that it solved.' How far do you agree with this view? [20]

2 Interpretations A and B both focus on the Elizabethan Religious Settlement. How far do they differ and what might explain any differences? [12]

> **Interpretation A – D. MacCulloch, *The Later Reformation in Tudor England***
>
> From this story of confusion and changing direction emerged a Church which has never subsequently dared define its identity decisively as Protestant or Catholic and which has decided in the end that this is a virtue rather than a handicap.

> **Interpretation B – C. Haigh, *The Reign of Elizabeth I***
>
> By the time Parliament closed in mid May 1559, the Elizabethan Religious Settlement had taken a permanent form … Not everyone was satisfied with it …

Elizabeth I and Spain, 1558–1587

AQA

1 Explain why England and Spain went to war in 1585. [8]

2 Write an account of England's relationship with Spain between 1558 and 1572. [8]

1 ...main cause of the war with Spain from 1585.' How far do you agree? Explain
y...

You may use the following in your answer:
- Religious differences
- The relationship between Elizabeth and Philip

You **must** also use information of your own. [16]

2 Describe **two** features of England's relationship with Spain between 1568 and 1572. [4]

Eduqas

1 Why was Spain a significant Catholic threat to Elizabeth? [12]

2 Explain the connections between **TWO** of the following that are to do with the relationship between England and Spain between 1558 and 1587:

- Philip II
- Elizabeth I
- Trade links
- Catholic plots [10]

OCR B

1 'England's intervention in the Netherlands was the most important reason why they went to war with Spain in 1585.' How far do you agree with this view? [20]

2 'Elizabeth's actions were more to blame than Philip II of Spain for war with Spain in 1585.' How far do you agree with this view? [20]

Elizabeth I and Mary, Queen of Scots

AQA

1 Explain the significance of Mary, Queen of Scots' marriage to Lord Darnley in helping to bring about her downfall in Scotland. [8]

2 Write an account of Mary, Queen of Scots' execution in 1587. [8]

Edexcel

1 Explain why Mary, Queen of Scots was a threat to Elizabeth I.

You may use the following in your answer:
- She was the Catholic heir to the throne of England
- Catholic plotters wanted Mary to replace Elizabeth as Queen of England

You **must** also use information of your own. [12]

2 Describe **two** features of the imprisonment of Mary, Queen of Scots between 1568 and 1587. [4]

Eduqas

1 Why was Mary, Queen of Scots a significant threat to the position of Elizabeth I as Queen of England? [12]

2 Explain the connections between **TWO** of the following that are to do with Mary, Queen of Scots:

- English Catholics
- The Northern Rebellion
- The Babington Plot
- The Throckmorton Plot [10]

OCR B

1 'Mary, Queen of Scots marrying the Earl of Bothwell was her greatest mistake.' How far do you agree with this view? [20]

2 In Interpretation A, Mary, Queen of Scots is shown as a martyr. Identify and explain how the artist does this. [3]

Interpretation A – Execution of Mary, Queen of Scots by Robert Inerarity Herdman, painted in 1867

The Attack of the Spanish Armada, 1588

AQA

1 Explain the differences between the English and Spanish forces in the attempted Spanish invasion of England in 1588. [8]

2 Explain why the Spanish Armada attacked England. [8]

Edexcel

1 'Bad weather was the main reason why the Spanish Armada was defeated.' How far do you agree? Explain your answer.

You may use the following in your answer:
- Impact of bad weather
- Impact of fireships

You **must** also use information of your own. [16]

2 Explain why Philip II attempted to invade England in 1588.

You may use the following in your answer:
- Angered by Elizabeth's actions in the Netherlands and Drake's Cadiz raid
- Had a clear plan of action

You **must** also use information of your own. [12]

Eduqas

1 Study the sources below and then answer the question which follows.

Source A

> The Spanish ships were on the whole much slower and less manoeuvrable than the English.

[Richard Rex, *The Tudors*]

Source B

> The English were overwhelmingly superior in long range guns – 497 guns to 172.

[Felipe Fernandez-Armesto, *The Spanish Armada*]

What can be learnt from Sources A and B about the Spanish Armada? [4]

2 Why did the Spanish Armada fail? [12]

OCR B

1 In Interpretation A, the artist shows that England had a great victory over the Spanish Armada. Identify and explain how the artist does this. [3]

Interpretation A – The Armada Portrait by George Gower, painted in 1588.

2 Interpretations A and B both focus on why the Spanish Armada was defeated. How far do they differ and what might explain these differences? [12]

> **Interpretation A – Philip II in 1588**
>
> I sent my fleet against men, not against the wind and waves.

> **Interpretation B – Francisco de Bobadilla, the Spanish general in charge of Spanish forces in the Armada, 1588**
>
> We found that many of the enemy's ships held great advantage over us in combat, both in the design and in their guns.

Threats posed to Elizabeth I, 1558–1601

AQA

1 Explain the extent of the Catholic opposition to Elizabeth I. [8]

2 Write an account of the Earl of Essex Rebellion of 1601. [8]

Edexcel

1 'Religion was the main cause of the Throckmorton Plot.' How far do you agree? Explain your answer.

You may use the following in your answer:
- Catholic unrest
- Foreign influences, such as from Spain and the Vatican

You **must** also use information of your own. [16]

2 Explain **two** features of the Ridolfi Plot. [4]

Eduqas

1 Study the sources below and then answer the question which follows.

Source A

[*Coded messages sent by Anthony Babington*]

Source B

> **A letter allegedly by Mary and endorsing Anthony Babington's plot to murder Elizabeth was intercepted by Walsingham.**

[Barbara Mervyn, *The Reign of Elizabeth*]

What can be learnt from Sources A and B about the Babington Plot? [4]

2 Why did the Puritans grow in significance in their opposition to Elizabeth? [12]

OCR B

1 Interpretations A and B look at the actions of the Earl of Essex in the late 1590s. How far do they differ and what might explain any differences? [12]

> **Interpretation A – Testimony from Rowland White, an eyewitness, made in 1599**
>
> My Lord Essex made all haste to the Queen's bedchamber ... he kneeled unto her, kissed her hands and had some private speech with her.

> **Interpretation B – Andy Harmsworth, *Elizabethan England***
>
> Against the Queen's wishes, the Earl of Essex made peace with Tyrone. He also rewarded many of his supporters by making them knights. Elizabeth was furious.

2 'The main consequence of the Babington Plot was the deterioration of the relationship between England and Spain.' How far do you agree with this view? [20]

Elizabethan Society

AQA

1 Explain the reasons for the widening of educational opportunities in Elizabethan England. [8]

2 Write an account of how Elizabeth's government attempted to deal with poverty. [8]

Edexcel

1 Describe **two** features of Elizabethan education. [4]

2 Explain why education opportunities grew in Elizabethan England.

You may use the following in your answer:
* Growth in the use of the printing press
* Influence of the Renaissance

You **must** also use information of your own. [12]

Eduqas

1 Why did the gentry grow in significance in Elizabethan society? [12]

2 Explain the connections between **TWO** of the following that are to do with poverty in Elizabethan England:

* Local government
* Vagabonds
* Law and order
* Elizabethan Poor Law [10]

OCR B

1 'Elizabeth's government was successful in dealing with poverty.' How far do you agree with this view? [20]

2 In Interpretation A, the artist shows the Elizabethan family to be religious. Identify and explain how the artist does this. [3]

Interpretation A – A Family Saying Grace before a Meal by Anthuenis Claeissens, painted c. 1585

Elizabethan Culture

AQA

1 Explain the reasons for the popularity of the theatre in Elizabethan England. [8]

2 Write an account of the key features of the Elizabethan theatre. [8]

Edexcel

1 Explain **two** features of Elizabethan entertainment for the rich. [4]

2 Explain why there was opposition towards theatres in Elizabethan England.

You may use the following in your answer:
- Source of disorder and lawlessness
- Standards within plays were deemed vulgar by some

You **must** also use information of your own. [12]

Eduqas

1 Study the sources below and then answer the question which follows.

Source A

> The blast of a trumpet will call a thousand people to see a filthy play... an hour's tolling of a bell would only bring a hundred people to a sermon.

[John Stockwood, preaching a sermon at St. Paul's Cross in 1576]

Source B

> In the playhouses at London it is the fashion of youths to go first into the yard, and to carry their eye through every gallery, then they go and sit as near to the fairest as they can.

[Stephen Gossen, *The School of Abuse*, 1579]

What can Sources A and B tell the historian about attitudes towards the Elizabethan theatre?   [4]

2 Explain the connections between **TWO** of the following that are to do with entertainment in Elizabethan England:

- Fashion
- Taverns
- Miniatures
- Blood sports   [10]

OCR B

1 'Entertainment was different for the poor compared with the rich.' How far do you agree with this view?   [20]

2 In Interpretation A the artist shows the Elizabethan theatre to be popular. Identify and explain how the artist does this.   [3]

Interpretation A – An illustration of the Rose Theatre

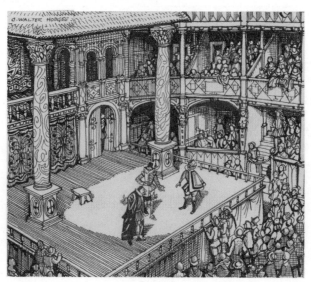

AQA

1 Write an account of Raleigh's Virginia mission. [8]

2 Explain the impact of Drake's world voyage. [8]

Edexcel

1 'The pursuit of wealth was the most successful of Elizabethan voyages.' How far do you agree? Explain your answer.

You may use the following in your answer:
- Attacking of Spanish treasure ships
- Role of Drake and Hawkins

You **must** also use information of your own. [16]

2 Describe **two** features of the Virginia missions of the 1580s. [4]

OCR B

1 In Interpretation A, the artist shows the extent of exploration during Elizabethan England. Identify and explain how the artist does this. [3]

Interpretation A – A map showing trade routes during the Elizabethan era

2 'Trade routes developed significantly under Elizabeth.' How far do you agree with this view? [20]

Exam-style Questions: Health and Medicine

Medieval Medicine (Middle Ages) 1

AQA

1 How useful is Source A to a historian Studying Galen's work? [8]

Source A (An artist's impression of Galen performing a dissection on a pig)

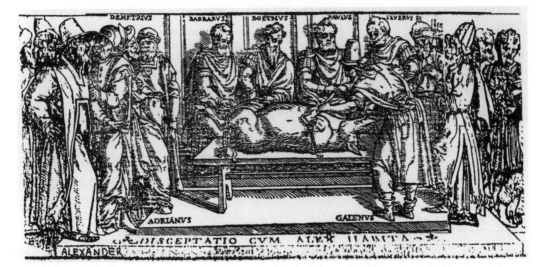

2 Explain the significance of Galen in the history of medicine. [8]

Edexcel

1 Explain **one** way in which Islamic religion had an impact on medical beliefs in the medieval period. [4]

2 Explain why hospitals had limited success in treating the ill during the medieval period. [12]

Eduqas

1 Study Sources A and B and answer the question that follows.

Source A

[An artist's impression of the care received by a patient in a medieval hospital]

Source B

> **No lepers, lunatics or persons having the falling sickness or other contagious disease, and no pregnant women or sucking infants and no intolerable persons, even though they be poor and infirm are to be admitted.**

[From the rules of the hospital of St John Bridgwater in the south of England, 1219]

Which of the two sources is more reliable to a historian studying hospitals in the Middle Ages? In your answer you should refer to the content and authorship of the sources and use your own knowledge and understanding of the wider historical context. [6]

2 Explain why there were few developments in treatments during the Middle Ages. [8]

OCR B

1 Write a clear and organised summary of the role of hospitals in the Middle Ages. [9]

2 Why did hospitals have a limited impact on improving people's health in the Middle Ages? [10]

AQA

1 Study Source A. How useful is Source A to a historian studying symptoms of the Black Death? [8]

Source A

2 Compare the Black Death in the Middle Ages with the cholera epidemics in the nineteenth century. In what ways are they similar? Explain your answer with reference to both the Black Death and the cholera epidemics. [8]

Edexcel

1 'There was little progress in medicine in Britain during the Middle Ages because of the impact of religion.' How far do you agree? Explain your answer. [16]

2 Explain why there was limited success in treating people with the Black Death in the Middle Ages. [12]

Eduqas

1 Study Sources A and B and answer the question that follows.

Source A

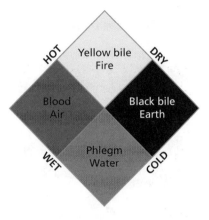

Source B

God was responsible for all illnesses. Therefore people would whip themselves for their sins and pray to God for forgiveness. People believed there was little point in trying to heal themselves as this power remained with God.

[Extract from a modern historian]

Use Sources A and B to identify one similarity and one difference in beliefs about illness between the Roman and medieval periods. [4]

2 Describe the beliefs about the causes of the Black Death in the Middle Ages. [5]

OCR B

1 How far do you agree that the most important reason for poor public health in the medieval period was due to the role of the Church? Give reasons for your answer. [18]

2 Write a clear and organised summary of people's beliefs about the Black Death in the medieval period. [9]

Renaissance Medicine (1400s–1600s) 1

AQA

1 Explain the significance of Vesalius' work in the history of medicine. [6]

2 Compare Andreas Vesalius and William Harvey.

In what ways are they similar?

Explain your answer with reference to both Vesalius and Harvey. [8]

Edexcel

1 Study Sources A and B. How useful are Sources A and B for an enquiry into the impact William Harvey made in medicine during the Renaissance period? Explain your answer using Sources A and B and your own knowledge of the historical context.

Source A – Diagram from Harvey's book *Exercitatio anatomica de motu cordis 1628*

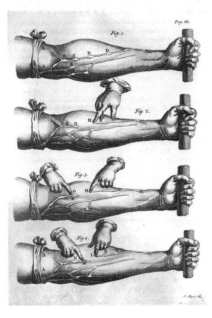

Source B – *The Works of William Harvey*, published in 1989

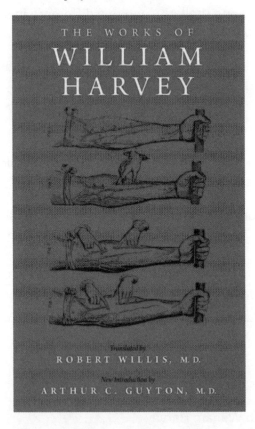

[8]

2 How could you follow up on Source B to find out more about the impact Harvey made in medicine during the Renaissance period?

[4]

Eduqas

1 Study sources A and B and answer the question that follows.

Source A

> I am not accustomed to saying anything with certainty, after only one or two observations.

[A quote from Vesalius]

Source B

> The Flemish physician Andreas Vesalius is widely considered to be the founder of the modern science of anatomy. He was a major figure of the Scientific Revolution. Vesalius' book "On the Structure of the Human Body" is one of the most important works about human anatomy.

[From a modern website entitled 'Famous Scientists – the art of genius']

Which of the two sources is more reliable to a historian studying Andreas Vesalius? In your answer you should refer to the content and authorship of the sources and use your own knowledge and understanding of the wider historical context. **[6]**

2 To what extent was the role of the individual the most influential factor in improving medical understanding in the Renaissance period? **[16]**

OCR B

1 'Technology was the most important factor in improving medical understanding in the Renaissance period.' How far do you agree with this statement? Give reasons for your answer. **[18]**

2 Why did the work of individuals in the field of medical knowledge not improve people's health in the Renaissance period? **[10]**

AQA

1 Study Sources A and B. What different attitudes to hospitals do these two sources show? [4]

Source A

> Throughout the late 1500s and early 1600s, voluntary charity was the means by which many hospitals were funded. Equally, although many poor and ill people required medical care, admission to hospitals was not always guaranteed. In most cases it was reserved for the 'deserving poor', those judged to be hard-working people who led 'respectable' lives.

Source B – An interview with a modern historian, who was promoting her book, *The Renaissance Revolution*

> The improvement in hospitals between the medieval period and Renaissance period should not be underestimated. A huge increase in the size of hospitals meant more patients could receive help. The increase in number of hospitals also allowed this to increase. Some hospitals even started to admit patients who were infected with diseases – this was a momentous, positive change.

2 Explain the significance of government intervention in medicine during the Renaissance period. [6]

Edexcel

1 Explain why there was not rapid change in the treatment of illness in Britain despite medical progress during the Renaissance period. [12]

2 Explain **one** way in which people's reactions to the Plague were similar in the fourteenth and seventeenth centuries. [4]

Eduqas

1 How useful is Source A to a historian studying hospitals in the Renaissance period? [8]

> The improvement in hospitals between the medieval period and Renaissance period should not be underestimated. A huge increase in the size of hospitals meant more patients could receive help. The increase in number of hospitals also allowed this to increase. Some hospitals even started to admit patients who were infected with diseases – this was a huge, positive change.

[Source A – An interview with a modern historian who was promoting her book, *The Renaissance Revolution*.]

2 Describe the development of government intervention in medicine and public health during the Renaissance period. [6]

OCR B

1 How far do you agree that the dissolution of the monasteries was the most important reason for the improvements in hospitals during the Renaissance period? Give reasons for your answer. [18]

2 Write a clear and organised summary of the preventions used by people to stop the Plague during the Renaissance period. [9]

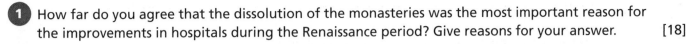

Industrial Medicine (1700s–1900) 1

AQA

1 Study Source A. How useful is Source A to a historian studying attitudes to government involvement in public health? [8]

Source A – Part of a letter in *The Times* newspaper, 1 August 1854, where the author is describing the work of Edwin Chadwick and the government.

> The Board of Health has fallen. We prefer to take our chances with cholera than be bullied into health. Everywhere the board's inspectors were bullying, insulting and expensive.

2 Compare the Plague in the Renaissance period and the cholera epidemics in the nineteenth century. In what ways are they similar? [8]

Edexcel

1 Explain why there were not rapid improvements in public health during the Industrial period. [12]

2 Explain **one** way in which treatments in the Industrial period were different to treatments in the Renaissance period. [4]

Eduqas

1 Explain why developments in public health were not successful during the Industrial period. [8]

2 Study Sources A and B and answer the question that follows.

Source A

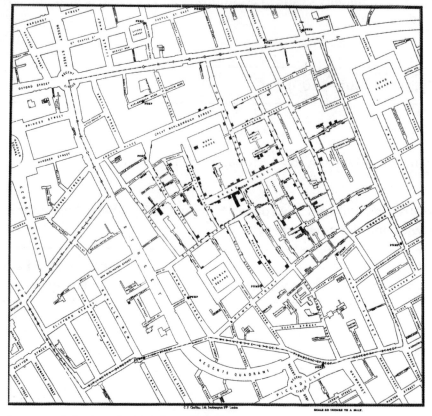

[John Snow's map of cholera in London, 1854]

Source B

[A cartoon called 'Death's Dispensary', published in 1860]

Which of the two sources is more reliable to a historian studying public health in the Industrial Revolution? In your answer you should refer to the content and authorship of the sources and use your own knowledge and understanding of the wider historical context. [6]

OCR B

1 Why did government attempts to improve public health have a limited impact during the Industrial period? Support your answer with examples. [10]

2 Write a clear and organised summary of the progress and limitations of scientific development during the Industrial period. [9]

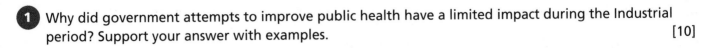

Industrial Medicine (1700s–1900) 2

AQA

1 Explain the significance of Edward Jenner in the history of medicine. [8]

2 Was the role of the individual the main factor in the development of medicine during the Industrial period?

Explain your answer. [16]

Edexcel

1 'Jenner's vaccination against smallpox was a major breakthrough in the prevention of disease in Britain during the period C1700–C1900.' How far do you agree? Explain your answer. [16]

2 Explain **one** way in which people's reactions to scientific development were similar in the Renaissance and Industrial periods. [4]

Eduqas

1 Study Sources A and B.

Source A

[Image of a medieval hospital]

Source B

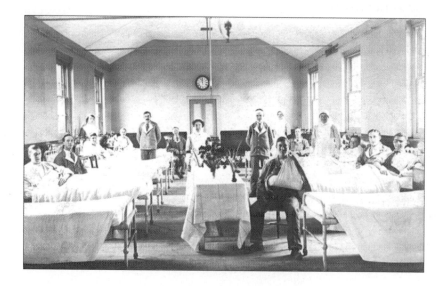

[Photograph taken of St Thomas' Hospital during the late Industrial Revolution period]

Use Sources A and B to identify one similarity and one difference in hospitals during the medieval period and the Industrial Revolution.

[4]

2 To what extent was the discovery of chloroform the most important factor in improving surgery in the Industrial Revolution?

[16]

OCR B

1 Why were there still problems with the role of, and care given in, hospitals in the industrial period? Support your answer with examples. [10]

2 How far do you agree that Jenner's discovery was the most important discovery of the Industrial period? Give reasons for your answer. [18]

Modern Medicine (1900s–Present) 1

AQA

1 Study Source A. How useful is Source A to a historian studying the importance of Alexander Fleming's work in relation to the development of penicillin? [8]

> **Source A – Extract from Alexander Fleming's Nobel Prize for Physiology and Medicine, 1945**
>
> I studied it as far as I could as a bacteriologist. I had a clue that here was something good but I could not possibly know how good it was and I had not the team, especially the chemical team, necessary to concentrate and stabilise the penicillin… It was ten years later that Florey and Chain made up a complete team at Oxford which succeeded in this and showed the marvellous chemotherapeutic properties of penicillin.

2 Explain the significance of World War One in the history of medicine. [6]

Edexcel

1 Study Sources A and B. How useful are the sources for an enquiry into the problems involved in performing operations on the Western Front? Explain your answer, using Sources A and B and your own knowledge of the historical context. [8]

Source A – An account by Reverend Pearson, who was the army Chaplain at Casualty Clearing Station 44 during the Battle of the Somme (1916)

> I spent most of my time giving anaesthetics. I have no right to be doing this because I had no medical qualifications, but we were simply so rushed. We couldn't get the wounded into the hospital quickly enough and the journey from the battlefield was simply terrible for these poor lads. It was a question of operating as quickly as possible… many died. We all simply had to help and do anything that was needed.

Source B – From the diary of Oswald Robertson, written on 30 November 1917. He was an army surgeon working on the Western Front during the First World War.

> Men were horribly mutilated – many were dying when brought into the ward. All the beds were full and we began putting stretchers on the floor. Blood everywhere – clothes soaked in blood, pools of blood in the stretchers, streams of blood dropping from the stretchers to the floor. All we could do was try to stop the bleeding and get the patients as comfortable as possible. I could only transfuse an occasional patient. The majority had to take their chance and go through the operation as best they could.

2 'Scientific treatment improved in the modern era because of people's willingness to accept new ideas'. How far do you agree? Give reasons for your answer. [16]

Eduqas

1 To what extent was the First World War the most important factor in improving surgery during the twentieth century? [16]

2 Study Sources A and B and answer the question that follows.

Source A

Crick: What a great breakthrough we made!
Watson: The two of us will be remembered for generations to come!

[A cartoon created by a fellow graduate of Cambridge University. Franklin, Crick and Watson were all previous graduates of Cambridge University.]

Source B

> In 1962, Crick and Watson, alongside Maurice Wilkins, won the Nobel Prize in Medicine for having discovered the structure of DNA. This was probably one of the most significant scientific discoveries of the 20th century and has allowed unlimited developments to take place.

[An extract from a modern historian]

Which of the two sources is more reliable to a historian studying Crick and Watson's work? In your answer you should refer to the content and authorship of the sources and use your own knowledge and understanding of the wider historical context. [6]

OCR B

1 Write a clear and organised summary of the development of the understanding of DNA during the twentieth century. [9]

2 How far do you agree that the role of the USA was the most important reason for the development and use of penicillin in the twentieth century? Give reasons for your answer. [18]

AQA

 Compare the impact of the Liberal Reforms 1906–1918 to the creation of the NHS, 1948. In what ways were they similar? Explain your answer in relation to both events. [8]

2 'War was the main factor in the development of medicine during the twentieth century.' How far do you agree? Give reasons for your answer. [16]

Edexcel

1 Explain why some people believe there are limitations to the success of the NHS in Britain. [12]

2 Explain **one** way in which people's health was improved by the Liberal reforms. [4]

Eduqas

1 Describe the development of the NHS in the twentieth century. [5]

2 Study Sources A and B and answer the question that follows.

Source A

[A British leaflet from the Liberal Party, highlighting the impact of the National Health Insurance Act of 1911]

[A photograph from 1910 showing Lloyd George meeting some old age pensioners]

2 Which of the two sources is more reliable to a historian studying the impact of the Liberal reforms? In your answer you should refer to the content and authorship of the sources and your own knowledge and understanding of the wider historical context. [6]

OCR B

1 Write a clear and organised summary of the successes of the Liberal reforms in relation to improving the public's health. [9]

2 How far do you agree that the most important changes in public health in Britain took place in the twentieth century? Give reasons for your answer. [18]

Modern Medicine (1900s–Present) 3

AQA

1 Study Source A. How useful is source A to a historian studying attitudes to scientific development? [8]

> **Source A – A quote from Dr Stephen Hawking, a physicist diagnosed with motor neurone disease**
>
> Stem cell research is the key to developing cures for degenerative conditions like Parkinson's and motor neurone disease from which I and many others suffer. The fact that the cells may come from embryos is not an objection, because the embryos are going to die anyway.

2 Explain the significance of the role of the government in scientific development between the 1960s and the present day. [8]

Edexcel

1 Study Sources A and B. How useful are Sources A and B for an enquiry into the problems of scientific development in the modern era? Explain your answer, using Sources A and B and your own knowledge of the historical context.

Source A – An extract from the Science Museum's website

> The thalidomide disaster is one of the darkest episodes in pharmaceutical research history. The drug was marketed as a mild sleeping pill safe even for pregnant women. However, it caused thousands of babies worldwide to be born with malformed limbs. The damage was revealed in 1962. Before then, every new drug was seen as beneficial. Now there was suspicion and rigorous testing.

Source B – An extract from the UK Health Centre website

> Churches such as the Catholic Church oppose all in vitro treatment (procedures outside of the body), again because they believe that infertility is God's will and to go against it is wrong. Many other religions echo this belief, and there is in fact further objection because of the number of embryos involved in IVF.

[8]

2 How could you follow up Source B to find out more about the problems of scientific development in the modern era? [4]

Eduqas

1 Explain why developments in antibiotics have not always been successful in the twentieth century. [9]

2 To what extent was the role of the government the most effective factor in improving people's health during the twentieth century? Explain your answer. [16]

OCR B

1 Why have there been limitations in the success of scientific developments during the twentieth century? [10]

2 How far do you agree that the most important reason for improvements in people's health during the twentieth century was the increasing role of the government? Give reasons for your answer. [18]

Exam-style Questions: Crime and Punishment

Edexcel

1 Describe **two** key features of Anglo-Saxon law enforcement. [4]

2 'The creation of new crimes was the most important change to English law and order made by the Normans.' How far do you agree? Explain your answer.

You may use the following in your answer:
- The Forest Laws
- The Normans abolished wergild.

You **must** also use information of your own. [16]

Eduqas

1 Describe the role of Saxon Laws. [5]

2 Explain why gangs of outlaws were feared during this period. [9]

OCR B

1 (a) Name **one** common crime in the medieval period. [1]

(b) Name **one** illegal act introduced by the Forest Laws. [1]

(c) Give **one** problem suffered by peasants during the medieval period. [1]

2 Write a clear and organised summary describing why outlaws were feared during the medieval period. Support your summary with examples. [9]

1000–1500: Punishment

Edexcel

1 Describe **two** key features of punishments used during the Middle Ages. [4]

2 Explain how and why Trial by Ordeal was carried out in the Middle Ages.

You may use the following in your answer:
- Trials took place in public
- Trial by ordeal was abolished in 1215

You **must** also use information of your own. [12]

Eduqas

1 Describe two main features of how law and order was enforced during the medieval period. [8]

2 Outline how far methods of punishing crime changed from Saxon times to the beginning of the Tudor period. [16]

OCR B

1 (a) Name **one** type of official responsible for maintaining law and order in the medieval period. [1]

(b) Describe **one** feature of the role of Parish Constable. [1]

(c) Give **one** example of Church authority in the medieval period. [1]

2 Write a clear and organised summary of methods of trial during the medieval period. Support your summary with examples. [9]

1500–1700: Crime

Edexcel

1 Describe **two** reasons why the crime rate increased after 1500. [4]

2 'Vagrants posed a serious threat to law and order in the Tudor period.' How far do you agree? Explain your answer.

You may use the following in your answer:
- Elizabeth I passed laws against begging
- Beggars could be classed as sturdy or deserving

You **must** also use information of your own. [16]

Eduqas

1 Explain why opportunities for crime increased during the Tudor period. [9]

2 Study Sources A and B below and answer the question that follows.

Source A

> Most vagabonds were not criminals or devious beggars, they were genuinely poor and unemployed people looking for work. The increasing movement of the population towards towns and cities in search of work, made many people fearful of strangers.

[An extract from a modern school textbook]

Source B

> ...the infinite numbers of idle, wandering people and robbers of the land are the chief cause of the problem, because they labour not. They lie idly in the alehouses day and night drinking. The most dangerous are the wandering soldiers and other stout rogues.

[An extract taken from a letter sent by Edward Hext, a Justice of the Peace in Somerset, to Lord Burghley, Queen Elizabeth's chief minister in 1596]

Which of the two sources is more reliable to a historian studying the crime of vagrancy in the Tudor period?

In your answer you should refer to the content and authorship of the sources and use your own knowledge and understanding of the wider historical context. [6]

OCR B

1 What caused the increase in crime between 1500 and 1700? Explain your answer. [10]

2 How far do you agree that vagrancy was the most serious crime between 1500 and 1750? Give reasons for your answer. [18]

Edexcel

1 Study Sources A and B. How useful are Sources A and B for an enquiry into the effectiveness of the methods used to catch criminals in this period?

Explain your answer, using Sources A and B and your knowledge of the historical context.　　[8]

Source A – An extract from a modern textbook describing the role of watchmen in London

> The beats of many watchmen were so short that they only lasted 5 minutes, which if done twice an hour, meant that the watchmen would spend at least 50 minutes relaxing in his watch-box. Frequently, two or three watchmen would meet up together in conversation in order to pass the time. They were employed to shut up shops, go on errands, or go into public houses with prostitutes. Also from the practice of being fixed in a certain watch-box for many years, there is no doubt some of them received bribes from criminals.

Source B – Thief taker Jonathon Wild apprehending a criminal to collect money from the victim

2 Study Source A. How could you follow up Source A to find out more about the effectiveness of the methods of catching criminals?

In your answer, you must give the question you would ask and the type of source you could use.　　[4]

Eduqas

1 Look at the three sources below, which show methods of catching criminals in the Tudor period and answer the question that follows.

Source A

[Thief taker Jonathon Wild apprehending a criminal to collect money from the victim]

Source B

[Watchmen patrolling the street]

Source C

> **Parish constables patrolled the streets, they were unpaid and mostly dealt with petty crimes. They often inflicted punishments on criminals, such as whipping vagabonds.**

[Taken from a modern school textbook]

Use Sources A, B and C to identify one similarity and one difference in the methods of catching criminals. [4]

2 Outline how far the Bloody Code had been successfully introduced by the beginning of the eighteenth century. [16]

OCR B

1 Write a clear and organised summary of methods of policing during the period 1500–1750. Support your summary with examples. [9]

2 How far do you agree that the introduction of the Bloody Code was successful during this period? Give reasons for your answer. [18]

1700–1900: Crime

Edexcel

1 'Smuggling was the most serious crime affecting Britain between 1700 and 1850.' How far do you agree? Explain your answer.

You may use the following in your answer:
* Smuggling was very difficult to prevent
* The Tolpuddle Martyrs were arrested in 1833

You **must** also include information of your own. [16]

2 Describe **two** reasons for the increase in crime during the period 1700–1900. [4]

Eduqas

1 Explain why opportunities for crime had increased by the end of the nineteenth century. [9]

2 Describe why protest increased in the eighteenth century. [5]

OCR B

1 Write a clear and organised summary describing why smuggling became an important crime. Support your summary with examples. [9]

2 (a) Name **one** group of protesters during this period. [1]

(b) Name **one** type of crime the authorities were concerned about. [1]

(c) Give **one** example of why changes in society affected the crime rate. [1]

Edexcel

1 Explain why there were reforms in the prison system between 1750 and 1850.

You may use the following in your answer:
- John Howard
- Hard labour

You **must** also use information of your own. [12]

2 Describe **two** key features of the Metropolitan Police Force. [4]

Eduqas

1 Explain why prison reform was a significant change in punishment of criminals in the eighteenth and nineteenth centuries. [12]

2 Outline how far the methods of policing had developed between 1700 and 1900. [16]

OCR B

1 How far do you agree that the introduction of the Bow Street Runners was the most important change to law and order during this period? Give reasons for your answer. [18]

2 What factors led to the need for prison reform during this period? Explain your answer. [10]

Edexcel

1 Explain why crime rates began to rise after 1950.

You may use the following in your answer:
- Methods of recording crime have improved
- Violent crime has risen to 6%

You **must** also use information of your own. [12]

2 Describe **two** new crimes that have developed in the twentieth century. [4]

Eduqas

1 Outline how far the types of crimes have changed between the nineteenth and twentieth centuries. [16]

2 Describe the reasons for crime rates having risen since 1950. [5]

OCR B

1 (a) Give **one** example of a common crime in the twentieth century. [1]

(b) Give **one** reason why victims of crime are more likely to report it during this period. [1]

(c) Give **one** example of a technology change that affected policing. [1]

2 Write a clear and organised summary describing the development of new crimes in this period. Support your summary with examples. [9]

Edexcel

1 'The development of technology was the most important factor affecting law enforcement after 1900.' How far do you agree? Explain your answer.

You may use the following in your answer:
- Improved methods of crime detection
- Specialisation of the police

You **must** also use information of your own. [16]

2 Describe **two** key features of new punishments developed in the twentieth century. [4]

Eduqas

1 Explain why the use of technology was important in developing policing methods in the twentieth century. [9]

2 Explain why there has been a significant change in the nature of punishment during the twentieth century. [12]

OCR B

1 Explain how the police force has developed during this period. [10]

2 How far do you agree that the most important changes in the punishment of offenders took place in the twentieth century? Give reasons for your answer. [18]

Case Studies

Edexcel

1 Explain why witchcraft trials began to decline after the Civil War.

You may use the following in your answer:
- Matthew Hopkins and his work as the Witchfinder General
- There was an increase in scientific understanding and rational explanations

You **must** also use information of your own. [12]

2 Explain why conscientious objectors refused to fight during the First and Second World Wars.

You may use the following in your answer:
- Conscription was introduced in 1916 for men aged 18–41
- Military tribunals were set up to determine if claims were genuine

You **must** also use information of your own. [12]

Eduqas

1 Describe **two** main features of witchcraft tests. [8]

2 Describe **two** main features of punishments for conscientious objectors. [8]

OCR B

1 Write a clear and organised summary describing why accusations of witchcraft increased during this period. Support your summary with examples. [9]

2 Write a clear and organised summary describing attitudes towards conscientious objectors during the twentieth century. Support your summary with examples. [9]

Answers

Please note that these answers are not intended to be full or model answers. They are intended to offer guidance on the kind of points you would be expected to include in your answer.

Norman England – pages 188–197

Page 188: Anglo-Saxon Society on the Eve of Conquest

Edexcel

1.

In answers candidates have shown...	Marks (2 for each descriptor)
Relevant points.	0 / 1 / 2
Explanation of points.	0 / 1 / 2

4 mark answers could include: Hundred courts would listen to cases – explain the king gave powers to local officials to hear cases; entire families could be punished for the actions of one individual; a person's solemn oath was given a high level of importance; trials by ordeal were used to ascertain innocence or guilt – explain what the trials were; wergild was paid to victims' families; explain – if this was not paid then a blood feud could be pursued.

2.

In answers candidates have shown...	Level	Mark
No rewardable material.		0
Simple, undeveloped and unorganised statements with limited knowledge and understanding.	1	1–3
Basic statements which are relevant to the question. Some knowledge and understanding. Limited analysis.	2	4–6
Some explanation which is relevant to the question. Good knowledge and understanding. Some analysis.	3	7–9
Developed explanation and analysis which is well structured. Excellent knowledge and understanding is portrayed.	4	10–12

Level 4 answers should include: Trial by ordeal – not fair because ordeals did not take into account evidence of a person's innocence or guilt; water trial – if a person sank they were innocent, if they survived the water did not want them because they were impure (guilty); iron ordeal, totally dependent on how well a person's skin healed (supposedly linked to God healing them); entire families being punished – collective responsibility was not fair, innocent people punished for another person's actions due to family ties; own information – if the wergild could not be paid then a blood feud could be pursued, this wasn't fair because ordinary people did not have a lot of money in order to pay the wergild.

OCR B

1.

In answers candidates have shown...	Mark
Relevant points identified from the source.	1
Basic explanation.	1
Developed explanation.	1

3 mark answers should include: Source detail – people from the royal household with hereditary right to rule were usually successors; the Witan could choose a successor from the royal household if succession was unclear/debated; developed explanation linked to the source – usually the heir would be the eldest son of the current king; there had to be a strong family connection in order to have an unchallenged claim to the throne; it was important for Saxon kings to have the support of the Witan; these men were responsible for helping the king run the kingdom and had great power in Anglo-Saxon society.

2.

In answers candidates have shown...	Level	Mark
No response or irrelevant comments.		0
Basic comments to answer the question.	1	1
Relevant areas of further research identified and described.	2	2–3
Relevant areas of further research identified and understanding of second order concepts shown.	3	4–5

Level 3 answers could include: How certain Saxon kings were chosen (similarities and differences); how family blood lines were maintained throughout the period (continuity); whether kings were chosen and supported by blood line or the Witan (cause and consequence).

Page 188: The Succession Crisis of 1066

AQA

1.

In answers candidates have shown...	Level	Mark
No answer or irrelevant statements.		0
Straightforward account that demonstrates basic analysis of causes.	1	1–2
Structured account that demonstrates simple analysis of causes.	2	3–4
Well-ordered account that demonstrates developed analysis of causes.	3	5–6
Coherent account that demonstrates a range of developed analysis of causes.	4	7–8

Level 4 answers should include: Edward had no children; Edward had promised the throne to William and Harold Godwinson; Hardrada claimed that Edward had seized the throne from his father and therefore he was the rightful claimant.

2.

In answers candidates have shown...	Level	Mark
No answer or irrelevant statements.		0
Simple explanation using basic knowledge.	1	1–4
Simple explanation using specific knowledge.	2	5–8
Developed explanation using a range of accurate knowledge.	3	9–12
Complex explanation using detailed knowledge.	4	13–16

Level 4 answers should include: Reasons to explain why Edgar did have a strong claim to the throne in 1066 – he was a blood relative (great nephew) of Anglo-Saxon kings; no other close living relative; succession usually went to closest living relative; reasons to explain why he didn't have a strong claim – he was a child; he was not supported by the Witan; he was not in England; the other contenders.

Edexcel

1.

In answers candidates have shown...	Marks (2 for each descriptor)
Relevant points.	0 / 1 / 2
Explanation of points.	0 / 1 / 2

4 mark answers could include: Edward promised the throne to William – explain that William had sent soldiers to help when Edward returned to England to become king; Edward sent Harold Godwinson to Normandy to reaffirm his promise to William – explain how William viewed himself as Edward's rightful heir; Edward promised Harold Godwinson the throne on his deathbed – explain that this caused issues because it went against his earlier promise to William.

2.

In answers candidates have shown...	Level	Mark
No rewardable material.		0
Simple, undeveloped and unorganised statements with limited knowledge, understanding and analysis. No judgement to answer the question.	1	1–4
Basic statements which are relevant to the question but limited analysis. Some knowledge and understanding. A judgement but without supporting evidence.	2	5–8
Some explanation and analysis shown, which is relevant to the question. Good knowledge and understanding. A valid judgement with supporting evidence.	3	9–12
Developed explanation and analysis which is well structured. Excellent knowledge and understanding. A strong supported judgement.	4	13–16

Level 4 answers should include: William of Normandy – was promised the throne in 1051, William and Edward had spent time together in Normandy and so had developed a close relationship – William believed that because of this promise he was the rightful heir. William believed that Harold Godwinson would support his claim following Edward's death – by naming a Norman as his successor, Edward had opened up the prospect of invasion after his death; Harold Godwinson – had sworn an oath to William to support his claim to the English throne. Harold went back on his word and claimed the throne for himself – this plunged England into a crisis because William believed that Harold was a usurper; own information – Edward had no children – there was always going to be a crisis because each contender (including the claim made by Hardrada) would want to stake his claim to the throne; a conclusion to explain how far you agree.

OCR B

1.

In answers candidates have shown...	Level	Mark
No response or irrelevant comments.		0
Basic and undeveloped comments to answer the question.	1	1–4

In answers candidates have shown...	Level	Mark
Simple description to answer the question.	2	5–8
Simple explanation of relevant points and a basic conclusion.	3	9–12
Good explanation of relevant points and a sound conclusion.	4	13–16
Consistent and focused explanation to convey arguments with a good conclusion.	5	17–20

Level 5 answers: For these types of questions you can agree, disagree or be anywhere in the middle; ensure that you explain a variety of factors; these questions will focus on one or more of the second order concepts – this question focuses on cause and consequence; agree – Edward had not produced any children to be his heir; Edward had promised the throne to William and Harold; no single contender was in a position to take the throne without a crisis; due to these reasons the events of 1066 unfolded with various battles for the English crown; disagree – although Harold had promised William the throne in 1051, his deathbed decision should have over-ruled previous choices made; the Witan supported Godwinson's claim and so this should have made him the rightful heir; William and Hardrada were taking chances to further their power and status; a conclusion to explain how far you agree.

2.

In answers candidates have shown...	Level	Mark
No response or irrelevant comments.		0
Basic comments to answer the question.	1	1
Relevant areas of further research identified and described.	2	2–3
Relevant areas of further research identified and understanding of second order concepts shown.	3	4–5

Level 3 answers could include: The promises made to William and Harold (similarities and differences); why Edward changed his mind and the consequences of this (cause and consequence).

Page 189: The Rival Claimants to the Throne in 1066

AQA

1.

In answers candidates have shown...	Level	Mark
No answer or irrelevant statements.		0
Basic explanation of causes.	1	1–2
Simple explanation of one cause.	2	3–4
Developed explanation of causes.	3	5–6
Complex explanation of causes.	4	7–8

Level 4 answers should include: The king had spoken his wishes that Harold should succeed him – the king's wishes should be granted; this promise showed the king had changed his mind relating to William's claim; Harold was appointed by the king and the Witan supported him.

2.

In answers candidates have shown...	Level	Mark
No answer or irrelevant statements.		0
Basic analysis of source based on candidate's knowledge.	1	1–2
Simple evaluation of source based on candidate's knowledge.	2	3–4
Developed evaluation of source based on candidate's knowledge.	3	5–6
Complex evaluation of source with a judgement reached based on candidate's knowledge.	4	7–8

Level 4 answers should include: The boat is bringing news that King Edward had died and Harold Godwinson had been crowned king; William, being positioned in France, would have had to receive the news in this way; William sits next to his half-brother, Bishop Odo, when receiving the news; Bishop Odo helped William during the invasion and fought by his side in the Battle of Hastings – he supported William's claim to seize the throne from Harold. Conclusion – overall how convincing is it – not at all / partly / totally?

Edexcel

1.

In answers candidates have shown...	Level	Mark
No rewardable material.		0
Simple, undeveloped and unorganised statements with limited knowledge and understanding.	1	1–3
Basic statements which are relevant to the question. Some knowledge and understanding. Limited analysis.	2	4–6
Some explanation which is relevant to the question. Good knowledge and understanding. Some analysis.	3	7–9
Detailed explanation which is well structured. Excellent knowledge and understanding.	4	10–12

Level 4 answers should include: He was promised the throne by Edward on his deathbed. This was a direct and strong link that the previous king had wanted him to be heir. This made his claim strong; the Witan supported his claim. This was important because the Witan would help the king run the country and make decisions – kings needed the Witan's support in order to be successful; his location in England, which meant it was easy for him to lay claim to the throne and be crowned before any rival contender made a claim; his position as Earl of Wessex made him one of the most powerful men in England. This helped with his claim because there was no one in England that could realistically challenge his claim to the throne.

2.

In answers candidates have shown...	Level	Mark
No rewardable material.		0
Simple, undeveloped and unorganised statements with limited knowledge, understanding and analysis. No judgement to answer the question.	1	1–4
Basic statements which are relevant to the question but limited analysis. Some knowledge and understanding. A judgement but without supporting evidence.	2	5–8

In answers candidates have shown...	Level	Mark
Some explanation and analysis which is relevant to the question. Good knowledge and understanding. A valid judgement with supporting evidence.	3	9–12
Developed explanation with analysis which is well structured. Excellent knowledge and understanding. A strong supported judgement.	4	13–16

Level 4 answers should include: He was English – this meant that England would not be invaded by a foreign country and England would have an English king; Earl of Wessex – this made him very powerful, he also had experience of running the country because he had helped Edward during his reign; other reasons to support why Harold had the strongest claim – Witan, the deathbed promise; other contenders' claims – William and Hardrada (Edgar?); a conclusion to explain how far you agree.

OCR B

1.

In answers candidates have shown...	Mark
Relevant points identified from the source.	1
Basic explanation	1
Developed explanation	1

3 mark answers should include: Source detail – Edward selected Harold to be his heir on his deathbed; Harold was elected by the English nobility to be king the day after Edward's death; Explanation linked to the source – Edward had changed his mind and promised the throne to Harold, this over-wrote his decision that William could be king; the support of the Witan was crucial in making a claim to the throne. The Witan supported Harold's claim to be the successor of Edward.

2.

In answers candidates have shown...	Level	Mark
No response or irrelevant comments.		0
Basic and undeveloped comments to answer the question.	1	1–4
Simple description to answer the question.	2	5–8
Simple explanation of relevant points and a basic conclusion.	3	9–12
Good explanation of relevant points and a sound conclusion.	4	13–16
Consistent and focused explanation to convey arguments with a good conclusion.	5	17–20

Level 5 answers: For these types of questions, you can agree, disagree or be anywhere in the middle; ensure that you explain a variety of factors; these questions will focus on one or more of the second order concepts – this question focuses on similarity and difference (between the contenders' claims); grounds for agreeing – he was promised the throne by Edward; the Witan supported his claim; he was English; his family had helped Edward run England during his reign and had proved their loyalty; grounds for disagreeing – Edward had promised William the throne before Harold; Harold had promised to support William's claim; Edgar was a blood relative; Hardrada claimed he was the rightful heir because of the promise made by Harthacnut to his father Magnus; a conclusion to explain how far you agree.

Page 190: The Battles of Fulford and Stamford Bridge

AQA

1.

In answers candidates have shown...	Level	Mark
No answer or irrelevant statements.		0
Simple explanation using basic knowledge.	1	1-4
Simple explanation using specific knowledge.	2	5-8
Developed explanation using a range of accurate knowledge.	3	9-12
Complex explanation using detailed knowledge.	4	13-16

Level 4 answers should include: Explanation of other events that were (perhaps more) significant in 1066 – Battle of Hastings which led to the change of king; Battle of Fulford which meant that the Saxon army was weakened before Stamford Bridge; explanation that Stamford Bridge was significant – it meant that Harold Godwinson had defeated Hardrada who was a mighty warrior; it was only William that now stood as the final claimant; the Saxon army was battered and bruised after this battle so their fighting at Hastings would not be as strong as it could have been; a conclusion to explain how far you agree.

2.

In answers candidates have shown...	Level	Mark
No answer or irrelevant statements.		0
Basic analysis of source based on candidate's knowledge.	1	1-2
Simple evaluation of source based on candidate's knowledge.	2	3-4
Developed evaluation of source based on candidate's knowledge.	3	5-6
Complex evaluation of source with a judgement reached based on candidate's knowledge.	4	7-8

Level 4 answers should include: The battle was fought near/on a bridge; legend states there was a Viking warrior on the bridge preventing the Saxons from crossing; the Vikings have axes; there is carnage as the battle is being fought; contextual knowledge to support – Harold's army surprised the Vikings; Vikings weren't well prepared; the story of the warrior on the bridge; the Viking army being split.

Edexcel

1.

In answers candidates have shown...	Marks (2 for each descriptor)
Relevant points.	0 / 1 / 2
Explanation of points.	0 / 1 / 2

4 mark answers could include: The earls in the north moved to defend York from Hardrada's invasion; Earls Morcar and Edwin led the Saxon defensive forces; the Saxons tried to defend York by being based south of the city; the Saxons placed themselves on a narrow strip of land with marsh ground and a river to the side; the battle started well for the Saxons – they held off the Vikings and pushed them into the marshland; as more Viking troops arrived the Saxon forces were pushed backwards; explain – due to Hardrada having the higher ground the Viking army could see that the Saxons were being pushed towards a natural pit; the Saxons became trapped and were slaughtered by the Vikings; explain – the path to York lay open for Hardrada.

2.

In answers candidates have shown...	Level	Mark
No rewardable material.		0
Simple, undeveloped and unorganised statements with limited knowledge and understanding.	1	1–3
Basic statements which are relevant to the question. Some knowledge and understanding. Limited analysis.	2	4–6
Some explanation which is relevant to the question. Good knowledge and understanding. Some analysis.	3	7–9
Developed explanation and analysis which is well structured. Excellent knowledge and understanding.	4	10–12

Level 4 answers should include: The Viking army had not expected the Saxons to arrive so quickly – this meant that some Vikings had left their chainmail and were not well prepared. This helped Saxon forces because Vikings were easier targets without their protection; Hardrada was killed – this meant victory for Godwinson because without a king there was no point in the Vikings continuing to fight and the surviving Vikings fled home to Norway; the Saxons (according to legend) had killed the Viking warrior who had blocked the bridge, which enabled the Saxons to get access to the main body of the Viking army and engage them in battle, from which they were defeated.

OCR B

1.

In answers candidates have shown...	Mark
Relevant points identified from the source.	1
Basic explanation	1
Developed explanation	1

3 mark answers could include: Source detail – part of the army was cut off from the main defending force and retreated to the city; the army defending the beck was forced off by the Norwegians; a third front was created by the Vikings, and the Saxons could not continue fighting; explanation linked to the source — Earls Morcar and Edwin led the Saxon forces at Fulford; this was not the main body of the Saxon army; the Saxons were pushed back by continuous arrivals of Vikings and were forced further back; the Saxons ended up in a natural pit where the Vikings slaughtered them; the Vikings had the advantage of height and could see this tactic working to their advantage.

2.

In answers candidates have shown...	Level	Mark
No response or irrelevant comments.		0
Simple identification of similarities and/or differences.	1	1–3
– Ways in which the interpretations are similar or different. – Attempt to explain why the interpretations are similar or different. – A basic conclusion.	2	4–6
– Analysis of the interpretations. – Detailed explanations of why the interpretations are similar or different. – A conclusion focusing on 'how far' the interpretations are similar or different.	3	7–9

In answers candidates have shown...	Level	Mark
– Analysis of the interpretations. – Developed explanations of why the interpretations are similar and/or different. – A valid and well-reached conclusion focusing on 'how far' the interpretations are similar or different.	4	10–12

Level 4 answers should include: Similarities – both interpretations mention the Vikings were defeated; both mention that the Vikings were fighting the Saxon forces. Differences – suggest different reasons for defeat; A mentions tactics and preparation being a causal factor and B mentions the morale and mental strength of the Saxon army. Explanation of differences – both could be correct for explaining why Vikings were defeated; the interpretations could have been focusing on different aspects of the battle – resources and preparation and so show different reasons; both factors work together to explain the defeat of the Vikings.

Page 192: The Battle of Hastings

AQA

1.

In answers candidates have shown...	Level	Mark
No answer or irrelevant statements.		0
A straightforward account that demonstrates basic analysis of causes.	1	1–2
Structured account that demonstrates simple analysis of causes.	2	3–4
Well-ordered account that demonstrates developed analysis of causes.	3	5–6
Coherent account that demonstrates a range of developed analysis of causes.	4	7–8

Level 4 answers should include: Harold's army being tired and weak from the start (following the long marches and the battle with Hardrada at Stamford Bridge); William's army was made entirely of professional soldiers, Harold's wasn't; William's tactics – pretending to retreat in order to weaken the Saxon shield wall.

2.

In answers candidates have shown...	Level	Mark
No answer or irrelevant statements.		0
Simple description using basic knowledge.	1	1–4
Simple explanation using specific knowledge.	2	5–8
Developed explanation using a range of accurate knowledge.	3	9–12
Complex explanation using detailed knowledge.	4	13–16

Level 4 answers should include: Inevitable – army was weak and wounded from the Battle of Stamford Bridge and the march north and back down south again; Harold's army was depleted which meant Harold had had to rely on the fyrd – these were no match for William's well trained and well prepared soldiers; Not inevitable – during the morning's fighting, Harold's army stood firm and the Norman army could not break through the shield wall; perhaps if some of the Saxon army had not broken rank to follow the retreating Normans, the outcome of the battle may have been different; a conclusion.

Edexcel

1.

In answers candidates have shown...	Level	Mark
No rewardable material.		0
Simple, undeveloped and unorganised statements with limited knowledge and understanding.	1	1–3
Basic statements which are relevant to the question. Some knowledge and understanding. Limited analysis.	2	4–6
Some explanation which is relevant to the question. Good knowledge and understanding. Some analysis.	3	7–9
Developed explanation and analysis which is well structured. Excellent knowledge and understanding.	4	10–12

Level 4 answers should include: William's army had been blessed by the Pope – gave a mental advantage and his men would have believed that victory for them was inevitable; William's tactics – pretending to retreat in order to weaken the Saxon shield wall; Harold's army being tired and weak from the start (following the long marches and the battle with Hardrada at Stamford Bridge); William's army was made entirely of professional soldiers, Harold's wasn't.

2.

In answers candidates have shown...	Level	Mark
No rewardable material.		0
Simple, undeveloped and unorganised statements with limited knowledge and understanding. No judgement to answer the question.	1	1–4
Basic statements which are relevant to the question but limited analysis. Some knowledge and understanding. A judgement but without supporting evidence.	2	5–8
Some explanation which is relevant to the question. Good knowledge and understanding. A valid judgement with supporting evidence.	3	9–12
Developed explanation with analysis which is well structured. Excellent knowledge and understanding. A strong supported judgement.	4	13–16

Level 4 answers should include: Saxon army was tired – battle with Hardrada and long marches to and from Stamford Bridge; William's army outnumbered the Saxons – William had brought with him plenty of soldiers and resources, Harold's army was depleted which meant Harold had had to rely on the fyrd; these were no match for William's well trained and well prepared soldiers; however, during the morning's fighting, Harold's army stood firm and the Norman army could not break through the shield wall (not inevitable); perhaps if some of the Saxon army had not broken rank to follow the Normans retreating, the outcome of the battle may have been different; a conclusion to explain how far you agree.

OCR B

1.

In answers candidates have shown...	Level	Mark
No response or irrelevant comments.		0
Simple identification of similarities and/or differences.	1	1–3
– Ways in which the interpretations are similar or different. – Attempt to explain why the interpretations are similar or different. – A basic conclusion.	2	4–6
– Analysis of the interpretations. – Detailed explanations of why the interpretations are similar or different. – A conclusion focusing on 'how far' the interpretations are similar or different.	3	7–9
– Analysis of the interpretations. – Developed explanations of why the interpretations are similar and/or different. – A valid and well-reached conclusion focusing on 'how far' the interpretations are similar or different.	4	10–12

Level 4 answers should include: Similarities – both mention that the Normans were victorious; both mention that William was an inspirational leader who evoked the best from his men; both mention the speeches William gave. Differences – suggest different reasons for victory: A, William's leadership was inspirational and he roused his men for one final push in which Harold was killed; B, it was God's plan that the Norman army would be victorious. Explanation of differences – A was written by a Norman and so it could be suggested that the writer wanted to lay the credit for victory firmly with the leadership from William; B was written many years after the battle; this source seems to give an overview of the battle rather than examination of specific events within the battle as in A.

2.

In answers candidates have shown...	Level	Mark
No response or irrelevant comments.		0
Basic comments to answer the question.	1	1
Relevant areas of further research identified and described.	2	2–3
Relevant areas of further research identified and understanding of second order concepts shown.	3	4–5

Level 3 answers could include: Why the Normans believed that God was on their side (continuity from the succession crisis); what effect the Pope's blessing had on the Norman army (consequences); the speeches that William made before and during the battle and the effect these had (cause and consequence).

Page 193: Anglo-Saxon Resistance and the Norman Response

AQA

1.

In answers candidates have shown...	Level	Mark
No answer or irrelevant statements.		0
Basic explanation of causes/consequences	1	1–2
Simple explanation of one cause/consequence.	2	3–4
Developed explanation of causes/consequences.	3	5–6
Complex explanation of causes and consequences of castle building programme.	4	7–8

Level 4 answers should include: Castles were built in strategic places to watch over and control the Saxons and to protect England's borders from invaders; villages were knocked down if it was thought it would be a good location for a castle; Saxon landowners had their land removed as rebellions became more frequent; loyal barons were placed in castles to act as a constant reminder that the Normans were in charge; barons had access to knights who would fight for them if necessary; William had loyal eyes and ears around England – rebellions could be dealt with quickly; the Saxons realised that fighting the Norman rule was dangerous and eventually impossible.

2.

In answers candidates have shown...	Level	Mark
No answer or irrelevant statements.		0
Basic explanation of reasons to answer the question.	1	1–2
Simple explanation to answer the question.	2	3–4
Developed explanation to answer the question.	3	5–6
Complex explanation to answer the question.	4	7–8

Level 4 answers should include: Rebellion was a serious threat to William's power and control; the North had allied with a foreign country (Denmark) and Edgar Aetheling. This could have resulted in a rival claimant to the throne seeking to rule England; if William had let the rebellion take shape then he could have faced a separate state in the north that was not under his control; William needed to teach the north a lesson and to set an example to the rest of the country not to rebel against him.

Edexcel

1.

In answers candidates have shown...	Marks (2 for each descriptor)
Relevant points.	0 / 1 / 2
Explanation of points.	0 / 1 / 2

4 mark answers could include: Hereward and Morcar attempted to rebel on the Isle of Ely; the earls were supported by an army sent by the Danish king; the rebels held their ground and made strides towards their goals; the rebellion came to a halt when monks betrayed the rebels and showed the Normans a secret pathway that would lead into their stronghold; the rebellion was crushed and Hereward escaped.

2.

In answers candidates have shown...	Level	Mark
No rewardable material.		0
Simple, undeveloped and unorganised statements with limited knowledge and understanding.	1	1–3
Basic statements which are relevant to the question. Some knowledge and understanding. Limited analysis is shown.	2	4–6
Some explanation which is relevant to the question. Good knowledge and understanding. Some analysis.	3	7–9
Developed explanation and analysis which is well structured. Excellent knowledge and understanding.	4	10–12

Level 4 answers should include: The rebellion was a serious threat to William's power and control; the North had allied with a foreign country (Denmark) and Edgar Aetheling. This could have resulted in a rival claimant to the throne seeking to rule England; William needed to teach the north a lesson and to set an example to the rest of the country not to rebel against him; if William had let the rebellion take shape then he could have faced a separate state in the north which was not under his control.

OCR B

1.

In answers candidates have shown...	Level	Mark
No response or irrelevant comments.		0
Basic and undeveloped comments to answer the question.	1	1–4
Simple description of points in order to answer the question.	2	5–8
Simple explanation of relevant points and a basic conclusion.	3	9–12
Good explanation of relevant points and a sound conclusion.	4	13–16
Consistent and focused explanation to convey their arguments with a good conclusion.	5	17–20

Level 5 answers could include: For these types of questions, you can agree, disagree or be anywhere in the middle; ensure that you explain a variety of factors; these questions will focus on one or more of the second order concepts – this question focuses on cause and consequence; agree – lots of people not directly involved in the rebellion were affected by William's actions; men, women and children were killed or starved; areas of the north were 'waste' for many years after this event – in the Domesday Book large parts of the north are described as 'waste'; disagree – William needed to establish control; he could not allow the north to make alliances with foreign countries; the people in the north were aware that there would have been some repercussions if their rebellion failed – they shouldn't have been surprised that William wanted to ensure it would not happen again; a conclusion to explain how far you agree.

2.

In answers candidates have shown...	Mark
Relevant points identified from the source.	1
Basic explanation.	1
Developed explanation.	1

3 mark answers could include: Source – villages destroyed, people killed, animals and crops burnt; explanation linked to the source – William needed to be sure that the north was taught a tough lesson – not to rebel against his rule. This would also act as a warning to other parts of England – by destroying villages, crops and animals the north was left so weak that it could not rebel again.

Page 194: Life Under Norman Control

AQA

1.

In answers candidates have shown...	Level	Mark
No answer or have made irrelevant statements.		0
Basic analysis of source based on candidate's knowledge.	1	1–2

In answers candidates have shown...	Level	Mark
Simple evaluation of source based on candidate's knowledge.	2	3–4
Developed evaluation of source based on candidate's knowledge.	3	5–6
Complex evaluation of source with a judgement reached based on candidate's knowledge.	4	7–8

Level 4 answers should include: The family are agricultural workers; the man/father has a tool to plough/harvest the land; the woman is collecting wood; the children are tending to the animals; contextual knowledge – ordinary people's lives centred around the land and animals; people would keep animals for food and in the winter would sell or slaughter them; wood would be used for fires – heat and cooking; the whole family would work together to ensure all of the daily jobs got completed.

2.

In answers candidates have shown...	Level	Mark
No answer or have made irrelevant statements.		0
Basic explanation of changes/continuities.	1	1–2
Simple explanation of changes/continuities.	2	3–4
Developed explanation of changes/continuities.	3	5–6
Complex explanation of changes/continuities.	4	7–8

Level 4 answers should include: all positions of power within government and the ruling classes were given to Normans; castles were built on a big scale – some villages were destroyed in the process; William put in place barons to ensure the Saxons remained loyal to the new Norman king; boundaries of earldoms were changed to reflect the areas controlled by the barons; however, much of the government remained unchanged; William was keen to keep things that had worked well in Edward's reign, e.g. Chancellor, taxation, administrative shires and sheriffs; law and order carried on in much the same way as Saxon times – the hundred courts, shire courts.

Edexcel

1.

In answers candidates have shown...	Marks (2 for each descriptor)
Relevant points.	0 / 1 / 2
Explanation of points.	0 / 1 / 2

4 mark answers could include: It was a land system; everyone knew their place; at the top was the king > barons > knights > peasants; each person owed loyalty and service to their lord (the person above them); land was lent down the chain; it helped William control England.

2.

In answers candidates have shown...	Level	Mark
No rewardable material.		0
Simple, undeveloped and unorganised statements with limited knowledge and understanding. No judgement to answer the question.	1	1–4
Basic statements which are relevant to the question but limited analysis. Some knowledge and understanding. A judgement but without supporting evidence.	2	5–8

In answers candidates have shown…	Level	Mark
Some explanation and analysis which is relevant to the question. Good knowledge and understanding. A valid judgement with supporting evidence.	3	9–12
Detailed explanation and analysis which is well structured. Excellent knowledge and understanding. A strong supported judgement.	4	13–16

Level 4 answers should include: Much of the government remained unchanged – William was keen to keep things that had worked well in Edward's reign, e.g. Chancellor, taxation, administrative shires and sheriffs; castles were built on a big scale, some villages and towns were destroyed in the process; William put in place barons to ensure the Saxons remained loyal to the new Norman king; boundaries of earldoms were changed to reflect the areas controlled by the barons; law and order carried on in much the same way as Saxon times – the hundred courts, shire courts; all positions of power within government and the ruling classes were given to Normans; a conclusion to explain how far you agree.

OCR B

1.

In answers candidates have shown…	Level	Mark
No response or irrelevant comments.		0
Simple identification of similarities and/or differences.	1	1–3
– Ways in which the interpretations are similar or different. – Attempt to explain why the interpretations are similar or different. – A basic conclusion.	2	4–6
– Analysis of the interpretations. – Detailed explanations of why the interpretations are similar or different. – A conclusion focusing on 'how far' the interpretations are similar or different.	3	7–9
– Analysis of the interpretations. – Developed explanations of why the interpretations are similar and/or different. – A valid and well-reached conclusion focusing on 'how far' the interpretations are similar or different.	4	10–12

Level 4 answers should include: Similarities – both suggest that the Normans were good at fighting, indeed William had won his place on the English throne as a result of a battle. Differences – A states that there was more continuity in England than change, B states that the Normans changed the world, suggesting innovative ways of ruling and consolidating their power and control. Explanation of differences – perhaps in government William was keen to keep things stable in England, this could be explained with the systems of Chancellor, taxation, law and order all continuing pretty much the same as in Saxon times, the big changes from the Normans came in the geographical sense in England – castle building and the feudal system, this can also be supported by the information collected for the Domesday Book.

2.

In answers candidates have shown…	Level	Mark
No response or irrelevant comments.		0
Basic comments to answer the question.	1	1
Relevant areas of further research identified and described.	2	2–3
Relevant areas of further research identified and understanding of second order concepts shown.	3	4–5

Level 3 answers should include: Areas that continued in the same way as Saxon times – government, Chancellor, taxation, law and order (continuity); areas that were changed after the conquest – The Forest and Murdrum Laws, the feudal system (change); the impact on the ordinary Saxon people (consequence).

Page 196: Norman Castles and the Domesday Book
AQA

1.

In answers candidates have shown…	Level	Mark
No answer or have made irrelevant statements.		0
Basic analysis of source based on candidate's knowledge.	1	1–2
Simple evaluation of source based on candidate's knowledge.	2	3–4
Developed evaluation of source based on candidate's knowledge.	3	5–6
Complex evaluation of source with a judgement reached based on candidate's knowledge.	4	7–8

Level 4 answers should include: There are two people sitting at a table gathering information; there is one man who seems to be answering questions (giving information); the exchange is taking place in a village – there are animals and agricultural tools in the image; contextual knowledge – William sent two sets of commissioners to ask the question to ensure that the information recorded was accurate; William wanted to know all about the land, money, people and animals. The inclusion of these things in the image suggests that this is what the questions are about; William sent his commissioners to towns and villages to gather this information.

2.

In answers candidates have shown…	Level	Mark
No answer or have made irrelevant statements.		0
Basic analysis of source based on candidate's knowledge.	1	1–2
Simple evaluation of source based on candidate's knowledge.	2	3–4
Developed evaluation of source based on candidate's knowledge.	3	5–6
Complex evaluation of source with a judgement reached based on candidate's knowledge.	4	7–8

Level 4 answers should include: There is a castle keep on top of a hill; there is a fenced yard at the bottom of the hill with buildings in it; the buildings are near to woodland; contextual knowledge – the castle keep was built on a mound of earth, this was called the motte. This would be the last line of defence if the castle was being attacked; the keep was built high so that the people inside could have the viewpoint advantage of height and the added protection this gave; the lower fenced section was called the bailey. This was where soldiers, food, weapons and resources would be kept; the castle seems to be constructed of wood – early Norman castles were built of wood because they were prefabricated and wood was easy to get; the forest nearby provided wood, food and resources to the people inside the castle. Castles like this would be used for organising the running of villages/ collecting taxes/points of trade, which is shown with people coming into bailey.

Edexcel

1.

In answers candidates have shown...	Level	Mark
No rewardable material.		0
Simple, undeveloped and unorganised statements with limited knowledge and understanding. No judgement to answer the question.	1	1–4
Basic statements which are relevant to the question but limited analysis. Some knowledge and understanding. A judgement but without supporting evidence.	2	5–8
Some explanation and analysis which is relevant to the question. Good knowledge and understanding. A valid judgement with supporting evidence.	3	9–12
Developed explanation and analysis which is well structured. Excellent knowledge and understanding. A strong supported judgement.	4	13–16

Level 4 answers should include: The Norman castle building programme was vast – the look of England changed as a result of the castles; villages were destroyed to make way for some castles; this changed the geographical contours of England; barons were placed in the castles to keep an eye on the Saxons; the old earldom borders were changed to make way for areas run by barons; this linked in with the castles. There were other big changes too – the feudal system cemented the Saxons at the bottom of the social hierarchy; the replacement of Saxon people with power and responsibility (such as governmental jobs) with Norman counterparts ensured that the Norman control was firmly established; a conclusion to explain how far you agree.

2.

In answers candidates have shown...	Marks (2 for each descriptor)
Relevant points.	0 / 1 / 2
Explanation of points.	0 / 1 / 2

4 mark answers could include: William sent commissioners around England to ask questions; the questions focused on land, money, people and animals; two sets of commissioners would visit each village/town; this was to ensure that people told the truth and the commissioners did their job properly; the information was collated and written into a book.

OCR B

1.

In answers candidates have shown...	Level	Mark
No response or irrelevant comments.		0
Simple identification of similarities and/or differences.	1	1–3
– Ways in which the interpretations are similar or different. – Attempt to explain why the interpretations are similar or different. – A basic conclusion.	2	4–6
– Analysis of the interpretations. – Detailed explanations of why the interpretations are similar or different. – A conclusion focusing on 'how far' the interpretations are similar or different.	3	7–9
– Analysis of the interpretations. – Developed explanations of why the interpretations are similar and/or different. – A valid and well-reached conclusion focusing on 'how far' the interpretations are similar or different.	4	10–12

Level 4 answers should include: Similarities – both mention that the French took ownership of areas of land in England, both mention that money was accounted for in the survey; Differences – A focuses mainly on York and who owns which parts of the area and how much revenue the people pay, B gives an overview of why William wanted the survey to be compiled; Explanation of differences – A is an extract from Domesday and so focuses on one area, York; B examines what William wanted to gain from the survey; you would expect to find answers to the areas identified in B if interpretation A was examined as a whole (from the Domesday Book) and across various areas in England.

2.

In answers candidates have shown...	Level	Mark
No response or irrelevant comments.		0
Basic and undeveloped comments to answer the question.	1	1–4
Simple description of points in order to answer the question.	2	5–8
Simple explanation of relevant points and a basic conclusion.	3	9–12
Good explanation of relevant points and a sound conclusion.	4	13–16
Consistent and focused explanation to convey arguments with a good conclusion.	5	17–20

Level 5 answers could include: For these types of questions, you can agree, disagree or be anywhere in the middle; ensure that you explain a variety of factors; these questions will focus on one or more of the second order concepts – this question focuses on change; agree – the Norman castle building programme was vast; the look of England changed as a result of the castles; villages were destroyed to make way for some castles, this changed the geographical contours of England; barons were placed in the castles to keep an eye on the Saxons; the old earldom borders were changed to make way for areas run by barons, this linked in with the castles. disagree – there were other big changes too: the feudal system cemented the Saxons at the bottom of the social hierarchy; the replacement of Saxon people with power and responsibility with Norman counterparts ensured that Norman control was firmly established; a conclusion to explain how far you agree.

Page 197: The Norman Church and the Death of William I

AQA

1.

In answers candidates have shown...	Level	Mark
No answer or irrelevant statements.		0
Basic explanation of changes/continuities.	1	1–2
Simple explanation of one change/continuity.	2	3–4
Developed explanation of changes/continuities.	3	5–6
Complex explanation of changes/continuities.	4	7–8

Level 4 answers should include: Everybody was religious, people believed that the only way to get to heaven was to follow the teachings of the church; the church was wealthy – wealth equated to power; clergy were dealt with in special church courts – these were outside the power of the king; no one (including medieval kings) wanted to be excommunicated – this gave the Pope huge power and influence. The scenario of the Investiture Controversy could be used as an example to show how the church had greater influence than the king in some aspects.

2.

In answers candidates have shown...	Level	Mark
No answer or irrelevant statements.		0
A straightforward account that demonstrates basic analysis of causes.	1	1–2
Structured account that demonstrates simple analysis of causes.	2	3–4
Well-ordered account that demonstrates developed analysis of causes.	3	5–6
Coherent account that demonstrates a range of developed analysis of causes.	4	7–8

Level 4 answers should include: William had decided to go against Norman tradition by splitting his kingdom between his sons; William did not leave all of his kingdom to Robert (his eldest son); William gave William Rufus the throne in England; this decision had annoyed Robert who felt he was the rightful king of England following the death of his father; Robert joined forces with Bishop Odo to claim the English throne; Archbishop Lanfranc secured Saxon support for William Rufus' claim to the English throne.

Edexcel

1.

In answers candidates have shown...	Level	Mark
No rewardable material.		0
Simple, undeveloped and unorganised statements with limited knowledge and understanding. No judgement to answer the question.	1	1–4
Basic statements which are relevant to the question but limited analysis. Some knowledge and understanding. A judgement but without supporting evidence.	2	5–8
Some explanation and analysis, which is relevant to the question. Good knowledge and understanding. A valid judgement with supporting evidence.	3	9–12

In answers candidates have shown...	Level	Mark
Developed explanation with analysis which is well structured. Excellent knowledge and understanding. A strong supported judgement.	4	13–16

Level 4 answers should include: No one (including medieval kings) wanted to be excommunicated; this gave the Pope huge power and influence. The scenario of the Investiture Controversy could be used as an example – Henry IV Holy Roman Emperor backed down and said sorry to the Pope; the church was wealthy – wealth equated to power. The monasteries held huge areas of land and people paid money (tithes) to the church; everybody was religious, people believed that the only way to get to heaven was to follow the teachings of the church, this showed that the church was very powerful; clergy were dealt with in special church courts, these were outside the power of the king; if kings were careful and did not upset the Pope then excellent church–state relations could be maintained – Archbishop Lanfranc ensured that the English church remained as independent as possible from the Pope; Archbishop Lanfranc showed how the church could be manoeuvred so that the Pope was kept happy but day-to-day business in the country could be independent; a conclusion to explain how far you agree.

2.

In answers candidates have shown...	Level	Mark
No rewardable material.		0
Simple, undeveloped and unorganised statements with limited knowledge and understanding.	1	1–3
Basic statements which are relevant to the question. Some knowledge and understanding. Limited analysis.	2	4–6
Some explanation which is relevant to the question. Good knowledge and understanding. Some analysis.	3	7–9
Detailed explanation and analysis which is well structured. Excellent knowledge and understanding.	4	10–12

Level 4 answers should include: William had decided to go against Norman tradition by splitting his kingdom between his sons; William did not leave all of his kingdom to Robert (his eldest son); William gave William Rufus the throne in England; This decision had annoyed Robert who felt he was the rightful king of England following the death of his father; Archbishop Lanfranc supported William I's decision not to leave everything to Robert; Archbishop Lanfranc secured Saxon support for William Rufus' claim to the English throne; Robert joined forces with Bishop Odo to claim the English throne; Bishop Odo thought that Robert was the weaker brother and with Robert on the throne his power would be strengthened.

Elizabethan England – pages 198–209

Page 198: Elizabeth I and Her Government

AQA

1.

In answers candidates have shown...	Level	Mark
Points without detail.	1	0–2
Details to support each point.	2	3–5
Three or more points each with supporting details.	3	6–8

Level 3 answers should include: Many in government wanted Elizabeth to marry quickly to ensure smooth succession; Elizabeth was worried that marrying someone from the English nobility, such as Robert Dudley, would deepen factional splits in her government; Elizabeth was worried that marrying someone from another country would commit her to an alliance she did not want and could lead to war with opposing countries; she confirmed her closest relative, her cousin's son James, as succcessor.

2.

In answers candidates have shown...	Level	Mark
One reason but no detail.	1	0–2
Two reasons with some detail.	2	3–5
Reasons with detail and linked them together.	3	6–8

Level 3 answers should include: Elizabeth used portraits extensively to promote her image and the message that she was the rightful Queen of England; Elizabeth used her coronation ceremony to push the message of her legitimacy and rightful position as Queen; Elizabeth used progresses to travel around the country so many people could see her – although this was restricted to the south and midlands of England.

Edexcel

1.

In answers candidates have shown...	Level	Mark
A simple generalised answer lacking structure.	1	1–3
Explanation with limited analysis.	2	4–6
Explanation with own knowledge.	3	7–9
A sustained explanation and analysis.	4	10–12

Level 4 answers should include: Elizabeth was reluctant to name a successor because for much of her reign the rightful heir was Mary, Queen of Scots, who she saw as a rival and a Catholic threat; Elizabeth never married and avoided any marriage alliance – both domestic and foreign – because she did not want to commit herself to a single alliance and feared the divisions such an alliance would bring; also, Elizabeth may have avoided marriage for personal reasons.

2.

In answers candidates have shown...	Level	Mark
A simple undeveloped answer.	1	1–4
Accurate explanation with limited analysis.	2	5–8
Explanation with their own knowledge reaching a limited judgement.	3	9–12
A sustained analytical explanation with substantiated judgement.	4	10–16

Level 4 answers should include: England was still at war with France and the war was going badly – England had lost Calais; Catholics saw Elizabeth as the product of an illegal marriage (Henry VIII and Anne Boleyn) and, therefore, was illegitimate and should not be queen; England was nearly bankrupt in 1558 but was fighting an expensive war and had commitments, such as expanding the navy; other factors also faced Elizabeth – rising unemployment, rising inflation; a conclusion to explain how far you agree.

Eduqas

1.

In answers candidates have shown...	Level	Mark
Basic unsupported judgement.	1	1–3
Some judgement using source.	2	4–5
Explains judgement using source and contextual knowledge.	3	6–8

Level 3 answers should include: Source argues that prices had been constantly rising. Could apply the knowledge here of poor harvests in the 1550s led to prices accelerating upwards; wages could not keep up with rising prices and this meant that people could afford less and living standards declined.

2.

In answers candidates have shown...	Level	Mark
Basic unsupported links.	1	1–3
Some explanation of connections.	2	4–6
Explanation of connections within context.	3	7–8
Full explanation of connections within detailed context.	4	9–10

Level 4 answers could include: Suggested connections could be: Privy Council was the executive decision making body of Parliament; Lord Burghley was the most powerful minister who sat in the Privy Council; members of the House of Commons also sat in Parliament.

OCR B

1.

In answers candidates have shown...	Level	Mark
An imbalanced answer – looks at one side of the argument without detail.	1	0–4
Some explanation and looks at both sides of the argument.	2	5–10
Explanation and good knowledge – some imbalance between different parts of the argument.	3	11–16
Sustained explanation with applied knowledge and both sides of argument fully addressed.	4	17–20

Level 4 answers should include: William Cecil was an experienced minister who had served under Edward; held the highest offices and seen as very able; also, had strong anti-Catholic views in line with many in government at the time so was sympathetic to fighting Catholics who were a threat to Elizabeth. He was very loyal to the Queen; Sir Francis Walsingham was very important as he built up a strong spy network that helped stop plots against Elizabeth; a conclusion to explain how far you agree.

2.

In answers candidates have shown...	Level	Mark
Extraction of information from source.	1	0–1
An inference or two without support from the source but uses own knowledge well.	2	2
Two inferences supported by own knowledge and sources.	3	3

Level 3 answers should include: Reference to the clothes Elizabeth is wearing in the painting; reference to the objects Elizabeth is holding in the painting – the orb and sceptre, symbols of her authority.

Page 199: The Elizabethan Religious Settlement

AQA

1.

In answers candidates have shown…	Level	Mark
One reason but no detail.	1	0–2
Two reasons with some detail.	2	3–5
Reasons with detail and linked them together.	3	6–8

Level 3 answers should include: How strictly the Settlement was enforced; how it upset both Catholics and Protestants because it did not go far enough according to their perspective; all catholic bishops resigned; most of the clergy took oath of loyalty to the new church.

2.

In answers candidates have shown…	Level	Mark
Points without detail.	1	0–2
Details to support each point.	2	3–5
Three or more points, each with supporting details.	3	6–8

Level 3 answers should include: Act of Supremacy made Elizabeth the Supreme Governor of the Church of England. This meant that she was Head of the Church but had a title that was acceptable to most Catholics and Protestants; Act of Uniformity ensured that acts of worship and church decoration were all the same across all churches in England. The English Prayer Book was central to this change.

Edexcel

1.

In answers candidates have shown…	Level	Mark
One mark for each point.	1	1–2
Two points explained with details.	2	3–4

Level 2 answers should include: Act of Supremacy made Elizabeth the Supreme Governor of the Church of England. This meant that she was Head of the Church but had a title that was acceptable to most Catholics and Protestants; Act of Uniformity ensured that acts of worship and church decoration were all the same across all churches in England. The English Prayer Book was central to this change.

2.

In answers candidates have shown…	Level	Mark
A simple generalised answer.	1	1–4
Limited explanation and depth.	2	5–8
Some explanation.	3	9–12
A sustained explanation and analysis.	4	13–16

Level 4 answers should include: The vague position on the doctrine of the Church of England – to tackle inconsistencies, two documents were issued, which moved the doctrine closer to Protestant views; the problems caused by the mass resignation of the clergy – left gap of highly trained clergy; the reaction of Catholics and Puritans – Advertisements issued in 1566; a conclusion to explain how far you agree.

Eduqas

1.

In answers candidates have shown…	Level	Mark
Basic unsupported judgement.	1	1–3
Some judgement using source.	2	4–5
Good judgement using source and contextual knowledge.	3	6–8

Level 3 answers should include: Expansion on 'Elizabeth had her own religious views' and outline that much of her early life was Protestant influenced, such as her tutor, Roger Ascham; but powerful elements of English society remained Catholic, e.g. the clergy and the House of Lords; the Elizabethan Religious Settlement aimed to find a 'middle way' that was acceptable to most Protestants and Catholics. Therefore, some form of compromise was inevitable to please the majority of people. Although extreme Protestants and Catholics would find the settlement unacceptable.

2.

In answers candidates have shown…	Level	Mark
Basic unsupported links.	1	1–3
Some explanation of connections.	2	4–6
Explanation of connections within context.	3	7–8
Full explanation of connections within detailed context.	4	9–10

Level 4 answers should explain the connection between two, for example: The Acts of Uniformity and Supremacy together made up the Elizabethan Religious Settlement; the work of the clergy in the Church of England was defined by the Act of Uniformity, such as the wearing of vestments and the use of the English Prayer Book; recusants refused to accept the Acts of Uniformity and Supremacy. These people were fined if they did not accept these laws.

OCR B

1.

In answers candidates have shown…	Level	Mark
An imbalanced answer – looks at one side of argument without detail.	1	0–4
Some explanation and looks at both sides of the argument.	2	5–10
Explanation and good knowledge – some imbalance between different parts of the argument.	3	11–16
Sustained explanation with applied knowledge and both sides of argument fully addressed.	4	17–20

Level 4 answers should include: The Elizabethan Religious Settlement was very vague about doctrine and this confused the clergy and the people; further legislation was needed to clarify the doctrinal position of the Church of England; a number of clergy resigned and there was not enough Protestant clerics to replace those who resigned; this meant that the overall quality of clergy declined and this caused discontent within congregations; pressure emerged from the Puritans; Elizabeth as Head of the Church was opposed by many; eventually, the Pope would excommunicate her; a conclusion to explain how far you agree.

2.

In answers candidates have shown…	Level	Mark
Extraction of information – uses sources descriptively.	1	0–3
Use of sources – looking at both sides of the argument.	2	4–6
Explanation of sources with some analysis and good knowledge – some imbalance between different parts of the argument.	3	7–9
Both sides of argument fully addressed and sources analysed.	4	10–12

Level 4 answers should: Compare both sources, looking for similarities as well as differences; Source A comments that the

Church was inconsistent while in Source B the Settlement had taken a permanent form; Source A suggests the Church had a positive outcome; Source B says it did not satisfy everyone; both suggest that the Settlement provided a middle ground.

Page 200: Elizabeth I and Spain, 1558–1587

AQA

1.

In answers candidates have shown…	Level	Mark
One reason but no detail.	1	0–2
Two reasons with some detail.	2	3–5
Reasons with detail and links them together.	3	6–8

Level 3 answers should include: The religious differences – Elizabeth was Protestant; Philip of Spain was Catholic; Elizabeth was excommunicated; the impact of the execution of Mary, Queen of Scots; Elizabeth's intervention in the Netherlands – she secretly supported them; English explorers (e.g. Hawkins, Drake) attacked the Spanish empire; French civil war meant Spain no longer worried about an Anglo–French alliance.

2.

In answers candidates have shown…	Level	Mark
Points without detail.	1	0–2
Details to support each point.	2	3–5
Three or more points, each with supporting details.	3	6–8

Level 3 answers should include: The trade links England had with Spain – Spain owned Antwerp, which England's economy relied on; Spain needed route through English channel; the reasons why Elizabeth and Philip avoided direct confrontation in the late 1560s and early 1570s – Elizabeth had rejected Philip's marriage proposal; Spain and England wanted to be on good terms and had a solid friendship.

Edexcel

1.

In answers candidates have shown…	Level	Mark
A simple undeveloped answer.	1	1–4
Accurate explanation with limited analysis.	2	5–8
Explanation with own knowledge reaching a limited judgement.	3	9–12
A sustained analytical explanation with substantiated judgement.	4	13–16

England had emerged as a Protestant nation and this had angered Spain; particular actions which are relevant here are Elizabeth's intervention in the Netherlands supporting Protestant exiles and the Pope excommunicating Elizabeth and encouraging her assassination; Elizabeth's heir was Mary, Queen of Scots and the Spanish supported a number of plots to make her Queen of England, most notably the Ridolfi Plot; there was a personal element too in that Elizabeth rejected Philip II of Spain's hand in marriage in 1558. This offended Philip who never quite trusted her again; a conclusion to explain how far you agree.

2.

In answers candidates have shown…	Level	Mark
One mark for each point.	1	1–2
Two points explained with details.	2	3–4

Level 2 answers should include: The trade links England had with Spain – Spain owned Antwerp, which England's economy relied on; Spain needed route through English channel; the

reasons why Elizabeth and Philip avoided direct confrontation in the late 1560s and early 1570s – Elizabeth had rejected Philip's marriage proposal; Spain and England wanted to be on good terms and had a solid friendship.

Eduqas

1.

In answers candidates have shown…	Level	Mark
A simple general answer.	1	1–3
Some explanation but inconsistent.	2	4–6
Explanation and good knowledge.	3	7–9
Sustained explanation with applied knowledge.	4	10–12

Level 4 answers should include: Spanish resources dwarfed England's; Spain's military resources were more than double compared with England; Spain had been involved in a number of plots against Elizabeth, such as the Ridolfi and Throckmorton Plots; the Pope excommunicated Elizabeth in 1570 and ordered Catholics to overthrow her.

2.

In answers candidates have shown…	Level	Mark
Basic unsupported links.	1	1–3
Some explanation of connections.	2	4–6
Explanation of connections within context.	3	7–8
Full explanation of connections within detailed context.	4	9–10

Level 4 answers should explain the connection between two, for example: Philip II and Elizabeth I both competed for trade routes in the New World; Catholic plots targeted to remove Elizabeth I as Queen of England; both Philip II and Elizabeth I were monarchs and were related as Philip had married Elizabeth's older sister, Mary.

OCR B

1.

In answers candidates have shown…	Level	Mark
An imbalanced answer – looks at one side of argument without detail.	1	0–4
Some explanation and looks at both sides of the argument.	2	5–10
Explanation and good knowledge – some imbalance between different parts of the argument.	3	11–16
Sustained explanation with applied knowledge and both sides of argument fully addressed.	4	17–20

Level 4 answers should include: Examples of Elizabeth's intervention in the Netherlands – supplying money and arms, allowing Dutch ships to use English ports and sheltering Dutch exiles; Catholic threat – Papal Bull of excommunication, various plots, such as the Ridolfi Plot, and the presence of Mary, Queen of Scots as a Catholic heir to the throne, who Spain preferred over Elizabeth; the attacks on the Spanish empire in the New World; a conclusion to explain how far you agree.

2.

In answers candidates have shown…	Level	Mark
An imbalanced answer – looks at one side of argument without detail.	1	0–4
Some explanation and looks at both sides of the argument.	2	5–10
Explanation and good knowledge – some imbalance between different parts of the argument.	3	11–16
Sustained explanation with applied knowledge and both sides of argument fully addressed.	4	17–20

Level 4 answers should include: Elizabeth's actions included assisting Dutch rebels, attacking Spanish interests in the New World and antagonising Spain with the policy of harassment, such as the seizure of Spanish bullion; Spain's actions included trade embargo on England and supporting plots against Elizabeth, such as the Ridolfi plot; a conclusion to explain how far you agree.

Page 201: Elizabeth I and Mary, Queen of Scots

AQA

1.

In answers candidates have shown…	Level	Mark
One reason but no detail.	1	0–2
Two reasons with some detail.	2	3–5
Reasons with detail and links them together.	3	6–8

Level 3 answers should include: The impact of the marriage to Lord Darnley on Mary's reign; other reasons why Mary fell in Scotland – her marriage to Bothwell, relationship with the nobility, rising support for Protestantism in Scotland.

2.

In answers candidates have shown…	Level	Mark
Points without detail.	1	0–2
Details to support each point.	2	3–5
Three or more points each with supporting details.	3	6–8

Level 3 answers should include: Reasons why Mary was executed – the Babington plot, Mary on trial for treason and found guilty; the key stages of the events surrounding Mary, Queen of Scots; the consequences of her execution.

Edexcel

1.

In answers candidates have shown…	Level	Mark
A simple general answer.	1	1–3
Some explanation but inconsistent.	2	4–6
Explanation and good knowledge.	3	7–9
A sustained explanation with applied knowledge.	4	10–12

Level 4 answers should include: The differences in religion and the aims of Catholic plotters in wanting Mary as Queen of England – to liberate Mary and overthrow Elizabeth; family links with Mary being Elizabeth's closest relative; Mary declared Elizabeth I was a bastard and that Mary was rightful Queen of England.

2.

In answers candidates have shown…	Level	Mark
One mark for each point.	1	1–2
Two points explained with details.	2	3–4

Level 2 answers should include: Moved from place to place and imprisoned in houses that were in the centre of England so it would make it difficult for supporters to land in England from the sea and march on where Mary was imprisoned to free her; Mary was deliberately kept short of supplies, such as bedding and changes of clothes.

Eduqas

1.

In answers candidates have shown…	Level	Mark
A simple general answer.	1	1–3
Some explanation but inconsistent.	2	4–6
Explanation and good knowledge.	3	7–9
A sustained explanation with applied knowledge.	4	10–12

Level 4 answers should include: Mary was the rightful heir to the English throne but she was Catholic. Thus, she was a figurehead for any potential Catholic rebellion who wanted her as queen and not Elizabeth; Catholic foreign powers also wanted Mary to replace Elizabeth and any potential invasion would have this as an objective.

2.

In answers candidates have shown…	Level	Mark
Basic unsupported links.	1	1–3
Some explanation of connections.	2	4–6
Explanation of connections within context.	3	7–8
Full explanation of connections within detailed context.	4	9–10

Level 4 answers should explain the connection between two, for example: The Northern Rebellion was led by Catholic nobles in the north who wanted to get rid of Elizabeth as Queen of England; the Throckmorton Plot and the Northern Rebellion had the common objective of overthrowing Elizabeth and replacing her with Mary.

OCR B

1.

In answers candidates have shown…	Level	Mark
An imbalanced answer – looks at one side of the argument without detail.	1	0–4
Some explanation and looks at both sides of the argument.	2	5–10
Explanation and good knowledge – some imbalance between different parts of the argument.	3	11–16
A sustained explanation with applied knowledge and both sides of argument fully addressed.	4	17–20

Level 4 answers should include: Darnley was a poor choice of husband despite his Tudor family links; he was a drunk, a gambler and wildly jealous of Mary's professional relationship with her secretary, David Rizzio; Mary's marriage with Bothwell split the Scottish nobility, those who hated Bothwell led a rebellion which overthrew Mary as Queen of Scotland. Bothwell fled leaving Mary alone; Mary's escape to England was a misjudgement as she underestimated how far Elizabeth saw her as a threat and that Mary was not going to get the mercy she thought Elizabeth would give her; a conclusion to explain how far you agree.

2.

In answers candidates have…	Level	Mark
Described information from the source.	1	0–1
Made an inference from the source.	2	2
Made two inferences supported by own knowledge and sources.	3	3

Level 3 answers should include: The position of the people in the painting; how Mary is portrayed in the painting; the reaction of people to Mary in the painting.

Page 203: The Attack of the Spanish Armada, 1588

AQA

1.

In answers candidates have shown…	Level	Mark
One reason but no detail.	1	0–2
Two reasons with some detail.	2	3–5
Reasons with detail and links them together.	3	6–8

Level 3 answers should include: Comparison of the different ships – size, speed, shape, 200 English ships, 130 Spanish ships; English galleons smaller but very fast; comparison of the foot soldiers – projected numbers and quality of trained troops; 20000 English soldiers plus 14000 sailors (many untrained), 30000 trained Spanish men; comparison of strategies, for example, the Spanish crescent formation and how the English tried to break it.

2.

In answers candidates have shown…	Level	Mark
One reason but no detail.	1	0–2
Two reasons with some detail.	2	3–5
Reasons with detail and links them together.	3	6–8

Level 3 answers should include: Drake's Cadiz raid; the growing importance of religious differences; Elizabeth's support of the Netherlands against the Spanish; the execution of Mary, Queen of Scots.

Edexcel

1.

In answers candidates have shown…	Level	Mark
A simple undeveloped answer.	1	1–4
Accurate explanation with limited analysis.	2	5–8
Explanation with own knowledge reaching a limited judgement.	3	9–12
A sustained analytical explanation with substantiated judgement.	4	13–16

Level 4 answers should include: Bad weather sunk more ships in the Spanish Armada when it fled across the North Sea compared with the fighting it had undertaken with the English ships; fireships broke the Spanish Armada's crescent formation. When in the crescent formation, the Spanish Armada was unbeatable and the English navy had failed to penetrate the Armada. Fireships caused panic and fear and the Spanish Armada broke ranks and lost its discipline which the English capitalised upon; the plans of the Spanish Armada were deeply flawed, for example no ports were secured in the Netherlands or in England for them to land and pick up and unload soldiers; preparations of the attack were hampered by Drake's Cadiz raid which destroyed much of the supplies and ships that made up the Spanish Armada; many of the Spanish ships were transport ships ill-suited for fighting much faster and smaller English ships; a conclusion to explain how far you agree.

2.

In answers candidates have shown…	Level	Mark
A simple generalised answer lacking structure.	1	1–3
Explanation with limited analysis.	2	4–6
Explanation with own knowledge.	3	7–9
A sustained explanation and analysis.	4	10–12

Level 4 answers should include: Elizabeth's intervention in the Netherlands which increased through the 1570s and 1580s in terms of money and arms infuriated Philip; Philip had drawn up a clear plan of action and he had the resources to launch, in his eyes, a decisive strike on England; the execution of the Catholic heir and fellow monarch, Mary, Queen of Scots, antagonised Philip who saw Elizabeth's actions as illegal and a blow to the Catholic world. Philip wanted to make England back into a Catholic country and he now saw that under Elizabeth, this would never happen so she needed to be replaced.

Eduqas

1.

In answers candidates have shown…	Level	Mark
A generalised answer – does not refer to both sources.	1	1–2
An analysis and use of both sources.	2	3–4

Level 2 answers should include: the strengths and weaknesses of the Armada shown in the sources such as the Armada's use of the formidable crescent formation versus the large, slow transport ships they used; the English had more equipment/ were more suited to fighting.

2.

In answers candidates have shown…	Level	Mark
A simple general answer.	1	1–3
Some explanation but inconsistent.	2	4–6
Explanation and good knowledge.	3	7–9
A sustained explanation with applied knowledge.	4	10–12

Level 4 answers should include: The actions of the English ships – fireships, fending off the Spanish attack across the English Channel; the type of ships the English used; the factors that could be put down to bad luck – bad weather, for example; English had more naval experience; Spanish plan was unclear about where to land.

OCR B

1.

In answers candidates have shown…	Level	Mark
Extraction of information from source.	1	0–1
An inference or two without support from the source but uses own knowledge well.	2	2
Two inferences supported by own knowledge and sources.	3	3

Level 3 answers should include: Elizabeth's hand over a globe indicates her control of the world and that her power spreads far across the world – this may refer to her influence spreading to the New World; behind Elizabeth are ships in combat in one panel and in another Spanish ships defeated and sinking in the sea.

2.

In answers candidates have shown...	Level	Mark
Extraction of information – uses sources descriptively.	1	0–3
Use of sources and looking at both sides of the argument.	2	4–6
Explanation of sources with some analysis and good knowledge – some imbalance between different parts of the argument.	3	7–9
Both sides of argument fully addressed and sources are analysed.	4	10–12

Level 4 answers should include: Interpretation A blames the defeat of the Spanish Armada on the bad weather whereas Interpretation B looks at the alternative reason of the differing types of ships between the English and Spanish with the English ships more suited to combat; A was by Philip II, who probably did not want to accept that the English had fought better.

Page 204: Threats Posed to Elizabeth I, 1558–1601

AQA

1.

In answers candidates have shown...	Level	Mark
One reason but no detail.	1	0–2
Two reasons with some detail.	2	3–5
Reasons with detail and links them together.	3	6–8

Level 3 answers should include: The nature of Catholic opposition – plots and rebellions – Northern Rebellion, Ridolfi Plot, Throckmorton Plot, Babington Plot; the aims of Catholic opposition – to overthrow or murder Elizabeth and replace her with Mary.

2.

In answers candidates have shown...	Level	Mark
Points without detail.	1	0–2
Details to support each point.	2	3–5
Three or more points, each with supporting details.	3	6–8

Level 3 answers should include: Why Essex rebelled – personal slights – his major business interest was taken away from him; look at how close the rebellion was to succeeding – think about the extent of the rebellion and how many joined the Earl of Essex in his rebellion – 300 rebels; after arresting members of the Privy Council, they marched on the centre of London; after 12 hours, Essex was arrested.

Edexcel

1.

In answers candidates have shown...	Level	Mark
A simple undeveloped answer.	1	1–4
Accurate explanation with limited analysis.	2	5–8
Explanation with own knowledge reaching a limited judgement.	3	9–12
A sustained analytical explanation with substantiated judgement.	4	13–16

Level 4 answers should include: Religion was a growing threat from 1570 with the Papal Bull of excommunication; between then and the Throckmorton Plot, there had been the growth of seminary priests and Jesuits secretly entering England and conducting underground Catholic ceremonies. This threat intensified anti-Catholic government reaction but also increased the desire of some Catholics to remove Elizabeth, such as the Throckmorton Plot; the Vatican and the Spanish were becoming increasingly dissatisfied with Elizabeth's anti-Catholic measures, consequentially; their actions were becoming more confrontational, such as Spanish backing plots to remove Elizabeth; Throckmorton believed that he had the backing of foreign Catholics to remove Elizabeth; Mary, Queen of Scots was a figurehead for such Catholic rebellions and provided a realistic and acceptable monarch for many English Catholics; a conclusion to explain how far you agree.

2.

In answers candidates have shown...	Level	Mark
One mark for each point.	1	1–2
Two points explained with details.	2	3–4

Level 2 answers should include: A Catholic inspired plot which aimed to remove Elizabeth; had Spanish backing and finances; the main consequence was that it damaged Anglo-Spanish relations to the extent the Spanish Ambassador was sent home.

Eduqas

1.

In answers candidates have shown...	Level	Mark
A generalised answer – does not refer to both sources.	1	1–2
An analysis and use of both sources.	2	3–4

Level 2 answers should include: Source A was hard evidence Walsingham needed to present to Elizabeth of Mary's threat to England; source B uses the word allegedly, which may mean that that Mary may not have communicated with Babington.

2.

In answers candidates have shown...	Level	Mark
A simple general answer.	1	1–3
Some explanation but inconsistent.	2	4–6
Explanation and good knowledge.	3	7–9
A sustained explanation with applied knowledge.	4	10–12

Level 4 answers should include: The Puritans were more co-ordinated in their opposition to Elizabeth in Parliament; the Puritans never invited foreign invaders to support them or campaigned for the removal of Elizabeth, but rather a change in policies and a government clampdown on Catholics; this limited their physical threat to Elizabeth.

OCR B

1.

In answers candidates have shown...	Level	Mark
Extraction of information – uses sources descriptively.	1	0–3
Use of sources and looking at both sides of the argument.	2	4–6
Explanation of sources with some analysis and good knowledge – some imbalance between different parts of the argument.	3	7–9
Both sides of argument fully addressed and sources are analysed.	4	10–12

Level 4 answers should include: The sources show a differing attitude of Essex; in Source A, Essex is seen to be loyal, trusted enough to have a private audience and conversation with the Queen and was quick to attend to her when summoned; source B's interpretation is different in that he is seen to act against the Queen's instructions by making peace in Ireland as well as acting outside the boundaries of his authority by rewarding his supporters; these actions made Elizabeth furious.

2.

In answers candidates have shown...	Level	Mark
An imbalanced answer – looks at one side of argument without detail.	1	0–4
Some explanation and looks at both sides of the argument.	2	5–10
Explanation and good knowledge – some imbalance between different parts of the argument.	3	11–16
A sustained explanation with applied knowledge and both sides of argument fully addressed.	4	17–20

Level 4 answers should include: The main short term consequence of the Babington Plot was the execution of Mary, Queen of Scots; this in turn caused shockwaves in the Catholic world in Europe; Philip was already planning an invasion of England even before the Babington Plot was uncovered so one can argue that the Babington Plot made little difference; however, what the Babington Plot did was hasten the Spanish invasion as well as make Protestants even more suspicious and intolerant of Catholics; a conclusion to explain how far you agree.

Page 206: Elizabethan Society
AQA

1.

In answers candidates have shown...	Level	Mark
One reason but no detail.	1	0–2
Two reasons with some detail.	2	3–5
Reasons with detail and links them together.	3	6–8

Level 3 answers should include: The developments in universities and grammar schools; the rising number of schools for the poor increased desire to read / write (printing press); influence of Renaissance.

2.

In answers candidates have shown...	Level	Mark
Points without detail.	1	0–2
Details to support each point.	2	3–5
Three or more points, each with supporting details.	3	6–8

Level 3 answers should include: For much of the Elizabethan period, poverty was not high on central government's priority list; it was the responsibility of local government to deal with poverty and, therefore, such provision was inconsistent depending on the town or city where the poor lived; particularly strong areas of provision were places like Ipswich and Norwich; Parliament passed laws in 1572 and 1576 to provide some poor relief and to punish vagabonds; increased poor relief was passed with the Elizabethan Poor Law of 1601.

Edexcel

1.

In answers candidates have shown...	Level	Mark
One mark for each point.	1	1–2
Two points explained with details.	2	3–4

Level 2 answers should include: The poor went to petty schools which taught basic skills in English and Maths; the rich went to grammar schools, which taught skills, such as being able to read Latin, which prepared students to go to university – a growing element of the education system; most of the rich were educated at home by tutors and then sent their children to university.

2.

In answers candidates have shown...	Level	Mark
A simple generalised answer lacking structure.	1	1–3
Explanation with limited analysis.	2	4–6
Explanation with own knowledge.	3	7–9
A sustained explanation and analysis.	4	10–12

Level 4 answers should include: The combined influence of the Renaissance, the Protestant Reformation and the printing press led to the skill of being able to read and write being highly desirable; this led to a growing demand in education; developments in grammar schools and universities; rising number of schools for the poor.

Eduqas

1.

In answers candidates have shown...	Level	Mark
A simple general answer.	1	1–3
Some explanation but inconsistent.	2	4–6
Explanation and good knowledge.	3	7–9
A sustained explanation with applied knowledge.	4	10–12

Level 4 answers should include: The sale of land made available from the Dissolution of the Monasteries in the 1530s and 1540s was bought by new landowners, many from the gentry; this land was rented out to farmers and enclosed, making profits for the gentry; the gentry invested in overseas voyages and new trading companies which became very successful; increased opportunities to hold government posts, both at local and national level.

2.

In answers candidates have shown...	Level	Mark
Basic unsupported links.	1	1–3
Some explanation of connections.	2	4–6
Explanation of connections within context.	3	7–8
Full explanation of connections within detailed context.	4	9–10

Level 4 answers should explain the connection between two, for example: The Elizabeth Poor Law centralised provision for the poor previously the responsibility of local government; vagabonds were seen as a danger to law and order in the provinces and they were targeted in the Elizabeth legislation for the poor; it was the responsibility of local government to ensure law and order was carried in out in the areas they were responsible for.

OCR B

1.

In answers candidates have shown…	Level	Mark
An imbalanced answer – looks at one side of argument without detail.	1	0–4
Some explanation and looks at both sides of the argument.	2	5–10
Explanation and good knowledge – some imbalance between different parts of the argument.	3	11–16
A sustained explanation with applied knowledge and both sides of argument fully addressed.	4	17–20

Level 4 answers should include: Although Parliament and Privy Council discussed the impact of poverty, it was never a high priority for Elizabeth compared with religion and foreign policy; therefore, the problem of growing poverty was passed on to local government to deal with; local governments had an inconsistent approach to dealing with poverty; impressed with the work in Ipswich, Norwich and London and with food prices continuing to rise, Parliament passed laws in 1572 and 1576 to provide some poor relief and to punish vagabonds; this had a limited impact so increased poor relief was passed with the Elizabethan Poor Law of 1601 and was seen as the definitive act that governments used to control and provide provision for the poor; a conclusion to explain how far you agree.

2.

In answers candidates have shown…	Level	Mark
Extraction of information from source.	1	0–1
An inference or two without support from the source but uses own knowledge well.	2	2
Two inferences supported by own knowledge and sources.	3	3

Level 3 answers should include: The family are wearing dark clothes – probably Protestants; their hands are together in prayer before eating a meal.

Page 207: Elizabethan Culture

AQA

1.

In answers candidates have shown…	Level	Mark
One reason but no detail.	1	0–2
Two reasons with some detail.	2	3–5
Reasons with detail and links them together.	3	6–8

Level 3 answers should include: The theatre was a cheap form of entertainment and there were other attractions on offer, such as food and a place to be seen and make business contacts; there was an increase in high quality playwrights, such as William Shakespeare, who produced very popular plays.

2.

In answers candidates have shown…	Level	Mark
Points without detail.	1	0–2
Details to support each point.	2	3–5
Three or more points, each with supporting details.	3	6–8

Level 3 answers should include: Features of the Elizabethan theatre; a single stage surrounded by the groundlings, a standing area that was cheapest; surrounded by the galleries, which were covered and seated and cost more; design was based on 'inn yards'; built to control wandering groups of actors.

Edexcel

1.

In answers candidates have shown…	Level	Mark
One mark for each point.	1	1–2
Two points explained with details.	2	3–4

Level 2 answers could include: The growth of art – reference to the miniature; the growth of house building and the showing of wealth; literature – often political; music – religious/secular/male voice chairs.

2.

In answers candidates have shown…	Level	Mark
A simple generalised answer lacking structure.	1	1–3
Explanation with limited analysis.	2	4–6
Explanation with own knowledge.	3	7–9
A sustained explanation and analysis.	4	10–12

Level 4 answers should include: Theatres attracted large crowds that could be a source of social disorder; this was a particular problem because theatres were built outside the city walls and outside the control of the city authorities; Puritans thought theatres were the work of the Devil that produced vulgar plays which encouraged sinful behaviour.

Eduqas

1.

In answers candidates have shown…	Level	Mark
A generalised answer – does not refer to both sources.	1	1–2
An analysis and use of both sources.	2	3–4

Level 2 answers should include: Views of the critics of the theatre that plays are vulgar; how people were using the theatre as a meeting place and a place to show off, especially for the young.

2.

In answers candidates have shown…	Level	Mark
Basic unsupported links.	1	1–3
Some explanation of connections.	2	4–6
Explanation of connections within context.	3	7–8
Full explanation of connections within detailed context.	4	9–10

Level 4 answers should explain the connection between two, for example: Blood sports, such as bear baiting and cock fighting, were often held in the yards of taverns; popular fashions were on display in miniatures which showed wealthy people wearing the expensive fashions of the period.

OCR B

1.

In answers candidates have shown...	Level	Mark
An imbalanced answer – looks at one side of the argument without detail.	1	0–4
Some explanation and looks at both sides of the argument.	2	5–10
Explanation and good knowledge – some imbalance between different parts of the argument.	3	11–16
A sustained explanation with applied knowledge and both sides of argument fully addressed.	4	16–20

Level 4 answers should include: The most popular form of art for the rich was the miniature; the rich collected miniatures as a sign of wealth as well as looking fashionable; miniatures were extremely beautiful works of art showing a portrait of an important person; the most popular form of music for the rich was religious music although there was a growth of secular music, particularly featuring male voice choirs; in contrast, alehouses and drinking beer were very popular and often the best way to get a meal if you were poor; at alehouses, you could buy tobacco, gamble at cards, dice or cockfighting and watch a play in the yard; there was a boom in architecture as courtiers built bigger and better homes for Elizabeth to visit; looking fashionable was an important part of Elizabethan society; key fashions of the Elizabethan era for men were wearing clothes which would show off their legs in hose and to emphasise the torso with flashed doublets; for women, rich jewellery, often in the form of miniatures, was important with long flowing robes made out of silk; a conclusion to explain how far you agree.

2.

In answers candidates have shown...	Level	Mark
Extraction of information from source.	1	0–1
An inference or two without support from the source but uses own knowledge well.	2	2
Two inferences supported by own knowledge and sources.	3	3

Level 3 answers should include: There are a lot of people watching the play; the theatre is a large building and this reflects its importance in society.

Page 209: Elizabeth I and the Wider World

AQA

1.

In answers candidates have shown...	Level	Mark
Points without detail.	1	0–2
Details to support each point.	2	3–5
Three or more points, each with supporting details.	3	6–8

Level 3 answers should include: Walter Raleigh obtained a royal patent to establish a colony in America in 1584; Raleigh established a colony which he called Virginia, named after Elizabeth I – 'the Virgin Queen'; the area was believed to contain an inexhaustible supply of wine, oil, sugar and flax; the colony did not prosper mainly because of a divided crew, bad weather and a poor choice about where to land in North America; the Virginia voyages are credited with introducing tobacco to England.

2.

In answers candidates have shown...	Level	Mark
One reason but no detail.	1	0–2
Two reasons with some detail.	2	3–5
Reasons with detail and links them together.	3	6–8

Level 3 answers should include: Drake returned to a hero's welcome and was knighted and celebrated bringing great wealth home with him; Drake's voyage caused anger and jealousy from Spain, who saw him as a pirate and one who had threatened their interests in the New World.

Edexcel

1.

In answers candidates have shown...	Level	Mark
A simple undeveloped answer.	1	1–4
Accurate explanation with limited analysis.	2	5–8
Explanation with own knowledge reaching a limited judgement.	3	9–12
A sustained analytical explanation with substantiated judgement.	4	13–16

Level 4 answers should include: Wealth – investors, such as merchants and the royal court, became very wealthy; overseas trade – new trade routes opened up during the reign of Elizabeth I and were managed by successful companies, such as The East India Company; power – England became a great sea power in the world; the navy – England developed a very strong navy which used cutting edge technology; a conclusion to explain how far you agree.

2.

In answers candidates have shown...	Level	Mark
One mark for each point.	1	1–2
Two points explained with details.	2	3–4

Level 2 answers should include: Walter Raleigh obtained a royal patent to establish a colony in America in 1584; Raleigh established a colony which he called Virginia, named after Elizabeth I – 'the Virgin Queen'; the area was believed to contain an inexhaustible supply of wine, oil, sugar and flax; the colony did not prosper mainly because of a divided crew, bad weather and a poor choice about where to land in North America; the Virginia voyages are credited with introducing tobacco to England.

OCR B

1.

In answers candidates have shown...	Level	Mark
Extraction of information from source.	1	0–1
An inference or two without support from the source but uses own knowledge well.	2	2
Two inferences supported by own knowledge and sources.	3	3

Level 3 answers should include: The number of countries and continents Elizabethan trade routes covered; what kind of luxury goods the trade routes brought to England.

2.

In answers candidates have shown…	Level	Mark
An imbalanced answer – looks at one side of argument without detail.	1	0–4
Some explanation and looks at both sides of the argument.	2	5–10
Explanation and good knowledge – some imbalance between different parts of the argument.	3	11–16
A sustained explanation with applied knowledge and both sides of argument fully addressed.	4	17–20

Level 4 answers should include: Under Elizabeth I, trade links within Europe increased, for example – The Eastland Company was established in 1579 to import goods from the Baltic; more luxury goods, such as silks and spices, were imported from the Mediterranean region; Richard Hakluyt's book – *The Principal Navigations, Voyages and Discoveries of the English Nation* – encouraged English sailors to make exploration voyages; this book was extremely influential; wider developments also encouraged exploration, such as inventions to assist travel, such as the compass; key developments in widening trade routes were that it brought great wealth to a number of businessmen; more trade routes opened up; England became a great trading power and the navy developed significantly in this period; a conclusion to explain how far you agree.

Health and Medicine – pages 210–225

Page 210: Medieval Medicine (Middle Ages) 1

AQA

1.

In answers candidates have shown…	Level	Mark
No answer or have made irrelevant statements.		0
Basic analysis of source.	1	1–2
Simple evaluation of source based on content and or provenance.	2	3–4
Developed evaluation of source with sustained judgement based on content and provenance.	3	5–6
Complex evaluation of source with sustained judgement based on content and provenance.	4	7–8

Level 4 answers should include: Useful – show's Galen's practical work; shows he supported the dissection of animals; his work was considered noteworthy; reliable due to the source being a drawing of a first-hand observation; Not useful – only one observation therefore is not representative; only shows Galen dissecting a pig, not his process or reasoning behind it.

2.

In answers candidates have shown…	Level	Mark
No answer or have made irrelevant statements.		0
Aspects of significance identified.	1	1–2
One aspect of significance briefly explained.	2	3–4
Developed aspects of significance explained.	3	5–6
Complex aspect of significance explained.	4	7–8

Level 4 answers should include: The impact and longevity of Galen's work; his Theory of Opposites; Christianity and Islam's support of Galen; the impact he had on other individuals such as Vesalius.

Edexcel

1.

In answers candidates have shown…	Level	Mark
No answer or irrelevant statements.		0
General knowledge with limited understanding.	1	1–2
Good knowledge with understanding.	2	3–4

Level 2 answers could include: Muslims believed in Galen and Hippocrates' work; books written by Muslims influenced beliefs in Britain and the rest of the Western world; because of the Koran, Muslims believed it was wrong to oppose Galen, therefore beliefs were not questioned.

2.

In answers candidates have shown…	Level	Mark
No answer or irrelevant statements.		0
One general statement to answer the question with simple knowledge.	1	1–2
Limited explanation and some knowledge.	2	3–4
Explanation with some reasoning and good knowledge.	3	5–8
Good explanation with reasoning and wide ranging knowledge.	4	9–12

Level 4 answers should include: Hospitals focused on 'care not cure'; they were run by monks and nuns therefore there was no science behind treatments; they were not intent on improving people's health if they were ill, just people's wellbeing; one of the main treatments was prayer; they did not understand how to improve people's health.

Eduqas

1.

In answers candidates have shown…	Level	Mark
No answer or have made irrelevant statements		0
A generalised response which largely paraphrases the sources with little attempt at analysis and evaluation.	1	1–2
Some understanding with a partial attempt to analyse and evaluate the reliability of both sources. Some consideration of the content and authorship of both sources with an attempt to reach a judgement set within the appropriate historical context.	2	3–4
Detailed understanding to fully analyse and evaluate the reliability of both sources. Analysis of the content and authorship of both sources, producing a clear, well substantiated judgement set within the appropriate historical context.	3	5–6

Level 3 answers should include: Source detail: Source A is from an artist who was around during the period and may have seen the types of treatments given to patients; this would make the source reliable; however, we do not know the name of the artist and their purpose for drawing this so the painting may be less reliable; the source also only shows two ways in which people were treated in hospitals: through herbal medicine and rest; other treatments include prayer and superstition and these are not shown; the source only shows one patient being treated; the artist may have lied about what he or she could have seen; Source B shows rules from a medieval hospital; this would be reliable as it is evidence from a specific hospital at the time; but these are only rules from one hospital and may not represent all hospitals; therefore could be unreliable; contextual knowledge: Medieval hospitals did not usually admit people who were ill, but rather people who were old or needed rest; hospitals did have rules and these were displayed for patients.

2.

In answers candidates have shown…	Level	Mark
No answer or irrelevant statements.		0
One general statement to answer the question.	1	1–2
A brief explanation with some understanding.	2	3–5
Detailed understanding with explanation.	3	6–8

Level 3 answers should include: Lack of scientific knowledge in the development of treatments; lack of willingness in the change of attitudes; the importance of the Church in not allowing progress; the importance of Galen's beliefs; the importance of the public's religious beliefs; lack of understanding about what caused disease.

OCR B

1.

In answers candidates have shown…	Level	Mark
No answer or irrelevant statements.		0
Some knowledge that shows some understanding.	1	1–3
Range of knowledge that shows some understanding.	2	4–6
Range of well selected relevant knowledge throughout the answer that shows understanding.	3	7–9

Level 3 answers should include: Hospitals focused on 'care not cure'; the increase in number of hospitals in the medieval period; the belief of the Church that it was their duty to look after people; hospitals were run by monks and nuns; they were places of rest for the old or poor rather than people who were actually ill; focused on providing healthy food, rest and prayer to their patients; nuns would create herbal remedies for their patients and there was no science in their treatments.

2.

In answers candidates have shown…	Level	Mark
No answer or irrelevant statements.		0
Some knowledge and some understanding.	1	1–3
Good knowledge with some understanding of one or more points.	2	4–5
Good knowledge with good understanding of one or more points.	3	6–7
Strong knowledge with strong understanding of one or more points.	4	8–10

Level 4 answers should include: Hospitals focused on 'care not cure'; they were run by monks and nuns, therefore there was no science behind treatments; they were not intent on improving people's health if they were ill, just people's wellbeing; ill people were discouraged from going to hospital; one of the main treatments was prayer; they did not understand how to improve people's health.

Page 212: Medieval Medicine (Middle Ages) 2
AQA

1.

In answers candidates have shown…	Level	Mark
No answer or have made irrelevant statements.		0
Basic analysis of source.	1	1–2
Simple evaluation of source based on content and or provenance.	2	3–4
Developed evaluation of source with sustained judgement based on content and provenance.	3	5–6
Complex evaluation of source with sustained judgement based on content and provenance.	4	7–8

Level 4 answers should include: Useful – shows symptoms such as buboes, fever, fatigue; Not useful – doesn't show symptoms such as sweating and sickness; doesn't show pneumonic symptoms such as breathlessness.

2.

In answers candidates have shown…	Level	Mark
No answer or have made irrelevant statements.		0
Basic explanation of one similarity.	1	1–2
Simple explanation of one similarity.	2	3–4
Developed explanation of similarities.	3	5–6
Complex explanation of similarities.	4	7–8

Level 4 answers should include: Little understanding of the causes of the outbreaks; high death rates; disease and lack of sanitation increased death rates; government cleaned up the streets due to the outbreaks; conditions improved, although only very slightly in the Middle Ages.

Edexcel

1.

In answers candidates have shown…	Level	Mark
No answer or irrelevant statements.		0
A generalised answer with limited knowledge.	1	1–4
Explanation with limited analysis and some relevant information. Unsupported judgement.	2	5–8
Explanation with some analysis and a good range of relevant information. Judgement with some support.	3	9–12
Detailed explanation with analysis and a wide range of relevant information. Judgement with support.	4	13–16

Level 4 answers should include: Agree – the Christian church was in charge of healthcare in Britain; the Church did not like to contradict Galen so progress was not made; as people were taught that God caused illness, people prayed to be made better rather than search for treatments that would work; Disagree – the Roman public health system hadn't been maintained; people's attitudes were not progressive – they didn't try to find reasons for illness; the belief was that people should be cared for rather than cured; there was lack of scientific knowledge and understanding; a conclusion to explain how far you agree.

2.

In answers candidates have shown...	Level	Mark
No answer or irrelevant statements.		0
One general statement to answer the question with simple knowledge.	1	1–2
Limited explanation and some knowledge.	2	3–4
Explanation with some reasoning and good knowledge.	3	5–8
Good explanation with reasoning and wide ranging knowledge.	4	9–12

Level 4 answers should include: People did not understand the causes of the Black Death; preventions and 'cures' did not work. Preventions included: Flagellants would whip themselves in order to receive forgiveness from God; carrying sweet smelling herbs to avoid the bad air – it was believed if you can't smell it, it wouldn't make you ill; praying – people would pray to God to ask for forgiveness for their sins. They believed if they repented, God would have mercy on them and make them well; staying indoors and lighting fires – it was believed that if you lit a fire you would kill the 'bad air'; clearing up street rubbish – although this could have helped, people did not understand Germ Theory, therefore this was not enforced.

Eduqas

1.

In answers candidates have shown...	Level	Mark
No answer or irrelevant statements.		0
A general statement of either a similarity or difference.	1	1–2
Explanation of similarity and difference between both sources.	2	3–4

Level 2 answers should include: Similarity – beliefs about the cause of illness were based on incorrect views; Difference – source A shows that people believed that imbalances within the body caused illness whereas Source B shows that God was responsible for all illnesses; Source A shows the four humours and the idea that individuals should try to look after their health themselves; Source B shows that people did not need to worry about their health as this rested with God.

2.

In answers candidates have shown...	Level	Mark
No answer or irrelevant statements.		0
Weak, generalised knowledge to support description.	1	1
Good knowledge to support description.	2	2–3
Detailed knowledge to support description.	3	4–5

Level 3 answers should include: Religious – punishment for disobeying God/sinning; miasma: bad air (smells in the air from rubbish in the streets); planets – people believed that

if planets such as Mars and Jupiter were too close together, this would cause the Plague; strangers – Jews, strangers, witches or anyone considered an 'outsider' were met with suspicion.

OCR B

1.

In answers candidates have shown...	Level	Mark
No answer or irrelevant statements.		0
Some knowledge with some basic understanding. Unclear explanation with an unclear judgement.	1	1–3
Sound knowledge with some understanding. Limited explanation with a loosely supported judgement.	2	4–6
Strong knowledge with generally clear understanding. Attempted explanation with attempted supported judgement.	3	7–10
Strong knowledge with secure understanding. Convincing explanation in most parts with a supported judgement.	4	11–14
Strong knowledge with secure understanding. Convincing explanation throughout with a well supported judgement.	5	15–18

Level 5 answers should include: Agree – There was a lack of scientific knowledge because of the importance of religious beliefs; people did not believe that Galen was wrong because the Church and Islam supported his views; people did not try to find ways to improve their health as they believed poor health was caused by God; Disagree – People did not understand the cause of disease; lack of understanding meant people did not invest time and money into science; people agreed with and believed in Galen and Hippocrates' views which were limited in scientific knowledge; the Romans left Britain without a sewer system; the government did not try to improve people's health; people continued to believe in the idea of the four humours; people continued to believe in the Theory of Opposites; a conclusion to explain how far you agree.

2.

In answers candidates have shown...	Level	Mark
No answer or irrelevant statements.		0
Some knowledge that shows some understanding.	1	1–3
Range of knowledge that shows some understanding.	2	4–6
Range of well selected relevant knowledge throughout the answer that shows understanding.	3	7–9

Level 3 answers should include: Religious – punishment for disobeying God/sinning; miasma – bad air (smells in the air from rubbish in the streets); planets – people believed that if planets such as Mars and Jupiter were too close together, this would cause the Plague; strangers – Jews, strangers, witches or anyone considered an 'outsider' was met with suspicion.

Page 213: Renaissance Medicine (1400s–1600s) 1

AQA

1.

In answers candidates have shown...	Level	Mark
No answer or irrelevant statements.		0
One general statement to answer the question.	1	1–2
A brief explanation of one reason to answer the question.	2	3–4
A brief explanation of several reasons to answer the question.	3	5–6

Level 3 answers should include: The publication of his famous book *The Fabric of the Human Body* in 1543; this was the most influential text during the Renaissance period; he stole and dissected bodies of criminals in the middle of the night; he was an Italian Professor of Surgery at Padua; he found that Galen had made several mistakes such as there was only one jawbone, not two and there were no invisible holes in the septum; Vesalius was the first person to openly challenge Galen.

2.

In answers candidates have shown...	Level	Mark
No answer or have made irrelevant statements.		0
Basic explanation of one similarity.	1	1–2
Simple explanation of one similarity.	2	3–4
Developed explanation of similarities.	3	5–6
Complex explanation of similarities.	4	7–8

Level 4 answers should include: Published influential works – *The Fabric of the Human Body* and *An Anatomical Account of the Motion of the Heart and Blood in Animals*); both disproved Galen – Vesalius proved that there was only one jaw bone, not two; both made discoveries about blood; both received some hostility because they disproved Galen.

Edexcel

1.

In answers candidates have shown...	Level	Mark
No answer or irrelevant statements.		0
Simple judgement with limited support. Lack of understanding of the sources.	1	1–2
A judgement with support. Understanding of the sources with some analysis.	2	3–5
Developed judgement with support including own knowledge. Understanding of the sources with analysis.	3	6–8

Level 3 answers should include: Source A is useful – shows Harvey's discovery that veins had valves and that blood was carried around the body through veins; detailed diagram from Harvey's book so it should be factually correct in relation to his discovery; Source B is useful – supports Source A in relation to Harvey's discovery; written after the time so would have based its content on a range of sources; there is a 'new introduction' therefore its previous content could have been revised and made even more correct/new information added; title makes it sound comprehensive; Source A is not useful – doesn't tell us that people still did not understand everything about blood or that Harvey concluded that the heart could be acting as a pump for the blood in the body; Source B is not useful – from the title we could surmise that the book may

be one sided as it may want to show William Harvey in an extremely positive light.

2.

1 mark awarded for each of the following:	Mark
Selecting a detail from the source that could form the basis of a follow-up enquiry.	1
Creation of a question that is linked to this detail.	1
Identification of an appropriate source to use.	1
Explanation of how the identified source might help answer the chosen follow-up question.	1

4 mark answers should include: From the details of the author (1) we could look at their background to check their qualifications and knowledge about William Harvey (1); We could check the references within their book to ensure that they have acknowledged a range of sources (1), and then follow up one of these sources to check it has been used correctly (1).

Eduqas

1.

In answers candidates have shown...	Level	Mark
No answer or irrelevant statements.		0
One general statement with source descriptions.	1	1–2
Some understanding and comment about reliability of both sources.	2	3–4
Detailed understanding of reliability with a judgement.	3	5–6

Level 3 answers should include: Source A is from Vesalius and he is saying that he will only state beliefs with confidence if he has lots of proof; this is reliable as we know that Vesalius dissected many bodies to prove his statements about anatomy, and worked tirelessly to prove these; however, Source A is less reliable because Vesalius may want to preserve his reputation by making people believe he doesn't state things without lots of research; Source B is from a website that is publicising great scientists and that these scientists are geniuses; this source could be seen as less reliable as it would be one-sided in its content about Vesalius in order to support the website's title; Source B could be seen as reliable as we know that Vesalius did publish the book stated in 1543 and that he was the first person to challenge Galen, therefore leading to the suggestion that he is the 'founder of the modern science of anatomy'.

2.

In answers candidates have shown...	Level	Mark
No answer or irrelevant statements.		0
General statements about the key issue.	1	1–2
Some knowledge and some understanding of the key issue and/or other factors.	2	3–4
Knowledge and some understanding of the issue. Some knowledge and some understanding of other factors.	3	5–8
Accurate knowledge and understanding of the issue. Some analysis and evaluation of other factors.	4	9–12
Accurate knowledge and understanding of the issue. Analysis and evaluation of other factors that leads to a supported judgement.	5	13–16

Level 5 answers should include: Harvey concluded that the heart acts like a pump after seeing a pump used to extinguish a fire; Vesalius had the confidence to prove that Galen was wrong; Harvey and Vesalius published influential books such as *The Fabric of the Human Body* and *An Anatomical Account of the Motion of the Heart and Blood in* Animals; Fabricius proved that veins had valves; Paré helped change people's ideas about surgery and found how to heal wounds better; Paré found that catgut ligatures could be used to tie arteries when limbs were amputated, causing less pain; Paré published *Apology and Treatise* in 1575 which taught surgeons how to better treat their patients; but, the reduction in the importance of religion meant people were starting to become more interested in science and new ideas; the increase in importance of science and technology – the printing press, pumps and microscopes allowed understanding to develop more quickly; the discovery and creation of microscopes allowed people to discover capillaries that transport blood to veins from the arteries; the printing press allowed ideas to spread very quickly; changing attitudes – people were slowly starting to accept Galen was wrong.

OCR B

1.

In answers candidates have shown…	Level	Mark
No answer or irrelevant statements.		0
Some knowledge with some basic understanding. Unclear explanation with an unclear judgement.	1	1–3
Sound knowledge with some understanding. Limited explanation with a loosely supported judgement.	2	4–6
Strong knowledge with generally clear understanding. Attempted explanation with attempted supported judgement.	3	7–10
Strong knowledge with secure understanding. Convincing explanation in most parts with a supported judgement.	4	11–14
Strong knowledge with secure understanding. Convincing explanation throughout with a well-supported judgement.	5	15–18

Level 5 answers should include: Agree – the discovery and creation of microscopes allowed people to discover capillaries that transport blood to veins from the arteries; the printing press allowed ideas to spread very quickly; it is suggested that Harvey concluded that the heart acts like a pump after seeing a pump used to extinguish a fire; Disagree – reduction in importance of religion – people were starting to become more interested in science and new ideas; changing attitudes – people were slowly starting to accept Galen was wrong; a conclusion to explain how far you agree.

2.

In answers candidates have shown…	Level	Mark
No answer or irrelevant statements.		0
Some knowledge and some understanding shown.	1	1–3
Good knowledge with some understanding of one or more points.	2	4–5
Good knowledge with good understanding of one or more points.	3	6–7
Strong knowledge with strong understanding of one or more points.	4	8–10

Level 4 answers should include: Although people's understanding about anatomy increased, people's understanding of health and illness did not; explanation of

the types of discoveries made by Vesalius, Harvey, Fabricius and Paré could be explored and identified as not improving people's understanding of what caused disease; it took a long time for people to support the new discoveries.

Page 216: Renaissance Medicine (1400s–1600s) 2

AQA

1.

In answers candidates have shown…	Level	Mark
No answer or irrelevant statements.		0
Relevant information from the source to answer the questions.	1	1–2
Descriptions of the sources.	2	3–4

Level 2 answers should include: Source A displays a negative attitude as it states that hospitals were run on a voluntary basis and not for all of society; whereas Source B displays positive attitudes as it states that hospitals had improved by the medieval period as they had increased in size and number as well as now admitting patients with illnesses.

2.

In answers candidates have shown…	Level	Mark
No answer or irrelevant statements.		0
One general statement to answer the question.	1	1–2
A brief explanation of one reason to answer the question.	2	3–4
A brief explanation of several reasons to answer the question.	3	5–6

Level 3 answers should include: Significant – the government passed measures such as installing public toilets and baths, and laws that streets needed to be kept clean; fines for people who did not keep streets clean. Insignificant – these laws were largely unsuccessful; the government did not believe it was their role to intervene in people's health; because it was believed that God caused illness, people felt that it was a waste of their money to spend it on improving health.

Edexcel

1.

In answers candidates have shown…	Level	Mark
No answer or irrelevant statements.		0
One general statement to answer the question with simple knowledge.	1	1–2
Limited explanation and some knowledge.	2	3–4
Explanation with some reasoning and good knowledge.	3	5–9
Good explanation with reasoning and wide ranging knowledge.	4	10–12

Level 4 answers should include: Although people's understanding about anatomy increased, people's understanding of health and illness did not; it took a long time for people to support the new discoveries; many treatments in hospitals did not change; hospitals' focus was still 'care not cure'; herbal remedies were still the main type of treatment used for illness; the Church still dominated in the field of health; the government did not contribute money towards trying to improve treating illnesses; people were still very religious therefore believed there was no point in trying to find cures for illnesses as this was controlled by God.

2.

In answers candidates have shown...	Level	Mark
No answer or irrelevant statements.		0
General knowledge with limited understanding.	1	1–2
Good knowledge with understanding.	2	3–4

Level 2 answers could include: Praying to God; use of herbal remedies; use of quack methods.

Eduqas

1.

In answers candidates have shown...	Level	Mark
No answer or have made irrelevant statements.		0
Basic analysis of source.	1	1–2
Simple evaluation of source based on content and or provenance.	2	3–4
Developed evaluation of source with sustained judgement based on content and provenance.	3	5–6
Complex evaluation of source with sustained judgement based on content and provenance.	4	7–8

Level 4 answers should include: Useful – explains the improvements made during the Renaissance period; infers that people's attitudes to hospitals changed; as a historian, her work will be based on fact so will be trustworthy; Not useful – does not give details as to which types of diseases were treated or examples of hospitals that were created; as she is promoting her book, she may exaggerate the impact of change.

2.

In answers candidates have shown...	Level	Mark
No answer or have made irrelevant statements.		0
Limited knowledge to describe the issue.	1	1–2
Knowledge to partially describe the issue.	2	3–5
Detailed knowledge to describe the issue within the historical context.	3	5–6

Level 3 answers should include: Although the government didn't think it was their role to intervene in public health, they passed some measures because public health was worsening; installation of public toilets; installation of public baths, but there were very few of these; passing of laws by towns to keep streets clean; people who did not keep streets clean were fined.

OCR B

1.

In answers candidates have shown...	Level	Mark
No answer or irrelevant statements.		0
Some knowledge with some basic understanding. Unclear explanation with an unclear judgement.	1	1–3
Sound knowledge with some understanding. Limited explanation with a loosely supported judgement.	2	4–6

In answers candidates have shown...	Level	Mark
Strong knowledge with generally clear understanding. Attempted explanation with attempted supported judgement.	3	7–10
Strong knowledge with secure understanding. Convincing explanation in most parts with a supported judgement.	4	11–14
Strong knowledge with secure understanding. Convincing explanation throughout with a well supported judgement.	5	15–18

Level 5 answers should include: Agree – after the dissolution of the monasteries, many hospitals were closed down; new hospitals were created which relied less on the church and more on local people and councils, meaning they were slightly less reliant on religious beliefs. Disagree – population increased therefore the size of hospitals needed to increase; some hospitals in London and Edinburgh started to admit patients with infectious diseases; simple surgeries were carried out in hospitals; the majority of physicians and doctors in hospitals had been trained at university; observation and bedside practice were improved through the work of Thomas Sydenham; a conclusion to explain how far you agree.

2.

In answers candidates have shown...	Level	Mark
No answer or irrelevant statements.		0
Some knowledge that shows some understanding.	1	1–3
Range of knowledge that shows some understanding.	2	4–6
Range of well selected relevant knowledge throughout the answer that shows understanding.	3	7–9

Level 3 answers should include: Religious – praying, whipping (with explanation); semi-scientific: banning large crowds, boarding up houses, burning cats and dogs (with explanation); herbal – smelling sweet herbs, use of quack doctors (with explanation).

Page 217: Industrial Medicine (1700s–1900) 1

AQA

1.

In answers candidates have shown...	Level	Mark
No answer or have made irrelevant statements.		0
Basic analysis of source.	1	1–2
Simple evaluation of source based on content and or provenance.	2	3–4
Developed evaluation of source with sustained judgement based on content and provenance.	3	5–6
Complex evaluation of source with sustained judgement based on content and provenance.	4	7–8

Level 4 answers should include: Useful – shows hostility of the public to new ideas; supports the view that many people did not like Chadwick's conclusions as the changes would mean higher taxes; Not useful – the author is unknown, therefore the reliability of the source is questionable; it is only one point of view and therefore doesn't give insight into the majority of the public's attitudes; it may have been published in *The Times* to cause reaction.

2.

In answers candidates have shown…	Level	Mark
No answer or have made irrelevant statements.		0
Basic explanation of one similarity.	1	1–2
Simple explanation of one similarity.	2	3–4
Developed explanation of similarities.	3	5–6
Complex explanation of similarities.	4	7–8

Level 4 answers should include: Increased government intervention due to high death rate (e.g. First and Second Public Health Acts); lack of understanding of the causes of disease; increased death rate due to poor public health; slow changing attitudes to preventative methods put in place.

Edexcel

1.

In answers candidates have shown…	Level	Mark
No answer or irrelevant statements.		0
One general statement to answer the question with simple knowledge.	1	1–2
Limited explanation and some knowledge.	2	3–4
Explanation with some reasoning and good knowledge.	3	5–9
Good explanation with reasoning and wide ranging knowledge.	4	10–12

Level 4 answers should include: Increase in population and size of towns; new back-to-back style housing; little fresh drinking water; new diseases such as cholera, typhoid and smallpox; resistance to new ideas; poor working conditions in factories; lack of fresh food; Public Health Act of 1848 only gave advisory policies, not enforcement policies; lack of support for Chadwick's conclusions; belief in 'laissez-faire' style approach to government; no Public Health Act in the 1850s; further outbreaks of cholera in 1865; real improvements did not occur until the second Public Health Act in 1875.

2.

In answers candidates have shown…	Level	Mark
No answer or irrelevant statements.		0
General knowledge with limited understanding.	1	1–2
Good knowledge with understanding.	2	3–4

Level 2 answers should include: Increase in scientific treatments; increase in use of pharmacies, patent medicines, and pills; decrease in use of herbal remedies.

Eduqas

1.

In answers candidates have shown…	Level	Mark
No answer or have made irrelevant statements.		0
Descriptive response with some understanding of key features.	1	1-2
Explanation with detailed understanding of key features.	2	3-5
Detailed explanation with detailed understanding of key features.	3	6-8

Level 3 answers should include: Population increase; people still did not know about germs so developments did not have a big impact; people still left rubbish and sewage in the streets, still drank dirty water and let animals roam around towns; the government passed measures such as installing public toilets and baths, laws that streets needed to be kept clean and fines for people who did not keep streets clean; these were not successful as the government did not believe it was their role to intervene in people's health; it was believed that God caused illness, people felt that it was a waste of their money to spend it on improving public health.

2.

In answers candidates have shown…	Level	Mark
No answer or have made irrelevant statements.		0
A generalised response which largely paraphrases the sources with little attempt at analysis and evaluation.	1	1–2
Some understanding with a partial attempt to analyse and evaluate the reliability of both sources. Some consideration of the content and authorship of both sources with an attempt to reach a judgement set within the appropriate historical context.	2	3–4
Detailed understanding to fully analyse and evaluate the reliability of both sources. Analysis of the content and authorship of both sources, producing a clear, well substantiated judgement set within the appropriate historical context.	3	5–6

Level 3 answers should include: Source A is reliable as it shows the research by Snow; Snow found that more people died of cholera around the pump in Broad Street; the source supports this knowledge; Source B is reliable as it also supports our knowledge that drinking from water pumps causes death; additionally, it was published in 1860 and there were cholera outbreaks in this decade which also makes it more reliable; it could be argued that Source A is less reliable as it was a map created by Snow, therefore he would not publish results that did not support his hypothesis; Source B is less reliable because it is a cartoon, therefore the purpose is to entertain and not just inform. This could mean that the cartoon exaggerates to capture the audience's attention.

OCR B

1.

In answers candidates have shown…	Level	Mark
No answer or irrelevant statements.		0
Some knowledge and some understanding shown.	1	1–3
Good knowledge with some understanding of one or more points.	2	4–5
Good knowledge with good understanding of one or more points.	3	6–7
Strong knowledge with strong understanding of one or more points.	4	8–10

Level 4 answers should include: Increase in population and size of towns; new back-to-back style housing; little fresh drinking water; new diseases such as cholera, typhoid and smallpox; resistance to new ideas; poor working conditions in factories; lack of fresh food; Public Health Act of 1848 only gave advisory policies, not enforcement policies; lack of support for Chadwick's conclusions; belief in 'laissez-faire' style approach to government; no Public Health Act in the 1850s; further outbreaks of cholera in 1865; real improvements did not occur until the second Public Health Act in 1875.

2.

In answers candidates have shown...	Level	Mark
No answer or irrelevant statements.		0
Some knowledge that shows some understanding.	1	1–3
Range of knowledge that shows some understanding.	2	4–6
Range of well selected relevant knowledge throughout the answer that shows understanding.	3	7–9

Level 3 answers could include: Progress – patent medicines; creation of pill machines; decrease in the use of herbal remedies; inoculations discovered by Edward Jenner; Pasteur developed the Germ Theory in 1861; Robert Koch discovered which specific germs caused disease; Ignaz Semmelweis found that using chlorinated lime water reduced infection; discovery of anaesthetics by James Simpson; Lister's discovery of antiseptics through using carbolic acid; move from antiseptic to aseptic surgery through Koch's realisation that sterilisation would eliminate germs. Limitations – people still used herbal remedies; some patent medicines did not work; there was little government control over patent medicines initially; people were slow to change their attitudes; people were still very religious and believed inoculations and vaccinations were going against God's wishes; the Royal Society initially refused to publish Jenner's ideas; the black period of surgery occurred between the discovery of anaesthetics and antiseptics.

Page 219: Industrial Medicine (1700s–1900) 2
AQA

1.

In answers candidates have shown...	Level	Mark
No answer or irrelevant statements.		0
Aspects of significance identified.	1	1–2
One aspect of significance briefly explained.	2	3–4
Developed aspects of significance explained.	3	5–6
Complex aspects of significance explained.	4	7–8

Level 4 answers should include: Inoculation of people with cowpox – found they did not contract smallpox; in 1840 the government paid for people to receive vaccinations against smallpox; in 1853 it became compulsory to be vaccinated against smallpox; in 1979 smallpox was finally wiped out around the world.

2.

In answers candidates have shown...	Level	Mark
No answer or irrelevant statements.		0
One general statement to answer the question.	1	1–4
Detailed understanding with evidence to support or oppose the factor in the question.	2	5–8
Detailed understanding with evidence to support or oppose the factor in the question and other factor(s).	3	9–12
Evaluation with evidence to support or oppose the factor in the question and other factor(s).	4	13–16

Level 4 answers should include: The work of John Snow, Jenner, Pasteur, Koch, Emil von Behring and Nightingale

was all very important in development; But consider the government's change in attitudes; the role of the government with the 1848 and 1875 Public Health Acts; the public's change in attitudes (although slow) started to embrace changes such as inoculation and anaesthetics; could include that changes such as inoculation and anaesthetics would not have taken place without the role of the individual; the increasing role of science and technology, such as patent medicines and pill machines.

Edexcel

1.

In answers candidates have shown...	Level	Mark
No answer or irrelevant statements.		0
Generalised answer with limited knowledge.	1	1–4
Explanation with limited analysis and some relevant information. Unsupported judgement.	2	5–8
Explanation with some analysis and a good range of relevant information. Judgement with some support.	3	9–12
Detailed explanation with analysis and a wide range of relevant information. Judgement with support.	4	13–16

Level 4 answers should include: Agree – in 1796 Edward Jenner inoculated people with cowpox and found they did not contract smallpox; in 1840 the government paid for people to receive vaccinations against smallpox; in 1853 it became compulsory to be vaccinated against smallpox. Disagree – people were slow to change their attitudes; some people believed that giving a human an animal's disease would cause them to grow animal features; people were still very religious and they believed inoculations and vaccinations were going against God's wishes; the Royal Society initially refused to publish Jenner's ideas, although eventually published them in 1798; a conclusion to explain how far you agree.

2.

In answers candidates have shown...	Level	Mark
No answer or irrelevant statements.		0
General knowledge with limited understanding.	1	1–2
Good knowledge with understanding.	2	3–4

Level 2 answers should include: People were slow to change their attitudes; people were still very religious and therefore believed scientific development was going against God's wishes.

Eduqas

1.

In answers candidates have shown...	Level	Mark
No answer or irrelevant statements.		0
General statement of either a similarity or difference.	1	1–2
Explanation of similarity and difference between both sources.	2	3–4

Level 2 answers should include: Similarity – Sources A and B show bed rest took place during both periods; Sources A and B show women worked in hospitals during both periods. Differences – Source B is more advanced as it shows the use of heaters; shows that hospitals during the Industrial period had a greater understanding of hygiene due to the difference in bed linen compared to Source A; Source A shows more of a focus on religion – crucifix in centre of image.

2.

In answers candidates have shown...	Level	Mark
No answer or irrelevant statements.		0
General statements about the key issue.	1	1–2
Some knowledge and some understanding of the key issue and/or other factors.	2	3–4
Knowledge and some understanding of the issue. Some knowledge and some understanding of other factors.	3	5–8
Accurate knowledge and understanding of the issue. Some analysis and evaluation of other factors.	4	9–12
Accurate knowledge and understanding of the issue. Analysis and evaluation of other factors that leads to a supported judgement.	5	13–16

Level 5 answers should include: Agree – anaesthetics decreased panic among patients during operations and increased the likelihood of people willing to undergo surgery. Disagree – antiseptics such as carbolic acid reduced infection during surgery; the discovery of sterilisation by Koch meant that instruments could be rid of germs completely; (anaesthetics actually increased the death rate, this was known as the black period of surgery.)

OCR B

1.

In answers candidates have shown...	Level	Mark
No answer or irrelevant statements.		0
Some knowledge and some understanding.	1	1–3
Good knowledge with some understanding of one or more points.	2	4–5
Good knowledge with good understanding of one or more points.	3	6–7
Strong knowledge with strong understanding of one or more points.	4	8–10

Level 4 answers should include: Key focus of hospitals remained 'care not cure'; the majority were unclean; lots of hospitals were set up by charities, meaning they were quite disorganised; Nightingale didn't support Pasteur's Germ Theory so developments in hygiene weren't fully effective.

2.

In answers candidates have shown...	Level	Mark
No answer or irrelevant statements.		0
Some knowledge with some basic understanding. Unclear explanation with an unclear judgement.	1	1–3
Sound knowledge with some understanding. Limited explanation with a loosely supported judgement.	2	4–6
Strong knowledge with generally clear understanding. Attempted explanation with attempted supported judgement.	3	7–10
Strong knowledge with secure understanding. Convincing explanation in most parts with a supported judgement.	4	11–14
Strong knowledge with secure understanding. Convincing explanation throughout with a well-supported judgement.	5	15–18

Level 5 answers should include: Agree – inoculations meant people no longer contracted smallpox; the government supported this by paying for people to receive vaccinations against smallpox; by 1853 it became compulsory to be vaccinated against smallpox meaning health improved; by 1979 smallpox was finally wiped out around the world; Disagree – people were slow to change their attitudes about smallpox and Jenner's vaccinations; the Royal Society initially refused to publish Jenner's ideas, although eventually published them in 1798; Pasteur developed his Germ Theory; Robert Koch discovered which specific germs caused disease; Emil von Behring used Koch and Pasteur's work to discover the way in which antibodies worked; Behring developed a cure for diphtheria; James Simpson's discovery of chloroform meant people no longer panicked during operations; Lister's discovery of antiseptics meant infection during surgery decreased; Koch's discovery of aseptic surgery meant infection during surgery would decrease further; a conclusion to explain how far you agree.

Page 221: Modern Medicine (1900s–Present) 1

AQA

1.

In answers candidates have shown...	Level	Mark
No answer or have made irrelevant statements.		0
Basic analysis of source.	1	1–2
Simple evaluation of source based on content and or provenance.	2	3–4
Developed evaluation of source with sustained judgement based on content and provenance.	3	5–6
Complex evaluation of source with sustained judgement based on content and provenance.	4	7–8

Level 4 answers should include: Useful – explains the importance of team work in the development of penicillin; explains the contribution of Florey and Chain's work; it is from Fleming himself so he will be an expert in this field; Not useful – as the source is from Fleming himself, commenting on receiving the Nobel Prize, he could be being modest in response to his prize, downplaying the importance of his discovery; or as it is an extract from a Nobel prize speech, Fleming could be exaggerating aspects in order for his speech to be more entertaining.

2.

In answers candidates have shown...	Level	Mark
No answer or irrelevant statements.		0
One general statement to answer the question.	1	1–2
A brief explanation of one reason to answer the question.	2	3–4
A brief explanation of several reasons to answer the question.	3	5–6

Level 3 answers should include: Importance of World War One regarding blood transfusions, and also mention clotting, skin grafts, surgery (including plastic surgery), mobile X-ray machines, transplant surgery and prosthetic limbs.

Edexcel

1.

In answers candidates have shown...	Level	Mark
No answer or irrelevant statements.		0
Simple judgement with limited support. Lack of understanding of sources.	1	1–2

In answers candidates have shown...	Level	Mark
Judgement with support. Understanding of the sources with some analysis.	2	3–5
Developed judgement with support including own knowledge. Understanding of the sources with analysis.	3	6–8

Level 3 answers should include: Sources A and B are useful because Source A shows that people giving anaesthetics and completing operations were not qualified, meaning that problems such as a high death rate occurred because there was a lack of staff; Source B shows that there were problems with blood transfusions and operations as not many people could be operated on and that there was a lack of confidence in the outcomes of these operations because of the conditions in which they were performed; Source B is also written by an army surgeon, who would have seen lots of operations take place, therefore there would be a reliable source; Sources A and B are not useful as they are only accounts by two individuals; we do not know if the conditions at Clearing Station 44 were representative of all Clearing Stations, additionally Source B is only from one army surgeon so we don't know if his experiences are representative; Own knowledge: There was lots of blood loss during wartime surgery, and this was a catalyst for the speed of developments in blood transfusions, therefore Sources A and B are representative.

2.

In answers candidates have shown...	Level	Mark
No answer or irrelevant statements.		0
Generalised answer with limited knowledge.	1	1–4
Explanation with limited analysis and some relevant information. Unsupported judgement.	2	5–8
Explanation with some analysis and a good range of relevant information. Judgement with some support.	3	9–12
Detailed explanation with analysis and a wide range of relevant information. Judgement with support.	4	13–16

Level 4 answers should include: Agree – ideas such as skin grafting, blood transfusions, genetics, stem cell research and magic bullets were accepted; less support for a laissez-faire style government – the government and the public were willing to accept the idea of more government intervention. Disagree – government intervention such as the USA's involvement in mass-producing penicillin; funding of the NHS; development of science and technology such as patent medicines and technologies such as refrigeration; the role of the individual such as Gilles, Franklin, Crick and Watson, Fleming; war was a turning point in speeding improvements in scientific treatment; a conclusion to explain how far you agree.

Eduqas

1.

In answers candidates have shown...	Level	Mark
No answer or irrelevant statements.		0
General statements about the key issue.	1	1–2
Some knowledge and some understanding of the key issue and/or other factors.	2	3–4
Knowledge and some understanding of the issue. Some knowledge and some understanding of other factors.	3	5–8

In answers candidates have shown...	Level	Mark
Accurate knowledge and understanding of the issue. Some analysis and evaluation of other factors.	4	9–12
Accurate knowledge and understanding of the issue. Analysis and evaluation of other factors that leads to a supported judgement.	5	13–16

Level 5 answers should include: Speeded up the developments and improvements in surgery, e.g. plastic surgery, use of mobile X-ray machines; blood transfusions without the problem of clotting; transplant surgery and prosthetic limbs. But, also consider the role of the individual – Harold Gilles, Marie Curie; Karl Landsteiner made his discovery of blood groups before the outbreak of war; Richard Weil, Rous and Turner; scientific development; changing attitudes.

2.

In answers candidates have shown...	Level	Mark
No answer or irrelevant statements.		0
One general statement with source descriptions.	1	1–2
Some understanding and comment about reliability of both sources.	2	3–4
Detailed understanding of reliability with a judgement.	3	5–6

Level 3 answers should include: Source A is reliable as it has been created by a fellow graduate of Cambridge meaning he would have no reason to negatively portray Crick and Watson; however, Blake is showing that Crick and Watson are not working as hard as Franklin, who was also from Cambridge; this is not a one-sided view; Source B is reliable as it is from a modern historian so they would have had conducted research into this topic in order to make their conclusions; Source A is not reliable as it is a cartoon therefore its purpose is to entertain so Blake may have exaggerated, e.g. Crick having a drink while Franklin works; Source B may be one-sided as it is from a page entitled 'Historical Figures' meaning it would portray Crick and Watson as extremely influential.

OCR B

1.

In answers candidates have shown...	Level	Mark
No answer or irrelevant statements.		0
Some knowledge that shows some understanding.	1	1–3
Range of knowledge that shows some understanding.	2	4–6
Range of well selected relevant knowledge throughout the answer that shows understanding.	3	7–9

Level 3 answers should include: Lack of understanding at the beginning of the nineteenth century; through experiments and research, Crick and Watson discovered the presence of DNA in human cells; this led to further understanding of genetics; Maurice Wilkins devised X-ray crystallography; Franklin discovered the double helix structure of DNA; stem cell research and Down's Syndrome can now be understood.

2.

In answers candidates have shown...	Level	Mark
No answer or irrelevant statements.		0
Some knowledge with some basic understanding. Unclear explanation with an unclear judgement.	1	1–3
Sound knowledge with some understanding. Limited explanation with a loosely supported judgement.	2	4–6
Strong knowledge with generally clear understanding. Attempted explanation with attempted supported judgement.	3	7–10
Strong knowledge with secure understanding. Convincing explanation in most parts with a supported judgement.	4	11–14
Strong knowledge with secure understanding. Convincing explanation throughout with a well-supported judgement.	5	15–18

Level 5 answers should include: Agree – USA's involvement meant antibiotics could be mass-produced because of the USA's funding; this helped wounded soldiers during the Second World War; without the USA's funding all previous work in the development of antibiotics would not have had an impact on patients; previously the development of antibiotics had been so slow due to lack of funding; Britain did not have the time or space to develop penicillin so needed the USA's help; Disagree – Fleming discovered antibiotics in 1928 through experiments; Florey and Chain's testing allowed governments to support the drug as it worked on humans; without the NHS, many people would not be able to afford penicillin; a conclusion to explain how far you agree.

Page 223: Modern Medicine (1900s–Present) 2

AQA

1.

In answers candidates have shown...	Level	Mark
No answer or have made irrelevant statements.		0
Basic explanation of one similarity.	1	1–2
Simple explanation of one similarity.	2	3–4
Developed explanation of similarities.	3	5–6
Complex explanation of similarities.	4	7–8

Level 4 answers should include: Both improved people's health; contributed to the welfare state; improved health of children, e.g. through 1906 School Meals Act and creation of NHS family doctors; gave help to older people e.g. 1908 Old Age Pensions Act and free access to prescriptions; both had a limited impact e.g. in both cases there was some opposition due to the need to increase taxes to fund the changes; some people still believed in a laissez-faire approach.

2.

In answers candidates have shown...	Level	Mark
No answer or irrelevant statements.		0
Answers that have basic description and/or some basic reasoning.	1	1–4
Answers that focus on the factor in the question or another factor.	2	5–8
Answers that focus on the factor in the question and another factor(s).	3	9–12
Answers that focus on the factor in the question and another factor(s) with evaluation.	4	13–16

Level 4 answers should include: Agree – war was a turning point/catalyst that speeded up improvements in scientific treatment; developments such as skin grafting, blood transfusions, and mobile X-rays all developed quickly because of the First World War; the Second World War highlighted problems in health, leading the NHS to be developed. Disagree – change in attitudes such as the acceptance of blood transfusions; less support for a laissez-faire style government – the government and the public were willing to accept the idea of more government intervention; government intervention such as the USA's involvement in mass producing penicillin; funding of the NHS; development of science and technology such as patent medicines and technologies such as refrigeration; the role of the individual such as Gilles, Franklin, Crick and Watson, Fleming; a conclusion to explain how far you agree.

Edexcel

1.

In answers candidates have shown...	Level	Mark
No answer or irrelevant statements.		0
One general statement to answer the question with simple knowledge.	1	1–2
Limited explanation and some knowledge.	2	3–4
Explanation with some reasoning and good knowledge.	3	5–9
Good explanation with reasoning and wide ranging knowledge.	4	10–12

Level 4 answers should include: Dislike for increase in taxes to fund the NHS; initially doctors thought they were being controlled too heavily by the government; some people still believed in a laissez-faire approach; initially charities and councils felt they were no longer needed for healthcare; the NHS is becoming extremely expensive; parts of the NHS are becoming privatised meaning people still need to pay for treatments; 'two-tier system' where the more wealthy receive better treatment due to the option of 'going private'.

2.

In answers candidates have shown...	Level	Mark
No answer or irrelevant statements.		0
General knowledge with limited understanding.	1	1–2
Good knowledge with understanding.	2	3–4

Level 2 answers should include one of the following: School meals had a positive impact on children's health; health visitors monitored young children and their mothers to check general health and wellbeing; Old Age Pensions Act gave financial support to elderly which improved their health; National Insurance Act gave workers some sick pay, support for the unemployed and medical treatment to those in work.

Eduqas

1.

In answers candidates have shown...	Level	Mark
No answer or irrelevant statements.		0
Weak, generalised knowledge to support description.	1	1
Good knowledge to support description.	2	2–3
Detailed knowledge to support description.	3	4–5

Level 3 answers should include: World War Two and evacuation highlighted Britain's poor public health; the 1944

William Beveridge report on the 'Five Evils' in Britain that the government needed to tackle, including disease and squalor; in 1948 Aneurin Bevan set up the National Health Service.

2.

In answers candidates have shown...	Level	Mark
No answer or have made irrelevant statements		0
A generalised response which largely paraphrases the sources with little attempt at analysis and evaluation.	1	1–2
Some understanding with a partial attempt to analyse and evaluate the reliability of both sources. Some consideration of the content and authorship of both sources with an attempt to reach a judgement set within the appropriate historical context.	2	3–4
Detailed understanding to fully analyse and evaluate the reliability of both sources. Analysis of the content and authorship of both sources, producing a clear, well substantiated judgement set within the appropriate historical context.	3	5–6

Level 3 answers should include: Source A – Reliable as it supports own knowledge – 1911 National Insurance Act gave sick benefit to workers who couldn't work; created by the Liberal Party to persuade the public to support the reforms; many were against the reforms as they believed in laissez-faire government; the National Insurance Act only covered men, not women, therefore this was not a 'dawn of hope' for all. Source B – reliable as it is a photograph meaning we can see what is actually happening rather than a drawing as in Source A; supports own knowledge – many old people were extremely happy with the impact of the Old Age Pensions Act; not reliable as its purpose is to persuade; created by the Liberal Party to highlight the benefits of their reforms; the photograph could be staged; many people did not support the reforms.

OCR B

1.

In answers candidates have shown...	Level	Mark
No answer or irrelevant statements.		0
Some knowledge that shows some understanding.	1	1–3
Range of knowledge that shows some understanding.	2	4–6
Range of well selected relevant knowledge throughout the answer that shows understanding.	3	7–9

Level 3 answers should include: School meals had a positive impact on children's health; health visitors monitored young children and their mothers to check general health and wellbeing; Old Age Pensions Act gave financial support to elderly which improved their health; National Insurance Act gave some workers sick pay, support for the unemployed and medical treatment to those in work.

2.

In answers candidates have shown...	Level	Mark
No answer or irrelevant statements.		0
Some knowledge with some basic understanding. Unclear explanation with an unclear judgement.	1	1–3

In answers candidates have shown...	Level	Mark
Sound knowledge with some understanding. Limited explanation with a loosely supported judgement.	2	4–6
Strong knowledge with generally clear understanding. Attempted explanation with attempted supported judgement.	3	7–10
Strong knowledge with secure understanding. Convincing explanation in most parts with a supported judgement.	4	11–14
Strong knowledge with secure understanding. Convincing explanation throughout with a well-supported judgement.	5	15–18

Level 5 answers should include: Agree – Liberal reforms; creation of the NHS; Beveridge's 'Five Evils'; evacuation highlighted poor public health; welfare state created universal improvements in public health; government took responsibility for public health; Disagree – Change in attitudes towards the end of the nineteenth century; the 1975 Second Public Health Act; Snow's discovery of the cause of cholera; the Renaissance period showed some developments such as attempts to clear streets, although these were not enforcement policies; the changes in public health that took place during previous centuries were small steps and contributed to the changes we see now; a conclusion to explain how far you agree.

Page 224: Modern Medicine (1900s–Present) 3

AQA

1.

In answers candidates have shown...	Level	Mark
No answer or have made irrelevant statements.		0
Basic analysis of source.	1	1–2
Simple evaluation of source based on content and or provenance.	2	3–4
Developed evaluation of source with sustained judgement based on content and provenance.	3	5–6
Complex evaluation of source with sustained judgement based on content and provenance.	4	7–8

Level 4 answers should include: Useful – gives a scientific explanation for why people supported its development; represents a scientific view point; Not useful – as it is from Dr Stephen Hawking, a scientist, who would therefore support scientific development, it is a one sided argument; as Hawking also suffers from motor neurone disease it would be within his own personal interest to support scientific development to try to find a cure.

2.

In answers candidates have shown...	Level	Mark
No answer or have made irrelevant statements.		0
Aspects of significance identified.	1	1–2
One aspect of significance briefly explained.	2	3–4
Developed aspects of significance explained.	3	5–6
Complex aspects of significance explained.	4	7–8

Level 4 answers should include: Anti-smoking campaigns; campaigns to reduce alcohol consumption; Change4Life; flu campaigns; national anti-drug campaigns; candidates could acknowledge the importance of the NHS and its funding to support an increasing population.

Edexcel

1.

In answers candidates have shown...	Level	Mark
No answer or irrelevant statements.		0
Simple judgement made with limited support. Lack of understanding of sources.	1	1–2
Judgement made with support. Understanding of the sources with some analysis.	2	3–5
Developed judgement made with support including own knowledge. Understanding of the sources with analysis.	3	6–8

Level 3 answers should include: Source A is useful as it mentions the problems that occurred during the 1960s with the thalidomide drug; shows that a lack of scientific understanding can negatively impact development; as Source A is from the Science Museum's website it is useful as we would expect it to support scientific development, but it doesn't, so this evidence is more substantial; Source A is less useful because it only mentions one reason for problems in scientific development. It does not mention problems such as people's moral or religious objections or the lack of understanding of some diseases such as AIDS or Ebola; Source B is useful as it mentions religious reasons why people are against scientific developments. This can also link in to some people's moral beliefs; it is also useful as it is from the UK Health Centre website meaning that we would expect it to support scientific development; however, it is not useful as it only highlights religious reasons for being against scientific development, and only Catholic reasons; it does not mention other religions or mistakes and errors such as the problems with thalidomide in the 1960s or lack of understanding of some diseases such as AIDS or Ebola.

2.

1 mark awarded for each of the following:	Mark
Selecting a detail from the source that could form the basis of a follow-up enquiry.	1
Creation of a question that is linked to this detail.	1
Identification of an appropriate source to use.	1
Explanation of how the identified source might help answer the chosen follow-up question.	1

4 mark answers should include: Following up 'because they believe that infertility is God's will and to go against it is wrong'; creating a question such as 'do all Catholics believe infertility is God's will?'; identification of source: Bible, Catholic Church website, Catholic priest, Catholic member of the public; explanation: to verify the statement and get further evidence.

Eduqas

1.

In answers candidates have shown...	Level	Mark
No answer or irrelevant statements.		0
One general statement to answer the question.	1	1–2

In answers candidates have shown...	Level	Mark
A brief explanation with some understanding.	2	3–5
Detailed understanding with explanation.	3	6–9

Level 3 answers should include: Lack of immediate impact; lack of funds so Fleming couldn't continue his work; Britain did not have the time and space needed to grow the mould required for penicillin in the 1930s and 40s due to being involved in World War Two; the USA initially refused to fund the development of antibiotics; antibiotics were expensive.

2.

In answers candidates have shown...	Level	Mark
No answer or irrelevant statements.		0
General statements about the key issue.	1	1–2
Some knowledge and some understanding of the key issue and/or other factors.	2	3–4
Knowledge and some understanding of the issue. Some knowledge and some understanding of other factors.	3	5–8
Accurate knowledge and understanding of the issue. Some analysis and evaluation of other factors.	4	9–12
Accurate knowledge and understanding of the issue. Analysis and evaluation of other factors that lead to a supported judgement.	5	13–16

Level 5 answers should include: Less support for a laissez-faire style government – the government and the public were willing to accept the idea of more government intervention; Liberal reforms; government intervention such as the USA's involvement in mass producing penicillin; creation and funding of the NHS; campaigns; war was a turning point/ catalyst that speeded up improvements; developments such as skin grafting, blood transfusions, and mobile X-rays all developed quickly because of the First World War; the Second World War highlighted problems in health, leading to the NHS being developed; change in attitudes such as the acceptance of blood transfusions; development of science and technology such as patent medicines and technologies such as refrigeration; the role of the individual such as Gilles, Franklin, Crick and Watson, Fleming.

OCR B

1.

In answers candidates have shown...	Level	Mark
No answer or irrelevant statements.		0
Some knowledge and some understanding shown.	1	1–3
Good knowledge with some understanding of one or more points.	2	4–5
Good knowledge with good understanding of one or more points.	3	6–7
Strong knowledge with strong understanding of one or more points.	4	8–10

Level 4 answers should include: Lack of funds e.g. Fleming; lack of knowledge, e.g. no magic bullets or vaccines developed to cure AIDS or Ebola; failures such as thalidomide causing babies to be born with disfigurements such as a lack of limbs in 1960s; not all people support scientific development, as they may have moral and religious objections; recently there has been a move to alternative medicines such as herbal remedies, acupuncture and meditation.

2.

In answers candidates have shown...	Level	Mark
No answer or irrelevant statements.		0
Some knowledge with some basic understanding. Unclear explanation with an unclear judgement.	1	1–3
Sound knowledge with some understanding. Limited explanation with a loosely supported judgement.	2	4–6
Strong knowledge with generally clear understanding. Attempted explanation with attempted supported judgement.	3	7–10
Strong knowledge with secure understanding. Convincing explanation in most parts with a supported judgement.	4	11–14
Strong knowledge with secure understanding. Convincing explanation throughout with a well-supported judgement.	5	15–18

Level 5 answers should include: Agree – less support for a laissez-faire style government – the government and the public were willing to accept the idea of more government intervention; Liberal reforms; government intervention such as the USA's involvement in mass-producing penicillin; creation and funding of the NHS; campaigns; Disagree – war was a turning point/catalyst that speeded up improvements; developments such as skin grafting, blood transfusions, and mobile X-rays all developed quickly because of the First World War; the Second World War highlighted problems in health, leading to the NHS being developed; change in attitudes such as the acceptance of blood transfusions; development of science and technology such as patent medicines and technologies such as refrigeration; the role of the individual such as Gilles, Franklin, Crick and Watson, Fleming; a conclusion to explain how far you agree.

Crime and Punishment – pages 226–235

Page 226: 1000–1500: Crime

Edexcel

1.

In answers candidates have shown...	Level	Mark
No answer or irrelevant points.		0
Relevant points.	1	1–2
Explanation of points.	2	3–4

Level 2 answers should include: A key feature such as the use of the wergild; information about an aspect of Anglo–Saxon law enforcement, including family loyalty or blood feuds; the use of tithings or trial by ordeal.

2.

In answers candidates have shown...	Level	Mark
No answer or irrelevant material.		0
Simple undeveloped and unorganised statements with limited knowledge and understanding. No judgement to answer the question.	1	1–4
Basic statements which are relevant to the question. Some knowledge and understanding. A judgement but without supporting evidence.	2	5–8

In answers candidates have shown...	Level	Mark
Some explanation which is relevant to the question. Good knowledge and understanding. A valid judgement with supporting evidence.	3	9–12
Detailed explanation which is well structured. Excellent knowledge and understanding. A strong supported judgement.	4	13–16

Level 4 answers should include: Detail about the amount of new crimes and new laws that were introduced following the Norman Conquest – Forest Laws; explanation of the role of royal courts and/or the role of the Church; explanation of different aspects of change in crime and punishment and identification of the extent of change in crime, trials, punishment and the court system; the Normans enforced laws more harshly than the Saxons; a conclusion to explain how far you agree.

Eduqas

1.

In answers candidates have shown...	Level	Mark
No response or irrelevant comments.		0
Limited knowledge to describe the issue.	1	1
Knowledge to partially describe the issue.	2	2–3
Detailed knowledge to fully describe the issue set within the historical context.	3	4–5

Level 3 answers should include: The need for a king to be able to defend his country from attacks, particularly as England was divided into kingdoms, each ruled by a warrior king; the need to protect landowners' property from theft or damage or protect people from violence and murder; the need to allow a victim of crime to claim compensation (wergild) if a crime was committed against them.

2.

In answers candidates have shown...	Level	Mark
No response or irrelevant comments.		0
Some knowledge and understanding, descriptive with limited explanation.	1	1–3
Detailed knowledge and understanding and partially explains the issue.	2	4–6
Detailed knowledge and understanding, fully explains the issue with a clear focus.	3	7–9

Level 3 answers should include: Outlaws roamed the country and would steal food, clothing or pots and pans and often targeting the poor; they would raid churches, because they contained valuable ornaments or money that was meant to be distributed to the poor; they would often use brutal methods, such as arson, extortion or violence and were difficult to capture.

OCR B

1. (a) 1 mark for any answer that offers a historically valid response. Answer may include theft of livestock, goods or money; **(b)** 1 mark for any answer that offers a historically valid response. Answer may include cutting down trees or owning a bow and arrow; **(c)** 1 mark for any answer that offers a historically valid response. Answer may include poverty, famine or bad harvests.

2.

In answers candidates have shown...	Level	Mark
No response or irrelevant comments.		0
Some knowledge of characteristic features and some general understanding.	1	1–3

In answers candidates have shown...	Level	Mark
A range of knowledge of characteristic features and a general understanding.	2	4–6
A well-selected range of valid knowledge and a clear understanding.	3	7–9

Level 3 answers should include: Outlaws roamed the country and stole from anyone, and were able to evade capture; churches were favourite targets for outlaws due to the valuable ornaments and money that they had; methods used by outlaws to commit crimes were often violent and could result in arson, extortion or murder.

Page 226: 1000–1500: Punishment

Edexcel

1.

In answers candidates have shown...	Level	Mark
No answer or have made irrelevant points.		0
Relevant points.	1	1–2
Explanation of points.	2	3–4

Level 2 answers should include: A key feature such as the stocks; information about an aspect of punishment such as the use of fines or the pillory; punishments were based on public humiliation or deterrence.

2.

In answers candidates have shown...	Level	Mark
No rewardable material.		0
A simple generalised answer, lacking development and only limited knowledge and understanding.	1	1–3
Basic statements which are relevant to the question, showing some knowledge and understanding of the period.	2	4–6
Some explanation, including accurate and relevant information demonstrating good knowledge and understanding.	3	7–9
Detailed explanation which is well structured. Accurate and relevant information is precisely selected, with excellent knowledge and understanding.	4	10–12

Level 4 answers should include: How trials by ordeal were used – trial by hot iron, hot water, cold water; clear detail about their purpose; certain trials were conducted by a priest or reserved for the clergy – trial by blessed bread; trials by ordeal took advantage of people's belief in God – it was believed that God helped innocent people and punished the guilty; abolished in 1215.

Eduqas

1.

In answers candidates have shown...	Level	Mark
No response or irrelevant comments.		0
General description with limited knowledge of two main features.	1	1–2
Some knowledge to describe two main features.	2	3–5
Detailed knowledge to fully describe two main features.	3	6–8

Level 3 answers should include two of the following: There was no police force, therefore the reliance was on friends or

family of the victim to ... age of twelve were ex... of the tithing broke the ... him to court; the hue and c... village were expected to hunt ...

2.

In answers candidates have show...		
No response or irrelevant comments.		
A basic narrative account, limited awareness of the process of change.		
Partial detail and structured narrative account, some awareness of the process of change.	2	5–7
Good detail and structured narrative account, good awareness of the process of change.	3	8–12
Excellent detail and a well-structured narrative account, secure awareness of the process of change.	4	13–16

Level 4 answers should include: Various methods of Saxon punishments including the use of the wergild, death penalty and blood feuds; the developments of punishments during the Norman Conquest such as whipping, blinding and mutilation, the decline of the wergild and blood feuds; the introduction of Royal, County and Church Courts to impose punishments for crimes; the death penalty for treason remained a constant punishment since Saxon times and by the beginning of the Tudor period this crime was increasing.

OCR B

1. **(a)** 1 mark for any answer that offers a historically valid response. Answer may include JP, Sheriff or Parish Constable; **(b)** 1 mark for any answer that offers a historically valid response. Answer may include to keep the peace, they were unpaid, the post was held only for a year; **(c)** 1 mark for any answer that offers a historically valid response. Answer may include the use of benefit of clergy, the right of sanctuary, church courts were set up.

2.

In answers candidates have shown...	Level	Mark
No response or irrelevant comments.		0
Some knowledge of characteristic features and some general understanding.	1	1–3
A range of knowledge of characteristic features and a general understanding.	2	4–6
A well-selected range of valid knowledge and a clear understanding.	3	7–9

Level 3 answers should include: Trials took place in front of local people, and Royal judges dealt with the most serious cases; trial by ordeal took advantage of the belief in God to decide upon guilt or innocence; the various different methods of trial by ordeal – trial by hot iron, hot water, cold water, trial by blessed bread (clergy and priests); why it was abolished in 1215.

Page 227: 1500–1700: Crime

Edexcel

1.

In answers candidates have shown...	Level	Mark
No answer or have made irrelevant points.		0
Relevant points.	1	1–2
Explanation of points.	2	3–4

...nclude: The Bloody Code introduced ...; feudalism decreased and the ... to increase in urban areas, leading to ...s known as 'footpads'; changes in people's ...beliefs lead to more people committing heresy.

In answers candidates have shown...	Level	Mark
No answer or irrelevant material.		0
Simple undeveloped and unorganised statements with limited knowledge and understanding. No judgement to answer the question.	1	1–4
Basic statements which are relevant to the question. Some knowledge and understanding. A judgement but without supporting evidence.	2	5–8
Some explanation which is relevant to the question. Good knowledge and understanding. A valid judgement with supporting evidence.	3	9–12
Detailed explanation which is well structured. Excellent knowledge and understanding. A strong supported judgement.	4	13–16

Level 4 answers should include: Examples that increasing unemployment and no system to help those in need meant an increase in the number of beggars; beggars were seen as a serious threat to society; they were hated and feared; begging became a crime in the 16th century and Elizabeth I passed laws against begging; punishments were harsh and included the stocks, pillory, whipping and branding; explanation that new crimes developed during this period including highway robbery, poaching and treason and these were punishable by death; beggars classed as deserving (allowed to beg) or sturdy (lazy and punished) after 1531; a conclusion to explain how far you agree.

Eduqas

1.

In answers candidates have shown...	Level	Mark
No response or irrelevant comments.		0
Some knowledge and understanding, descriptive with limited explanation.	1	1–3
Detailed knowledge and understanding and partially explains the issue.	2	4–6
Detailed knowledge and understanding, fully explains the issue with a clear focus.	3	7–9

Level 3 answers should include: The increase in population and decline of feudalism led to more people moving to urban areas, and larger towns; increasing unemployment, continued poverty and increasing trade meant begging, vagrancy and highway robbery became more common; tax rises and trade restrictions created a huge increase in the crime of smuggling.

2.

In answers candidates have shown...	Level	Mark
No response or irrelevant comments.		0
Some understanding but largely paraphrases the source.	1	1–2
Detailed understanding and attempts to analyse the reliability of both sources.	2	3–4
Detailed understanding and fully analyses both sources.	3	5–6

Level 3 answers should include: Source A is reliable because: it is a school textbook and should therefore have researched the issue of vagrancy in detail; it should take into account a number of interpretations in order to present the detail, including understanding the movement of the population and poverty of the era; however the content of Source A also states that although most vagrants were not criminals, it suggests that it may have still been an issue and that the crime may still be committed. Source B is reliable as it has been written by a JP responsible for helping to enforce law and order at the time, and they would have encountered cases of crime related to or involving vagrants and vagrancy; it describes the issue of fear and violence that would often be associated with the crime of vagrancy, and as this letter is sent to the Queen's chief minister, it would support the fact that laws against vagrancy had been established.

OCR B

1.

In answers candidates have shown...	Level	Mark
No response or irrelevant comments.		0
Some knowledge of characteristic features and some general understanding.	1	1–3
A range of knowledge of characteristic features and a general understanding.	2	4–5
A well-selected range of valid knowledge and a clear understanding.	3	6–7
Strong knowledge and secure understanding with well-supported explanations.	4	8–10

Level 4 answers should include: The increasing population; unemployment; decline of feudalism; changes in the nature of crime including heresy, treason and vagrancy; demonstrate understanding of how and why the increase was caused.

2.

In answers candidates have shown...	Level	Mark
No response or irrelevant comments.		0
Some knowledge of characteristic features and some general understanding, explanation or judgement is unclear.	1	1–3
A range of knowledge of characteristic features and a general understanding, explanation or judgement that is basic.	2	4–6
A well-selected range of valid knowledge and understanding, attempts to explain ideas.	3	7–10
Strong knowledge and secure understanding with a well-supported explanation and judgment.	4	11–14
Strong knowledge and very secure understanding with a consistently focused explanation and judgement.	5	15–18

Level 5 answers should include: Agree and demonstrate that increasing unemployment and no system to help those in need meant an increase in the number of beggars; agree and explain that beggars were seen as a serious threat to society; they were hated and feared and faced harsh punishment; disagree and explain that new crimes developed during this period including highway robbery, poaching and treason and these were punishable by death; a conclusion to explain how far you agree.

Page 229: 1500–1700: Punishment

Edexcel

1.

In answers candidates have shown...	Level	Mark
No response or irrelevant comments.		0
A simple judgement on usefulness, supported by a general comment on the content and/or provenance of the sources.	1	1–2
Judgements on usefulness, and supported by developed comment on the content and/or provenance of the sources.	2	3–5
Judgements on usefulness and supported by well-developed comments on the content and provenance of the sources.	3	6–8

Level 3 answers should include: Source A is useful in that it describes the role and functions expected of a watchman; the short length of the watchman's beat and the description that they tended to work alone gives useful information to suggest they were not particularly effective in catching criminals in the act; this is a modern interpretation from a textbook of one method of catching criminals. However, it does not mention the work of parish constables or thief takers and has a generally negative point of view of the success of catching criminals; the source suggests that prevention of crime rather than solving of crime was more important during this period. Source B is useful as it suggests that thief takers such as Jonathon Wild were successfully able to capture criminals. The artist's impression shows Wild apprehending a criminal; the source also demonstrates that thief takers tended to work in a group and that this may potentially lead to a more successful outcome of apprehending criminals; the source does suggest that perhaps the reason that thief takers were successful is because they were paid rewards and therefore had an incentive to catch criminals; the source is an artist's impression of the work of thief takers and may have been deliberately exaggerated, in order to glamorise success.

2.

In answers candidates have shown...	Level	Mark
No answer or have made irrelevant points.		0
Relevant points.	1	1–2
Explanation of points.	2	3–4

1 mark for a detail in Source A that could form the basis of a follow-up enquiry and 1 mark for a question that is linked to it. For example, detail in Source A: the indication that the watchman patrolled his beat alone; question to ask: how many watchmen were there on patrol in London?

1 mark for identification of an appropriate source and 1 mark for an answer that shows how it might help answer the chosen follow up question. For example, what type of source to use: local records giving the details of watchmen employed in the city of London; how might this help answer the question: it would show whether there were enough watchmen to patrol the area effectively.

Eduqas

1.

In answers candidates have shown...	Level	Mark
No response or irrelevant comments.		0
Use of the sources to identify either one similarity or difference.	1	1–2
Use of the sources to identify both a similarity and difference.	2	3–4

Level 2 answers should include: Similarities – A and B both show the use of equipment to catch criminals; B and C both describe patrolling the streets. A and C both show the use of violence. Differences – A shows a group of thief takers, whereas B shows a parish constable patrolling on his own; B uses a stick, C describes whipping; A describes that thief takers got paid to catch criminals; C shows parish constables were unpaid.

2.

In answers candidates have shown...	Level	Mark
No response or irrelevant comments.		0
A basic narrative account demonstrates limited awareness of the process of change.	1	1–4
Partial detail and structured narrative account. Demonstrates some awareness of the process of change.	2	5–7
Good detail and structured narrative account, demonstrates good awareness of the process of change.	3	8–12
Excellent detail and a well-structured narrative account, demonstrates secure awareness of the process of change.	4	13–16

Level 4 answers should include: The number of crimes punishable by death increased from 50 to more than 200 for example, stealing a rabbit or damaging a tree became hanging offences; the punishments were usually brutal, physical and public in order to shame the criminal and to deter others; fewer people were hanged as juries did not want to give the death penalty and new crimes began to be developed, therefore new punishments were required.

OCR B

1.

In answers candidates have shown...	Level	Mark
No response or irrelevant comments.		0
Some knowledge of characteristic features and some general understanding.	1	1–3
A range of knowledge of characteristic features and a general understanding.	2	4–6
A well-selected range of valid knowledge and a clear understanding.	3	7–9

Level 3 answers should include: The role of watchmen or constables; explain that there was no national system or police force for catching criminals; thief takers such as Jonathon Wild were paid by the victim of the crime to catch the criminal and bring them to justice.

2.

In answers candidates have shown...	Level	Mark
No response or irrelevant comments.		0
Some knowledge of characteristic features and some general understanding, explanation or judgement is unclear.	1	1–3
A range of knowledge of characteristic features and a general understanding, explanation or judgement is basic.	2	4–6
A well-selected range of valid knowledge and understanding, attempts to explain ideas.	3	7–10
Strong knowledge and secure understanding with a well-supported explanation and judgment.	4	11–14
Strong knowledge and very secure understanding with a consistently focused explanation and judgement.	5	15–18

Level 5 answers should include: Agree and demonstrate that the number of crimes punishable by death increased from 50 to more than 200 (e.g. to include stealing a rabbit and damaging a tree); Agree and explain that the punishments were usually brutal, physical and public in order to shame the criminal and to deter others. Disagree and explain that fewer people were hanged as juries did not want to give the death penalty; new punishments were developed; a conclusion to explain how far you agree.

Page 231: 1700–1900: Crime

Edexcel

1.

In answers candidates have shown...	Level	Mark
No answer or irrelevant material.		0
Simple undeveloped and unorganised statements with limited knowledge and understanding. No judgement to answer the question.	1	1–4
Basic statements which are relevant to the question. Some knowledge and understanding. A judgement but without supporting evidence.	2	5–8
Some explanation which is relevant to the question. Good knowledge and understanding. A valid judgement with supporting evidence.	3	9–12
Detailed explanation which is well structured. Excellent knowledge and understanding. A strong supported judgement.	4	13–16

Level 4 answers should include: Detail about the reasons for the increase in smuggling, including the high tax on imported goods, the large profits that could be made, and the difficulty in catching smugglers; crimes against authority such as the Tolpuddle Martyrs and Swing Riots also took place and this threatened the stability of the government; smugglers were seen as heroes fighting against the government; smuggling began to decline after 1850 as taxes on imported goods were cut; a conclusion to explain how far you agree.

2.

In answers candidates have shown...	Level	Mark
No response or irrelevant comments.		0
Relevant points.	1	1–2
Explanation of points.	2	3–4

Level 2 answers could include: Overcrowding in towns and cities made it more difficult to catch criminals; extreme poverty forced people to steal in order to survive; professional criminals operated in urban areas and were difficult to catch.

Eduqas

1.

In answers candidates have shown...	Level	Mark
No response or irrelevant comments.		0
Some knowledge and understanding, descriptive with limited explanation.	1	1–3
Detailed knowledge and understanding and partially explains the issue.	2	4–6
Detailed knowledge and understanding, fully explains the issue with a clear focus.	3	7–9

Level 3 answers should include: Increasing population and overcrowding in towns and cities meant it was easier to commit petty crime and avoid being caught; smuggling increased due to the large profits that could be made, and it was difficult for customs officers to prevent it; extreme poverty meant that many people were forced to steal in order to survive; this made the poor resentful of the wealthy.

2.

In answers candidates have shown...	Level	Mark
No response or irrelevant comments.		0
Limited knowledge to describe the issue.	1	1
Knowledge to partially describe the issue.	2	2–3
Detailed knowledge to fully describe the issue set within the historical context.	3	4–5

Level 3 answers should include: The French Revolution had made the government and upper classes fearful of rioting; many working people demanded reforms to improve working and living conditions; protesting due to the fear of extreme poverty, shortages of food and cuts in wages; protesting for the right to vote or strike.

OCR B

1.

In answers candidates have shown...	Level	Mark
No response or irrelevant comments.		0
Some knowledge of characteristic features and some general understanding.	1	1–3
A range of knowledge of characteristic features and a general understanding.	2	4–6
A well-selected range of valid knowledge and a clear understanding.	3	7–9

Level 3 answers should include: Describe the type of goods that were smuggled into Britain; explain that smuggling increased because tax on imported goods was so high; smuggling was difficult to prevent because of the number of people involved and the public belief that smugglers were heroes.

2. (a) 1 mark for any answer that offers a historically valid response. Answer may include the Chartists or the Luddites; (b) 1 mark for any answer that offers a historically valid response. Answer may include rioting, petty theft or public protest; (c) 1 mark for any answer that offers a historically valid response. Answer may include the impact of newspapers or increasing industrialisation.

Page 232: 1700–1900: Punishment

Edexcel

1.

In answers candidates have shown...	Level	Mark
No rewardable material.		0
A simple generalised answer, lacking development and only limited knowledge and understanding.	1	1–3
Basic statements which are relevant to the question, showing some knowledge and understanding of the period.	2	4–6
Some explanation, including accurate and relevant information demonstrating good knowledge and understanding.	3	7–9
Detailed explanation which is well structured. Accurate and relevant information is precisely selected, with excellent knowledge and understanding.	4	10–12

Level 4 answers should include: Growing demand for alternatives to corporal and capital punishment meant that prisons were no longer used just for debtors or to hold prisoners before trial; the influence of John Howard's and Elizabeth Fry's views on the purpose and condition of prisons; the emphasis on reforming the criminal rather than for retribution.

2.

In answers candidates have shown...	Level	Mark
No answer or irrelevant points.		0
Relevant points.	1	1–2
Explanation of points.	2	3–4

Level 2 answers should include two of the following: They were established in 1829, but only in London to begin with; recruits were carefully selected, well trained and it was a full-time job; by 1842 a detective department had been set up to solve crimes as well as prevent them.

Eduqas

1.

In answers candidates have shown...	Level	Mark
No response or irrelevant comments.		0
General explanation and analysis with limited reference to changes.	1	1–2
Some explanation and analysis with reference to changes.	2	3–5
Reasoned explanation and analysis with reference to changes.	3	6–8
Sophisticated and reasoned explanation and with reference to changes.	4	9–12

Level 4 answers should include: The death penalty became less acceptable as a method of punishment and transportation was viewed as an incredibly harsh punishment for minor crimes. It was abolished in 1868; the separate and silent system isolated prisoners in order to encourage self-reflection, however this was expensive to maintain; prison conditions improved following the work of reformers such as John Howard and Elizabeth Fry.

2.

In answers candidates have shown...	Level	Mark
No response or irrelevant comments.		0
A basic narrative account. Demonstrates limited awareness of the process of change.	1	1–4
Partial detail and structured narrative account. Demonstrates some awareness of the process of change.	2	5–7
Good detail and structured narrative account. Demonstrates good awareness of the process of change.	3	8–12
Excellent detail and a well-structured narrative account. Demonstrates secure awareness of the process of change.	4	13–16

Level 4 answers should include: The role of the Bow Street Runners and that they were introduced by local magistrates in an attempt to tackle the increase in crime; the introduction of the Metropolitan Police in 1829 had a greater impact, because they were carefully recruited, well-trained and full time; in 1856 it became compulsory for all counties to have a police force; a detective department was set up in 1842, and the police now attempted to solve crimes as well as prevent them.

OCR B

1.

In answers candidates have shown...	Level	Mark
No response or irrelevant comments.		0
Some knowledge of characteristic features and some general understanding, explanation or judgement is unclear.	1	1–3
A range of knowledge of characteristic features and a general understanding, explanation or judgement is basic.	2	4–6
A well-selected range of valid knowledge and understanding, attempts to explain ideas.	3	7–10
Strong knowledge and secure understanding with a well-supported explanation and judgment.	4	11–14
Strong knowledge and very secure understanding with a consistently focused explanation and judgement.	5	15–18

Level 5 answers should include: Agree and demonstrate that the introduction of the Bow Street Runners was an attempt to tackle the increase in crime; agree and explain that the Bow Street Runners were introduced by local magistrates, and further developed to include a horse patrol to prevent highway robbery; disagree and explain that the introduction of the Metropolitan Police had a greater impact because they were carefully recruited, well-trained and full time; a conclusion to explain how far you agree.

2.

In answers candidates have shown...	Level	Mark
No response or irrelevant comments.		0
Some knowledge of characteristic features and some general understanding.	1	1–3
A range of knowledge of characteristic features and a general understanding.	2	4–5
A well-selected range of valid knowledge and a clear understanding.	3	6–7
Strong knowledge and secure understanding with well-supported explanations.	4	8–10

Level 4 answers should include: The poor condition of prisons and the introduction of the separate and silent system; changes in the nature of punishment as the impact of transportation and the Bloody Code declined; the work of prison reformers such as John Howard and Elizabeth Fry.

Page 233: 1900–Present: Crime

Edexcel

1.

In answers candidates have shown…	Level	Mark
No rewardable material.		0
A simple generalised answer lacking development and only limited knowledge and understanding.	1	1–3
Basic statements which are relevant to the question, showing some knowledge and understanding of the period.	2	4–6
Some explanation, including accurate and relevant information demonstrating good knowledge and understanding.	3	7–9
Detailed explanation which is well structured. Accurate and relevant information is precisely selected, with excellent knowledge and understanding.	4	10–12

Level 4 answers should include: Victims of crime are more likely to report it, particularly due to insurance claims; there has been an increased trend towards violent crime and anti-social behaviour; old crimes such as theft and smuggling have increased due to new methods such as computers and cars being used by criminals; new laws such as the Race Relations Act and anti-terrorism laws have increased the number of actions now classed as crimes.

2.

In answers candidates have shown…	Level	Mark
No answer or have made irrelevant points.		0
Relevant points.	1	1–2
Explanation of points.	2	3–4

Level 2 answers could include two of the following: Car crime is now one of the largest categories of crime, particularly among teenage boys; cyber-crime such as hacking and phishing has increased rapidly due to the internet; people trafficking; hooliganism; modern terrorism.

Eduqas

1.

In answers candidates have shown…	Level	Mark
No response or irrelevant comments.		0
A basic narrative account, demonstrates limited awareness of the process of change.	1	1–4
Partial detail and structured narrative account, demonstrates some awareness of the process of change.	2	5–7
Good detail and structured narrative account, demonstrates good awareness of the process of change.	3	8–12
Excellent detail and a well-structured narrative account, demonstrates secure awareness of the process of change.	4	13–16

Level 4 answers should include: The development of new crimes, examples may include car theft, cyber-crime and hooliganism; many of these new crimes are similar in methods and motives to crimes committed in previous centuries – give examples from the nineteenth century; explain that the Race Relations Act was introduced in 1965 and discrimination of gender, race, sex or ethnicity has become a serious crime.

2.

In answers candidates have shown…	Level	Mark
No response or irrelevant comments.		0
Limited knowledge to describe the issue.	1	1
Knowledge to partially describe the issue.	2	2–3
Detailed knowledge to fully describe the issue set within the historical context.	3	4–5

Level 3 answers should include: More actions are now classified as crimes, such as race and sex discrimination; victims of crime are more likely to report it, particularly for insurance claims; methods of recording crime have improved with the use of computer technology.

OCR B

1. **(a)** 1 mark for any answer that offers a historically valid response. Answer may include car theft, burglary or vandalism; **(b)** 1 mark for any answer that offers a historically valid response. Answer may include for insurance purposes or improving methods of recording crime; **(c)** 1 mark for any answer that offers a historically valid response. Answer may include the introduction of CCTV, DNA testing or increasing use of computers.

2.

In answers candidates have shown…	Level	Mark
No response or irrelevant comments.		0
Some knowledge of characteristic features and some general understanding.	1	1–3
A range of knowledge of characteristic features and a general understanding.	2	4–6
A well-selected range of valid knowledge and a clear understanding.	3	7–9

Level 3 answers should include: The rise of car crime, hooliganism and people trafficking; and reasons why; the development of computers and the internet has led to a huge increase in cyber crimes, such as fraud and phishing; the Race Relations Act of 1965 made it illegal to discriminate against businesses or stir up racial hatred.

Page 234: 1900–Present: Punishment

Edexcel

1.

In answers candidates have shown…	Level	Mark
No answer or irrelevant material.		0
Simple undeveloped and unorganised statements with limited knowledge and understanding. No judgement to answer the question.	1	1–4
Basic statements which are relevant to the question. Some knowledge and understanding. A judgement but without supporting evidence.	2	5–8
Some explanation which is relevant to the question. Good knowledge and understanding. A valid judgement with supporting evidence.	3	9–12
Detailed explanation which is well structured. Excellent knowledge and understanding. A strong supported judgement.	4	13–16

Level 4 answers should include: Detail about specific technology developments such as DNA, fingerprinting and CCTV to aid the police; explanations of how communication and transport methods have improved, such as the use of walkie-talkies, radios and motorised transport; specialist police units have been set up in order for the police to focus on specific areas of crime and crime detection; the police regularly engage with the general public using a variety of methods such as Neighbourhood Watch schemes, PCSOs and social media; a conclusion to explain how far you agree.

2.

In answers candidates have shown...	Level	Mark
No answer or have made irrelevant points.		0
Relevant points.	1	1–2
Explanation of points.	2	3–4

Level 2 answers should include: New punishments were aimed at rehabilitation and reforming criminals to pay back society; the use of ASBOs and electronic tagging.

Eduqas

1.

In answers candidates have shown...	Level	Mark
No response or irrelevant comments.		0
Some knowledge and understanding, descriptive with limited explanation.	1	1–3
Detailed knowledge and understanding and partially explains the issue.	2	4–6
Detailed knowledge and understanding, fully explains the issue with a clear focus.	3	7–9

Level 3 answers should include: New crimes developed and the police needed to use more technology such as CCTV and computers to catch criminals; scientific developments such as DNA testing and fingerprinting have become vital for police investigation; motorised transport such as cars, motorbikes and helicopters allow the police to reach crimes scenes much quicker.

2.

In answers candidates have shown...	Level	Mark
No response or irrelevant comments.		0
General explanation and analysis with limited reference to changes.	1	1–2
Some explanation and analysis with reference to changes.	2	3–5
Reasoned explanation and analysis with reference to changes.	3	6–8
Sophisticated and reasoned explanation and with reference to changes.	4	9–12

Level 4 answers should include: New punishments such as community service, ASBOs and electronic tagging have been used as an alternative to prison; many changes have taken place in prisons including open or high security, and specific prisons for women and juvenile offenders; Prisons aim to reduce re-offending rates through education and rehabilitation; the death penalty was abolished in 1964, after a number of miscarriages of justice had taken place.

OCR B

1.

In answers candidates have shown...	Level	Mark
No response or irrelevant comments.		0
Some knowledge of characteristic features and some general understanding.	1	1–3
A range of knowledge of characteristic features and a general understanding.	2	4–5
A well-selected range of valid knowledge and a clear understanding.	3	6–7
Strong knowledge and secure understanding with well-supported explanations.	4	8–10

Level 4 answers should include: The changes in policing, including the development of motorised transport and improvements in science to aid crime detection; changes in the nature of the police force, including female officers and neighbourhood watch schemes; understanding of specialist police units and their purpose in investigating various forms of crime.

2.

In answers candidates have shown...	Level	Mark
No response or irrelevant comments.		0
Some knowledge of characteristic features and some general understanding, explanation or judgement is unclear.	1	1–3
A range of knowledge of characteristic features and a general understanding, explanation or judgement is basic.	2	4–6
A well-selected range of valid knowledge and understanding, attempts to explain ideas.	3	7–10
Strong knowledge and secure understanding with a well-supported explanation and judgement.	4	11–14
Strong knowledge and very secure understanding with a consistently focused explanation and judgement.	5	15–18

Level 5 answers should include: Agree and explain the abolition of corporal and capital punishment; agree and describe the changes in the nature of punishment, such as rehabilitation for offenders, community service and electronic tagging as alternatives to prison; disagree and explain that changes pre-1900 were more significant such as transportation and the Bloody Code; a conclusion to explain how far you agree.

Page 235: Case Studies

Edexcel

1.

In answers candidates have shown...	Level	Mark
No rewardable material.		0
A simple generalised answer, lacking development and only limited knowledge and understanding.	1	1–3
Basic statements which are relevant to the question, showing some knowledge and understanding of the period.	2	4–6
Some explanation, including accurate and relevant information demonstrating good knowledge and understanding.	3	7–9
Detailed explanation which is well structured. Accurate and relevant information is precisely selected, with excellent knowledge and understanding.	4	10–12

Level 4 answers should include: There was increased political stability following the Civil War, and people had become less suspicious of each other's actions; increased education and scientific understanding of the world helped to provide rational explanations for events; the Witchfinder General Matthew Hopkins disappeared in 1647 and witchcraft laws were eventually abolished in 1736.

2.

In answers candidates have shown...	Level	Mark
No rewardable material.		0
A simple generalised answer, lacking development and only limited knowledge and understanding.	1	1–3
Basic statements which are relevant to the question, showing some knowledge and understanding of the period.	2	4–6
Some explanation, including accurate and relevant information demonstrating good knowledge and understanding.	3	7–9
Detailed explanation which is well structured. Accurate and relevant information is precisely selected, with excellent knowledge and understanding.	4	10–12

Level 4 answers should include: Conscientious objectors would refuse to fight due to religious or moral beliefs; conscientious objectors believed that it was not right to be involved in conflicts where humans would kill each other; military tribunals were set up to decide whether claims were genuine; many conscientious objectors engaged in non-combat roles involving essential war work such as working on farms or in factories.

Eduqas

1.

In answers candidates have shown...	Level	Mark
No response or irrelevant comments.		0
General description with limited knowledge of two main features.	1	1–2
Some knowledge to describe two main features.	2	3–5
Detailed knowledge to fully describe two main features.	3	6–8

Level 3 answers could include any two of the following: If a person had unusual marks on their body such as spots, freckles or pimples, then these could be used as evidence of guilt; if the accused floated when they were thrown into the water during the 'floating test' they were regarded as guilty because the water was rejecting them; witness account, statements or confessions suggesting the person had committed evil deeds; these were often gained by torture.

2.

In answers candidates have shown...	Level	Mark
No response or irrelevant comments.		0
General description with limited knowledge of two main features.	1	1–2
Some knowledge to describe two main features.	2	3–5
Detailed knowledge to fully describe two main features.	3	6–8

Level 3 answers could include any two of the following: A conscientious objector could be put on trial, and if found guilty they could be sent to prison; conscientious objectors would have their voting rights taken away; non-combat roles such as working on farms or in factories could be given to those with partial exemption from war; they were often abused in the street, beaten up or sacked from their jobs.

OCR B

1.

In answers candidates have shown...	Level	Mark
No response or irrelevant comments.		0
Some knowledge of characteristic features and some general understanding.	1	1–3
A range of knowledge of characteristic features and a general understanding.	2	4–6
A well-selected range of valid knowledge and a clear understanding.	3	7–9

Level 3 answers should include: A number of factors including war and religion had a huge impact on the increase in accusations; changing attitudes towards the poor led to many old and vulnerable women being accused of witchcraft; powerful members of authority, including King James, believed in witches. He wrote a book about witchcraft called *Demonology*.

2.

In answers candidates have shown...	Level	Mark
No response or irrelevant comments.		0
Some knowledge of characteristic features and some general understanding.	1	1–3
A range of knowledge of characteristic features and a general understanding.	2	4–6
A well-selected range of valid knowledge and a clear understanding.	3	7–9

Level 3 answers should include: During the First World War the attitude from authority was harsh, including men being put on trial, placed in prison or having voting rights taken away; the general public resented conscientious objectors and they were often abused in the street, beaten up or sacked from their jobs; during the Second World War conscientious objectors were treated more leniently, and could avoid direct conflict by engaging in non-combat roles such as farming or factory work.

Notes

Notes

Acknowledgements

Image credits

Cover and P1 ©Shutterstock.com/Georgios Kollidas; ©Shutterstock.com/mishabender; ©Shutterstock.com/Morphart Creation

P.8 Harald Hardrada window © Colin Smith

P.23 © The Art Archive / Alamy Stock Photo

P.26 © The Art Archive / Alamy Stock Photo

P.29 Matt Chamberlain Illustration

P.50 © Stephen Dorey – Bygone Images / Alamy Stock Photo

P.52 © Rolf Richardson / Alamy Stock Photo

P.54 © The Art Archive / Alamy Stock Photo

P.54 © The Art Archive / Alamy Stock Photo

P.56 Medieval Windsor © Wessex Archaeology. All Rights Reserved.

P.189 © Chronicle / Alamy Stock Photo

P.190 The Battle of Stamford Bridge, September 25th, 1066. Illustration for Story of the British Nation (Hutchinson, c 1920). © Look and Learn

P.196 The Domesday Book. King William's officers question a farm tenant for the national survey known as the Domesday Book. © Look and Learn

P.208 Used by permission of the Folger Shakespeare Library under a Creative Commons Attribution-ShareAlike 4.0 International License.

P.214 Cover of The Works of William Harvey, translated by Robert Willis M.D., Edited by New introduction by Arthur C. Guyton M.D. © 1989. Reprinted with permission of the University of Pennsylvania Press.

P.218 © Mary Evans Picture Library / Alamy Stock Photo

P.220 © Classic Image / Alamy Stock Photo

P.224 Supplied by National Library of Wales/Llyfrgell Genedlaethol Cymru

P.229/230 © Chronicle / Alamy Stock Photo

P.230 © FromOldBooks.org / Alamy Stock Photo

All other images are ©Shutterstock.com or ©HarperCollinsPublishers Ltd.

Text Credits

P.50 Extract from The Anglo-Saxon Age: A Very Short Introduction by John Blair (2000): 14 words (p. 20). By permission of Oxford University Press.

P.189 Interpretation A – By historian Stephen Baxter. Reprinted by permission of Boydell & Brewer Ltd from Edward the Confessor and the Succession Question, edited by Richard Mortimer, Boydell Press, 2009, page 118.

P.190 Interpretation A – From the Britannica website. Reprinted with permission from Encyclopaedia Britannica, © 2015 by Encyclopaedia Britannica, Inc.

P.191 Interpretation A – from Wikipedia. From https://en.wikipedia.org/wiki/Battle_of_Fulford under the Creative Commons Attribution-ShareAlike License (http://creativecommons.org/licenses/by-sa/3.0/).

P.198 Source taken from Elizabethan England by Andy Harmsworth. Reproduced by permission of Hodder Education.

P.200 Source taken from Elizabethan England by Andy Harmsworth. Reproduced by permission of Hodder Education.

P.200 Interpretation A. Taken from Diarmaid MacCulloch, The Later Reformation in England 1547-1603, 1990, St. Martin's Press. Reproduced with permission of Palgrave Macmillan.

P.200 Interpretation B. Taken from Christopher Haigh (editor), The Reign of Elizabeth I, 1984, Macmillan. Reproduced with permission of Palgrave Macmillan.

P.203 Source A. Reprinted with permission from Amberley Books.

P.203 Source B. Taken from The Spanish Armada: The Experience of War in 1588 by Felipe Fernandez-Armesto (1988). By permission of Oxford University Press.

P.205 Source B. Taken from The Reign of Elizabeth by Barbara Mervyn. Reproduced by permission of Hodder Education.

P.206 Interpretation B. Taken from Elizabethan England by Andy Harmsworth. Reproduced by permission of Hodder Education.

P.211 Source B. Reprinted with permission from the Museum of London's Pocket Histories: London plagues 1348–1665 (http://www.museumoflondon.org.uk/sch/london-plagues).

P.216 Source A. Reprinted with permission from the Science Museum.

P.221 Source A. Taken from Sir Alexander Fleming's speech at the Nobel Banquet 1945. From Les Prix Nobel en 1945, Editor Arne Holmberg, [Nobel Foundation], Stockholm, 1946 Copyright © The Nobel Foundation 1945.

P.225 Source A. Reprinted with permission from the Science Museum.

P.225 Source B. Reprinted with permission from UK Health Centre.

P.228 Source A. Taken from OCR Crime and Punishment through time: An SHP development study by Christopher Culpin, Ian Dawson and Richard McFahn. Reproduced by permission of Hodder Education.

P.229 Source A. Taken from OCR Crime and Punishment through time: An SHP development study by Christopher Culpin, Ian Dawson and Richard McFahn. Reproduced by permission of Hodder Education.

P.230 Source C. Taken from Crime & Punishment Through Time: An SHP development study: Student's Book (Discovering the Past for GCSE) by Ian Dawson. Reproduced by permission of Hodder Education.

Revision Tips

Rethink Revision

Have you ever taken part in a quiz and thought '*I know this*!', but, despite frantically racking your brain, you just couldn't come up with the answer?

It's very frustrating when this happens, but in a fun situation it doesn't really matter. However, in your GCSE exams, it will be essential that you can recall the relevant information quickly when you need to.

Most students think that revision is about making sure you *know* stuff. Of course, this is important, but it is also about becoming confident that you can **retain** that *stuff* over time and **recall** it quickly when needed.

Revision That Really Works

Experts have discovered that there are two techniques that help with all of these things and consistently produce better results in exams compared to other revision techniques.

Applying these techniques to your GCSE revision will ensure you get better results in your exams and will have all the relevant knowledge at your fingertips when you start studying for further qualifications, like AS and A Levels, or begin work.

It really isn't rocket science either – you simply need to:

- **test yourself** on each topic as many times as possible
- **leave a gap** between the test sessions.

It is most effective if you leave a good period of time between the test sessions, e.g. between a week and a month. The idea is that just as you start to forget the information, you force yourself to recall it again, keeping it fresh in your mind.

Three Essential Revision Tips

1. **Use Your Time Wisely**
   - Allow yourself plenty of time.
   - Try to start revising six months before your exams – it's more effective and less stressful.
   - Your revision time is precious so use it wisely – using the techniques described on this page will ensure you revise effectively and efficiently and get the best results.
   - Don't waste time re-reading the same information over and over again – it's time-consuming and not effective!

2. **Make a Plan**
   - Identify all the topics you need to revise (this Complete Revision & Practice book will help you).
   - Plan at least five sessions for each topic.
   - One hour should be ample time to test yourself on the key ideas for a topic.
   - Spread out the practice sessions for each topic – the optimum time to leave between each session is about one month but, if this isn't possible, just make the gaps as big as realistically possible.

3. **Test Yourself**
   - Methods for testing yourself include: quizzes, practice questions, flashcards, past papers, explaining a topic to someone else, etc.
   - This Complete Revision & Practice book provides six practice opportunities per topic.
   - Don't worry if you get an answer wrong – provided you check what the correct answer is, you are more likely to get the same or similar questions right in future!

Visit our website to download your free flashcards, for more information about the benefits of these revision techniques, and for further guidance on how to plan ahead and make them work for you.

www.collins.co.uk/collinsGCSErevision